D1756334

Edinburgh University Library

University of Edinburgh

30150   025331023

Postmodern Cross-Culturalism and Politicization in U.S. Latina Literature

MODERN
AMERICAN
LITERATURE
New Approaches

Yoshinobu Hakutani
General Editor

Vol. 42

PETER LANG
New York • Washington, D.C./Baltimore • Bern
Frankfurt am Main • Berlin • Brussels • Vienna • Oxford

Fatima Mujčinović

Postmodern Cross-Culturalism and Politicization in U.S. Latina Literature

From Ana Castillo to Julia Alvarez

PETER LANG
New York • Washington, D.C./Baltimore • Bern
Frankfurt am Main • Berlin • Brussels • Vienna • Oxford

EDINBURGH UNIVERSITY LIBRARY

WITHDRAWN

Library of Congress Cataloging-in-Publication Data

Mujčinović, Fatima.
Postmodern cross-culturalism and politicization in U.S. Latina literature:
from Ana Castillo to Julia Alvarez / Fatima Mujčinović.
p. cm. — (Modern American literature; v. 42)
Includes bibliographical references (p.) and index.
1. American literature—Hispanic American authors—History and
criticism. 2. Women and literature—United States—History—20th
century. 3. American literature—Women authors—History and criticism.
4. American literature—20th century—History and criticism. 5. Hispanic
American women—Intellectual life—20th century. 6. Postmodernism
(Literature)—United States. 7. Hispanic American women
in literature. 8. Identity (Psychology) in literature. 9. Hispanic
Americans in literature. 10. Group identity in literature. 11. Exiles
in literature. I. Title. II. Series: Modern American
literature (New York, N.Y.); v. 42.
PS153.H56M85   810.9'9287'08968—dc22   2003025200
ISBN 0–8204–6929–7
ISSN 1078–0521

Bibliographic information published by **Die Deutsche Bibliothek**.
Die Deutsche Bibliothek lists this publication in the "Deutsche
Nationalbibliografie"; detailed bibliographic data is available
on the Internet at http://dnb.ddb.de/.

The paper in this book meets the guidelines for permanence and durability
of the Committee on Production Guidelines for Book Longevity
of the Council of Library Resources.

© 2004 Peter Lang Publishing, Inc., New York
275 Seventh Avenue, 28th Floor, New York, NY 10001
www.peterlangusa.com

All rights reserved.
Reprint or reproduction, even partially, in all forms such as microfilm,
xerography, microfiche, microcard, and offset strictly prohibited.

Printed in Germany

To my parents

TABLE OF CONTENTS

ACKNOWLEDGMENTS

I am grateful to many people for support during this project. First, I would like to thank my doctoral advisors, Dr. Carl Gutiérrez-Jones, Dr. Ellen McCracken, and Dr. María Herrera-Sobek, who provided an invaluable academic guidance, critique, and encouragement during and after my Ph.D. studies. I am particularly indebted to my family and friends, whose love and support have been steadfast throughout all of my endeavors.

During my dissertation writing, several departments and centers at the University of California, Santa Barbara, gave different forms of support without which my book project would not have materialized: Chicano/a Studies Department, Women's Studies Department, Comparative Literature Program, Spanish Department, Graduate Division, Chicano/a Center, and Women's Center.

I am also thankful to my colleagues in the English Department at Westminster College for their encouragement and understanding during my first year of teaching, when I was completing this manuscript. During the production stage, Carol Frankman, in the Faculty Technology Center, and Teresa Knight, an English senior, offered an invaluable assistance with the preparation of the final camera-ready copy.

Finally, I would like to acknowledge several journals for granting me permission to reprint my articles:

"Multiple Articulations of Exile in U.S. Latina Literature: Confronting Exilic Absence and Trauma," reprinted, by permission, from *MELUS* 28.4 (Winter 2003): 167-186.

"Hybrid Latina Identities: Critical Positioning In-Between Two Cultures," reprinted, by permission, from *CENTRO: Journal of the Center for Puerto Rican Studies* 13.1 (Spring 2001): 44-59.

"*In Search of Bernabé*: A Politicized Motherhood," copyright by *Ethnic Studies Review* (ESR), The National Association for Ethnic Studies, 24.1-3 (2001): 29-47.

INTRODUCTION

U.S. Latina Literature: Mobilizing and Reconfiguring Postmodern Subjectivity

The literary expression of Latino[1] groups in the U.S. has been focusing on identity problematics since its beginnings in the second half of the nineteenth century, when the U.S. annexations of the northern Mexican territories (1848) and the Puerto Rican island (1898) generated large diasporic communities of these distinct national groups.[2] Emerging at this point as individual literary expressions of Hispanic communities, rather than a unified and largely diversified literary production, U.S. Latino/a literary creativity was, nevertheless, consolidated by similar representations of the minority experience.[3]

Created at the margins of Anglo American culture and in reaction to the cultural exclusion and stigmatization of its people, U.S. Latino/a literature inevitably developed the modernist theme of a quest for identity.[4] Its early phase expressed both individual and communal struggles for self-definition in conditions of racism, colonialism, and nativism.[5] One of the first Mexican American novels, *The Squatter and the Don* by María Amparo Ruiz de Burton, foregrounds the question of minority identity in the mid-nineteenth century. Written in 1885, the novel chronicles the arrival of white settlers in California after the 1848 annexation and protests against the subsequent disenfranchisement of Californian Mexicans, who gained U.S. citizenship but lost their lands to the Anglo American citizens.[6] The novel also clearly exposes the contradiction and ambivalence of subject positioning that the Mexican Californians experienced with the arrival of Anglo colonialism. The incongruity between the Californios' newly acquired national identification and their centuries-old Mexican cultural identity marked the beginning of the problematic of bicultural selfhood that has troubled and invigorated Mexican American/Chicano quest for self-definition ever since.[7] Other Latino groups in the U.S. encountered similar ambiguity and instability of national, cultural, political, and linguistic identifications—an experience that has configured identity politics as a predominant concern of U.S. Latino/a literature.

In the 1960s, several social and literary movements of minority groups placed identity politics at the forefront of U.S. social arena. Demands for political power articulated by Chicano and Puerto Rican activists in this period were accompanied by appeals for a new, positive identity. Reaching for the glory of the American indigenous past, Chicano and Puerto Rican *indigenista* movements[8] affirmed a hybrid identity of their ethnic groups and asserted *mestizaje* as a means of self-defined and resistant subject formation. In their literary expressions they also integrated calls for alternative and exclusionary national identifications by returning to the pre-Colombian roots and re-imagining the ancient empires of Aztlán and Boricua as their homelands.[9] In the 1970s, U.S. Latino/a literature teemed with poetry and prose that resonated with the identity problematics of subaltern and diasporic positioning. Featuring numerous personal narratives and memoirs, literature of this period captured rural and urban experiences of Latino (im)migrants while echoing their feelings of cultural, sociopolitical, and geographic displacement.[10] In both decades, strategies of self-definition were primarily masculinist and exclusionary, reflecting Latinos' desire for a homogenous and solidified communal identity while counteracting their marginal social positions. These oppositional strategies were based on strong cultural and nationalist agendas, being formed in opposition to Anglo cultural hegemony and nationalism which had repressed cultural and political rights of U.S. Latino citizens.

The decades of the 1980s and the 1990s stimulated a literary boom in U.S. Latino/a literature, providing more autonomous and diversified literary representations. Latino/a literature of this latest phase has continued to probe identity issues by problematizing the politics of self-definition and subject-positioning in the context of minority experiences.[11] In addition, it has integrated previously ignored female writers, opening up more space for their engagement with identity politics and for their construction of gendered historical voices. Invested in a demystification of gender oppression, U.S.

Latina authors have brought to light the specificity of female subjectivity by exposing multiple forms of women's subjugation and providing feminist perspectives on the issues of self-definition and emancipation. In their examination of the problematics of female identity, these writers have also presented new possibilities for a successful assertion of female agency in the postmodern world.[12]

This book focuses on the contemporary U.S. Latina writing that investigates and reconfigures subject-constitution and subject-positioning in connection to the cultural and sociopolitical conditioning of postmodernity. I analyze several U.S. Latina novels, short stories, and autobiographical pieces as narratives that place self-definition in the spaces of biculturalism and geopolitics to suggest new forms of emancipated subjectivities, forms that Chela Sandoval identifies as "differential" for they represent identities that are politicized and invested in strategic and coalitional positioning.[13] These subjectivities depart from the previous nationalist and exclusive paradigms of self-imagining by embracing transnational and multiple identities. They also depart from the traditional humanist notions of identity as unified and stable[14] by insisting on the concepts of hybridity and mobility: the new identities are syncretic, multiple, diasporic, and ambiguous, reflecting the postmodern conditions of mass migrations, globalization, post-coloniality, and technological development. Exploring the postmodern conditioning of identity, the selected U.S. Latina narratives present minority selfhood as decentered and "deterritorialized,"[15] emerging in interstitial spaces and through what Donna Haraway calls "transgressed boundaries, potent fusions, and dangerous possibilities" (154). Their portrayal of interstitial subjectivities reveals the potential empowerment and hazard of self-positioning in the spaces of biculturalism and transnational geopolitics.

The multiple subjectivity presented in U.S. Latina literature is further defined in the specific context of a "third-world"[16] female experience, an experience marked by multiple forms of hegemony and violence—patriarchy, nationalism, racism, capitalism, and state authoritarianism. Thus, this particular multiplicity of female subjectivity is linked to manifold types of oppression that act upon subjects and mark their identity as gendered, classed, racialized, sexed, and geopoliticized. In this specific context, the agency of postmodern (female) subjects is asserted through resistance to patterns of oppression, signifying a becoming that conflicts with repressive protocols of dominant socioeconomic and geopolitical orders. As Chela Sandoval argues in her theory of oppositional methods in the postmodern world,[17] the dialectics of the postmodern condition manifests itself when the formation of subjectivities becomes marked by forces of oppression and at the same time receives the capacity for an oppositional and differential agency.

The new, postmodern subjectivities portrayed in the U.S. Latina texts included in this study engage in oppositional forms of enunciation, contesting and deconstructing dominant social discourses in order to ensure a progressive transfiguration and emancipation of the individual and the communal. The female protagonists in Ana Castillo's *The Mixquiahuala Letters* and Graciela Limón's *In Search of Bernabé*, for example, challenge patterns of objectification and oppression enacted by dominant social narratives, and in this process they emerge as agents of sociopolitical and cultural transformation at the intersection between the private and public spaces. Although they embrace and affirm their difference, these subjects also reach beyond their specific conditions to forge potent political alliances, insisting, as Chela Sandoval would argue, on the possibility of "affinity-through-difference."[18] This act of social alignment moves away from individualist notions of identity and argues for political affiliations, rather than essentialist and separatist unions. For example, although a Chicana writer, Graciela Limón writes about the civil war in El Salvador, condemning the brutal oppression of Central American civilians. Similarly, the main female protagonists in Ana Castillo's book transcend their racial and class differences to join in a common struggle against patriarchy.

Articulating these concerns in their writings, the U.S. Latina authors studied in this project portray minority identities that are constituted through different experiences of sociopolitical and cultural marginalization and are subsequently transformed into differential and politicized modes of being. Their texts reveal the possibilities of survival and transformation in postmodern conditions of objectification, displacement, and political oppression by presenting subjectivities based on hybrid, transnational notions rather than homogenous, nationalist paradigms. In addition, these writers do not advocate the form of agency that completely rejects power; instead, they promote political and emancipated forms of subjectivity that lead to individual and communal empowerment. Furthermore, while they engage their narrative protagonists in constant negotiations with the discourses of authority that are often oppressive and violent, they espouse an empowerment based on non-violent strategies, strategies that seek to establish agency apart from violence and force.

Another important intervention in these texts is their cross-national and geopolitical concern: all of the authors construct links between the U.S. and Latin America, insisting on a trans-American experience. As they examine gender and ethnic subject positioning in the space of biculturalism, they investigate both antagonistic and compatible intercultural patterns, which allows them to perform an astute cultural analysis and criticism. They also place primary attention on the geopolitical and historical dimensions of the trans-American connections, integrating Latin American history and politics in a U.S. context and presenting experiences that occur on both sides of geopolitical borders.

The significance of these narrative attempts to foreground inter-American links is multifaceted. In the context of individual and communal identity, the insistence on trans-national and diasporic subjectivity focuses attention on multiple cultural sources of U.S. Latino self-definition and thus expands notions of identity in relation to national, territorial, and geopolitical categories. Self-definition in multiple cultural and national terms allows for an inclusive Latino identity, while generating a fluid cross-cultural and international positioning. In the context of national culture and identity, the international dimension of these texts destabilizes the equivalency between nation and culture and exposes the fallacy of the projected cultural homogeneity. Their emphasis on the presence of other cultural and national histories in the U.S. underscores the heterogeneity of American culture and calls attention to ongoing processes of cultural hybridization. In addition, this rupture of the hegemonic moment provides alternative narratives which challenge dominant historiographic and political discourses and thus produce new knowledge.[19] The epistemological goal of this project is to raise awareness of local/global negotiations as well as to generate an oppositional political consciousness, or what Chela Sandoval terms "differential consciousness." Bringing Latin American history and politics into a U.S. context, these Latina texts challenge U.S. political hegemony in the region and reveal its role in immigrant influx and displacement. They expose the fact that political and economic instability in Latin America is related to U.S. geostrategic interests and that the processes of displacement inevitably affect both geopolitical realities.

I have limited my discussion of U.S. Latino literature to female authors, not only because of their departure from masculinist notions of minority identity, but also because of their postmodern reconfigurations of feminine subjectivity. Latina writers emphasize that female subjects are marked not only by gender but also by multiple and intersecting categories of class, ethnicity, sexuality, and geopolitics. Yet they accentuate the category of gender by utilizing it as a significant intervention in their narratives: many of their texts contest patriarchal forms of oppression through feminist methodologies of resistance. Furthermore, their gendered representations expose the frequently unacknowledged feminine agency in political insurgency and social transformation. As demonstrated in Latin American feminist theory,[20] when gendered subject-positioning is asserted in the social arena to confront oppressive state authority, it becomes a powerful tool of social transformation. U.S. Latina narratives, like many politically engaged Latin American texts, emphasize the multiple signification of gender, constructing it as a strategy that unmasks oppressive authority at both the domestic and national levels. In addition, their dialogue with Latin American feminism points out the necessity of women's international solidarity and the inclusion of the geopolitical category in U.S. feminist debates.

In the following discussion of identity politics, I engage a variety of primary texts by authors of different U.S. Latino groups. Ana Castillo, Graciela Limón, Demetria Martínez, and Helena María Viramontes are Chicana writers; Rosario Morales, Aurora Levins Morales, and Judith Ortiz Cofer are Puerto Rican, while Julia Alvarez is Dominican American and Cristina García Cuban American. Undeniably, U.S. Latina writers comprise a heterogeneous group that contains numerous inter-ethnic differences and, consequently, distinct concerns and positioning. However, the diversity of my selection is deliberate, governed by an intent to examine subject-constitution and positioning across specific ethnic groupings and thus to demonstrate multiple and different configurations of Latino/a identity in the U.S. At the same time, I hope to present U.S. Latina literature as a topos of solidarity and alliance. U.S. Latino/a literary texts demonstrate that, while each Latino group has emerged out of the specific historical circumstances of political and economic relation to the U.S. (see endnote 3), they all have undergone a similar marginalization and exclusion, which makes the process of their identity constitution and positioning comparable across ethnic specificities. This common experience of oppression is precisely the point that solidifies and brings together U.S. Latino/a literary expression and establishes necessary alliances and collectivity. I foreground the presence of cross-ethnic connections articulated by these writers, noticing that the presence of the Central American experience in Chicana narratives, for example, points toward the politics of coalition and differential social movement, where specific sociopolitical conditions are taken into account while demanding cross-national and cross-ethnic solidarity.

My intention is also to contribute to the growing body of literary criticism that has recently begun to study U.S. Latino/a literature as an inclusive and connected literary tradition,[21] as opposed to separate and unrelated analyses of individual Latino/a literary productions. Eliana Ortega and Nancy Saporta Sternbach's essay in the 1989 study *Breaking Boundaries: Latina Writing and Critical Readings*, edited by Asunción Horno-Delgado et al, was the first critical consideration of U.S. Latina literature as a unified literary discourse. However, while the book itself includes critical essays on literary works from different Latino backgrounds, the analyses are still grouped according to distinct ethnic groups, reflecting the editors' carefulness not to blur group differences (even though the literary differences may not be that divisive). In the last decades, there have been many groundbreaking and original studies on Chicano/a and Puerto Rican literature in English, and I hope that the criticism of Latino/a literature will follow their pace of production and dissemination.

Comparative studies are important because they indicate literary similarities and differences in a wide range of Latino/a writing while gaining a stronger ground for a successful generating of theories on and from Latino/a discursive practices. They also validate U.S. Latino/a literature as a complex and innovative literary production that significantly contributes to modern American literature and provides more autonomy and power of literary articulation to one of the largest minority groups in the U.S.[22] By extension, comparative and inclusive literary approaches help assert a more pronounced visibility and a more powerful presence of Latino influences in mainstream U.S. culture.

Cultural and Geopolitical Concerns in U.S. Latina Identity Politics

The first part of the book investigates the dynamics of sociocultural conditioning in identity formation by exploring articulations of selfhood in the polyvalent and ambiguous space of "biculturalism."[23] Latinos' cultural experience in the U.S. is inevitably marked by an encounter between their original cultural heritage and the dominant Anglo culture. This encounter is often troublesome, for it exposes the incompatibility and contradictions of different cultural signifiers. Gloria Anzaldúa remarks: "The coming together of two self-consistent, but habitually incompatible frames of reference, causes *un choque*, a cultural collision"(78). As they try to negotiate their marginalized ethnic cultures with the dominant cultural domain, U.S. Latinos face the perpetual dilemma of bicultural self-definition: "which collectivity to listen to?" and "how to reconcile different voices?" The pressure intensifies as the minority subjects become caught between the assimilationist demands of the dominant culture and the need to preserve their original cultural identity. The cultural hegemony of U.S. society further complicates their acceptance of bicultural identity by identifying cultural difference and diversity as "a serious threat" to national and cultural unity.[24]

This state of duality in the sociocultural arena that U.S. Latino subjects inhabit often becomes internalized as a psychological struggle, extending into a pathological condition generated by external forces. The self exposed to two different realities and contradictory demands may split in response to the anxiety and confusion arising out of biculturalism's polyvocality. As Anzaldúa notes in her study of *mestiza* identity, living in more than one culture results in an internalized conflict: "Cradled in one culture, sandwiched between two cultures, straddling all three cultures and their value systems, *la mestiza* undergoes a struggle of flesh, a struggle of borders, an inner war"(78).

The inability to deal with a multiplicity of cultural systems frustrates the self-definition of minority members, corresponding to the ambiguity of self-formation and self-differentiation explained by psychoanalytic theories:[25] enmeshed between conscious and unconscious drives, one's identity becomes internally split and placed in a perpetual struggle between two principles, the reality and the pleasure principle. Even when this internal strife becomes negotiated by the repression of the "other,"[26] the encounter with ambiguity continues as the residue of the split manifests itself in a desire for the never attainable self-totality. The search for wholeness of self is infinite, being continuously troubled by the "return of the repressed"[27] and its mark of otherness. "Who, then, is this other to whom I am more attached than to myself, since at the heart of my assent to my own identity, it is still he who agitates me?" asks Jacques Lacan in his discussion of the unconscious, articulating the dilemma of the split identity ("The Agency of the Letter" 172). The otherness of self is agitating because it is alien and different from the already recognized self-image.

The psychoanalytic explanations of the processes of identity splitting and repression introduce the notions of a partial, fractured identity that is constituted by the ambiguity and conflictual dualism between the I and the other. The concept of the other subverts the image of an autonomous identity, exposing it as fragmented and dissonant. Translated into a bicultural context, the presence of the "cultural Other" configures the subject definition always in relation to multiple and different cultural systems, propelling one into a constant negotiation of multiple realities. Lacan's explanation of the dialectical opposition between the I and the other is fitting to the discussion of the bicultural dynamics because it introduces the notion of an identity that is (re)constituted through the deferral, multiplicity, and ambiguity of meaning. Searching for a complete self-meaning and fulfillment, the self is placed in a perpetual movement along the "chain of signifiers"[28] since meaning cannot be contained within a single signifier, or representation. Consequently, one's identity is marked by absence and elision and an infinite multiplicity of reference.

Similarly, bicultural subjects are enmeshed between multiple cultural referents, and they often experience cultural conflict, as Anzaldúa articulates, as a struggle for self-meaning. They find themselves placed in different signifying systems, and in this state of a multiple being their selfhood is always informed by the alterity of the other. In this course, their subjectivity is often formed in the space of "in-betweenness,"[29] an interstitial location where distinct cultures converge and collide, forming both collaborative and conflictual processes. These processes may provoke either a sense of fluid subject-positioning or of agitating disorientation as they invalidate the singularity and stability of the cultural domain and complicate, as Lacan puts it, one's "assent to identity."

The U.S. Latina texts included in my study foreground identities that consciously situate themselves in the place of in-betweenness, engaging narrative protagonists in a constant negotiation between two cultures, two nations, and two geopolitical realities. They designate this location as a site that the protagonists deliberately inhabit in order to imagine and construct their selves in a new, affirmative way. As I argue throughout my project, these texts dramatize a resurgence of new subjectivities that embrace the space of biculturalism in its ambiguity, contradiction, and complexity in order to assert differential and politicized hybrid identities, affirming Homi Bhabha's notion of the 'in-between space' as a "terrain for elaborating new strategies of selfhood" (*The Location of Culture* 1). Being a locus where one culture contests and interacts with the other, this polyvalent and ambiguous terrain reveals alternative and critical modes of cultural practice and subject-positioning by resisting closure, singularity, and totality.

In the first chapter, I analyze the evolvement of gendered subjectivity and consciousness in the space of cultural in-betweenness. The analysis traces different patterns of the female identity formation in a bicultural context, where gender ideology and cultural hegemony are intensified. Subjected to patriarchal demands and expectations of two cultures, the female protagonists in Ana Castillo's *The Mixquiahuala Letters*, for example, experience a double weight of oppression and subjugation. They are forced to perform submissive roles in both Mexican and Anglo cultures and thus are entrapped in the web of patriarchal control cast between two cultural domains. However, this space of in-betweenness offers them a capacity for transformation when the women learn to claim it as a new cultural terrain that generates subversive strategies of emancipation and agency. They assert their hybrid identity and fluid positioning at the crossroads of distinct cultures, resisting cultural patriarchy while simultaneously synthesizing different liberating positions. Similarly, Rosario Morales and Aurora Levins Morales portray their gender positioning at the crossroads of Puerto Rican and Anglo American cultures, resisting patriarchy in both cultural domains and yet finding inspiration and affirmation in different experiences of womanhood across distinct cultures. In their co-authored autobiography *Getting Home Alive*, they present their bicultural identity as a heterogeneous site where many cultures converge (U.S., Puerto Rican, Jewish, and Eastern European). This allows them to diversify their subject-positioning and claim a fluid, hybrid self-definition. Finally, the young female protagonists in Julia Alvarez's *How The García Girls Lost Their Accents* engage in a critical negotiation of their native Dominican culture and the adopted Anglo culture in order to secure a positive and emancipated self-definition. They consciously embrace bicultural conditions and perform a subversive movement between two cultures and gender ideologies. In all of these texts, the intersection of two and/or more cultures translates from a site of entrapment into a space of liberation, generating multiple sources of identification and strategies of differential agency.

In the second chapter, I investigate the construction of ethnic and national identity in diasporic conditions. The formation of selfhood at the intersection of two national and cultural domains is defined by the perplexity and ambivalence of self-identification, as demonstrated in Judith Ortiz Cofer's creative autobiography *Silent Dancing*, Cristina García's *Dreaming in Cuban*, and Julia Alvarez's *How the García Girls Lost Their Accents* and *¡Yo!*. Marked by their experiences of exile and displacement, the protagonists in these narratives struggle with the condition of dislocation, which is reflected in their desire to find a place of belonging and reconnect with their past. In this search for affirmative and inclusive self-definition, they emerge as postmodern subjectivities, contesting the notions of identity based on the rootedness in a singular place and tied to the national structure. Attempting to negotiate their existence defined by multiple locations and shifting boundaries, they embrace cross-cultural identities as strategies of a dialogic and liberating self-creation. Focusing on diasporic self-positioning, these works challenge the limiting concept of nation while redefining identity as fluid and hybrid. This allows them to provide alternative paradigms for imagining the space of the social and the individual.

Both chapters investigate biculturalism as a space that initiates the emergence of differential subjectivity and oppositional consciousness.[30] The multiplicity and the ambiguity of cultural referents provide a space for identities that are grounded in partiality, fluidity, syncretism, and mutability. These forms of selfhood transcend static, essentialist paradigms and generate a consciousness that refuses loyalty to singularity and totality. The new identities are rooted in the politics of becoming, seeking to obtain knowledge and recognition of different influences in their self-formation, rather than to construct an image of the unified autonomous self.

It is important to note that, as Lacan argues, the process of becoming is different from and opposed to the process that attempts to establish what one is. The effort to know oneself is fruitless if there is no knowledge of how one has become, and, therefore, one's identity cannot be accepted if it is not explained in terms of its formation. 'Know thyself' is an empty adage, emphasizes Lacan, if it does not involve "reconsider[ing] the ways that lead to it" ("The Agency of the Unconscious" 174). This is a call for a search for self-knowledge that links the present with the past, echoing Freud's goal of "coming to the place where that was" (171). However, while Freud establishes the objective of replacing the unconscious ("that") with the conscious as a way of strengthening the ego, Lacan reinterprets the return to the place "where that was" as the return to the Other, to the point that precedes the subject and signifies what Freud names "the nucleus of one's being" (173).[31] The return to the locus of the Other traces back the formation of all identity and demonstrates the image of an autonomous identity as an illusion. However, this knowledge of becoming, posits Lacan, leads to personal "reintegration and harmony," and "even reconciliation," because it affirms one's being as partial, fluid, and plural, being always informed by the presence of the Other (171).

While accepting, rather than counteracting, the presence of the Other, this new epistemology of selfhood reveals the possibility of living on the shifting boundaries of the self and through ambiguity and plurality. Gloria Anzaldúa describes it as a new *mestiza* consciousness: "The new *mestiza* copes by developing a tolerance for contradictions, a tolerance for ambiguity. She learns to be an Indian in Mexican culture, to be Mexican from an Anglo point of view. She learns to juggle cultures. She has a plural personality, she operates in a pluralistic mode..."(79). Instead of signifying a crisis of identity, the hybrid and strategic subjectivity becomes a creative *modus operandi* in postmodern conditions, evolving into a potent political practice.

After exploring hybrid identity as an effect of and response to sociocultural conditioning, I focus on geopolitical conditions in the second part of the book, arguing that hybrid identity needs to be problematized via the complications of global political conditions. As the selected U.S. Latina narratives demonstrate, identity formation becomes marked not only by the complications of gender, ethnicity, and class but also by the traumatic experience of political oppression and authoritarianism. As illustrated in Helena María Viramontes' "The Cariboo Café," Julia Alvarez's *How the García Girls Lost Their Accents*, and Cristina García's *Dreaming in Cuban*—all discussed in Chapter Three—an articulation of subjectivity becomes frustrated when the complications of political migrations and exile come into play. Identity formation, then, includes new psychological negotiations: between home and exile, past and present, memory and forgetting, and danger and safety. Political immigrants portrayed in these texts are tormented by the feelings of loss and alienation experienced in exile, haunted by the memory of state violence in the present, and nostalgically tied to the past and the originary place. Consequently, their self-definition and positioning in the new, immigrant location is continually disrupted by their unhealed trauma, causing spatial and temporal dislocations. As Jean Franco reminds, "even for a Latina born in the U.S. there is an ancestral memory of violence and loss,"[32] and this internalized and obscured experience of trauma further complicates the evolvement of selfhood. Becoming a "stranded object,"[33] an internalized traumatic experience does not allow for a proper and necessary transition to healed positions as the past injury becomes further repressed. However, the haunting past always returns to displace and rupture the enunciative present, causing more perplexity in self-definition. The trauma becomes doubled and transmissible as political victimization intertwines with cultural oppression and this layering of trauma is passed on to new generations. In this fashion, the geopolitical conditioning continues to assert its mark in the process of identity formation in spite of temporal and spatial mediations.

Reinforcing this argument, the third chapter examines exilic identities as effects of geopolitical conditioning. I investigate how the trauma of exile causes a fractured identity and initiates the interplay between time and space in a negotiation of exilic experience. I explain that although exile is often considered in terms of spatial dislocation and nostalgia for home, its temporal aspect is also fundamentally important. In their imaginative recreations of home and their perpetual desire to return, the Latina and the Latino protagonists in these texts are portrayed as suffering from temporal displacements that condition their exilic experience and identity formation. The Central American mother in "The Cariboo Café," for example, is so traumatized by the brutal murder of her five-year-old son that she is unable to situate herself in the present, which leads to her tragic experience of exile. Lourdes Puente in *Dreaming in Cuban*, on the other hand, completely represses the traumatic past and obsessively invests herself in an escapist construction of the present and the future. I also pay attention to both female and male experiences of exile depicted in the novels, noticing different responses and coping strategies in relation to gender, age, and class. With these categories determining the patterns of adjustment, some of the characters learn to transform exilic conditions of absence and loss into creative tools of emancipation and self-affirmation, demonstrating multiple and diverse articulations of exile.

U.S. Latina texts of exile and displacement also draw attention to the fact that effects of political violence act upon victimized subjects even in the safety of exile: often a traumatic experience of political violence may become internalized in the victim's psyche and projected onto the new location. Furthermore, they demonstrate that political oppression cannot be contained within national borders since state violence affirms itself as a global phenomenon that evades restrictions of national insignias. This emphasis on political violence points out the necessity of a simultaneous liberation of the individual and the sociopolitical, a necessity that has been perceived by many Latin American feminist activists and theorists.[34] Following feminist claims, U.S. Latina authors also establish links between the private and public spaces. The texts by Demetria Martínez and Graciela Limón, for example, assert the intersection between the private and the public as the only viable location of political resistance in conditions of state authoritarianism. I analyze these texts in the final chapter, focusing on geopolitical identities that are forged at the intersection of the individual and the social.

Drawing on the Latin American experience, the U.S. Latina texts that explore subject constitution and positioning in conditions of authoritarianism expose the dialectical dependence between the individual and the collective as a relation that generates both destructive and liberating forces. *In Search of Bernabé* by Graciela Limón and *Mother Tongue* by Demetria Martínez highlight new forms of subjectivity that mobilize privatized modes of praxis in order to assert opposition and emancipation in a militarily sanctioned public space. In this process of political positioning, the protagonists gain a sociopolitical agency and identity that stand against individual and communal oppression.

This segment of U.S. Latina literature constructs the politics of liberation as a private and communal project that strives to engender individual emancipation through sociopolitical transformation. I relate this argument to the Latin American feminist theory that discusses individual emancipation in relation to social justice and national liberation. The fundamental principle of this project is identified in the notion of relational agency, where one is always positioned in relation to others and transformed through communal dynamics.

Latin American feminist discourse builds a strong connection between individual and sociopolitical spheres by relating the issues of women's marginalization and oppression to geopolitical issues. Its debate exposes the social and political nature of these conditions and exposes the continuum of the forceful exercise of male authority in the private and the public space. The awareness that individual emancipation is linked to national liberation arose in the specific historical moment when many Latin American countries experienced severe oppression by military and totalitarian dictatorships. This was precisely the time when women's resistance movements emerged to protest the destructive effects of totalitarianism on women's lives, subsequently transforming themselves into a powerful political force against the repressive state power. These gender-based protests of the 1970s and 1980s incorporated women's issues in claims for social liberalization and democratization, realizing that the transformation of gender politics was closely tied to the geopolitical transformation.[35]

Examining identity formation in the space of geopolitics, the Latina narratives presented in the second part of this project perform an important intervention by exposing direct links between authoritarianism and patriarchy. They demonstrate that state oppression and violence are, as Sonia Alvarez argues, the continuation and intensification of the patriarchal exercise of power.[36] The novels *In Search of Bernabé* and *Mother Tongue* criticize the interlaced power structures of authoritarianism and patriarchy by portraying gender abuse and political violence as effects of the same oppressive patriarchal authority. Their simultaneous challenge of patriarchal and sociopolitical authority points out, not only the oppressive reality that constitutes the female condition, but also the transgressive power of politicized female subjectivities formed under conditions of patriarchy and authoritarianism. Defying sexual, gender, class, national, and political conventions, female protagonists in these narratives emerge as a powerful insurgent force that transforms their own selves and social conditions that act upon them.

The chapters trace a transformation of subject-positioning from subjugated to emancipated positions. Gendered identity becomes transformed from the condition of an entrapment between two cultures to the state of differential and liberated subjectivity. National and ethnic self-identifications move away from unicultural and national definitions to cross-cultural diasporic negotiations. Exilic identity transcends the limitations of exilic uprootedness, absence, and alienation and embraces the creative potentiality of the new location. Geopolitical identity becomes a resistant positioning against the subjugation and oppression exercised by authoritarian states, turning into a locus of the integration between the personal and the public.

While presenting these transformations of identity in the context of cultural and geopolitical negotiations, the selected U.S. Latina texts also transfigure the notions of biculturalism and geopolitics: biculturalism is presented as a space of political practice, while geopolitics is constructed as a terrain for politicization of the private.

Often rendered in terms of cultural synthesis, biculturalism is presented in these narratives also as a site of contention, transgression, and transformation. The selected U.S. Latina texts show that, while it can be experienced as either a place of entrapment or a condition of mobility between different cultural domains, the oppressive aspects of biculturalism can be countered through a creative synthesis of empowering possibilities and a critical opposition to patterns of subjugation. In this fashion, the mediation in the ambiguous space of biculturalism expands the usual negotiation of cultural identity and takes on the meaning of survival and resistance in conditions of subjugation.

The geopolitical positioning foregrounded in the selected narratives emphasizes material conditions of political oppression that constitute identity and thus ties the politics of identity to the politics of liberation. As shown in the Latin American experience of military regimes, the geopolitical terrain often resignifies the individual as a site of sociopolitical meaning, marking the entrance of the personal into the public space as a political and oppositional movement. In this process, the exclusive sphere of sociopolitical interaction becomes infused with personal meaning and reconstructed through relational and communal agency.

Postmodern Narrative Strategies

In order to foreground the notion of differential and politicized hybrid identities, U.S. Latina literature adopts narrative strategies that reflect this thematic concern. Multiple narrative points of view, fragmented stories, nonlinear timelines, fusion of history and fiction, eclectic narrative styles, and occasional bilingualism—all challenge monologic and unified narrative structures. Rosario Morales and Aurora Levins Morales' lyrical autobiography *Getting Home Alive*, Judith Ortiz Cofer's memoir *Silent Dancing*, and Demetria Martínez's novel *Mother Tongue*, for example, constitute hybrid texts: in their introspective narrations the authors integrate poems, diary entries, photographs, personal essays, political announcements, recipes, newspaper clippings, and grocery lists. Along with Graciela Limón's *In Search of Bernabé*, Martínez's text also fuses history and fiction to provide an oppositional re-narrativization of the dominant sociopolitical text and foreground the dialectics between the subjective and the socio-historical. Similarly, Cristina García's multiple narrative points in *Dreaming in Cuban* develop a dialogic technique that challenges dominant social discourses and hegemonic constructions of sociopolitical meaning. Ana Castillo's epistolary novel, *The Mixquiahuala Letters*, too, opposes singular meaning and authority with its chronological dislocation and an invitation to read the letters in random order. Helena María Viramontes' short story "The Cariboo Café" exploits a technique of fragmented narration in order to convey temporal and spatial dislocations that displaced persons experience in the condition of exile. Finally, Julia Alvarez' *How the García Girls Lost Their Accents* develops a retrospective line of narration to portray a return to the originary place and trace the process of becoming, while *¡Yo!* includes sixteen different points of view in order to illustrate a multiple subjectivity and positioning of the central character.

This aesthetic experimentation emerges in U.S. Latina literature from the specific postmodern conditions that mark the authors' discursive and material realities: political and economic displacements, temporal and spatial discontinuities, cultural and linguistic hybridization, and an interdependence between the local and the global. The authors develop diverse textual strategies in an attempt to theorize the new postmodern subjectivities formed under these conditions. As they create fragmented and hybrid narrative structures to dramatize the dispersal and decenteredness of identity in the postmodern world, the selected U.S. Latina texts foreground the traumatic dislocation and disorientation that the minority self experiences in the contemporary historical moment. They emphasize that the reality of minority subjects cannot be represented in an orderly and linear narrative: the female condition in patriarchy or the experience of the oppressed under authoritarianism, for example, find the most powerful representation through ruptured and dislocated textual moments. Being inscribed by the patterns of rupture and dislocation—the models of repressive social practices—the narrative structure comes to speak of the social objectification and territorialization of the individual.

Seeking to represent minority experiences, U.S. Latina writers pluralize reality and thus destabilize the singularity and homogeneity of perception and actuality. They reveal the inevitable presence of the Other, affirming that reality is always ambiguous and multiple and that the self is always informed by alterity and deferral. This mode of representation points not only toward the minority subjects, who are enmeshed between different socio-cultural referents, but also toward (post)modern subjects in general, who are placed in a perpetual course of elision, layering, and displacement of meaning.

Developing narrative structures based on displacement, condensation, decentralization, disjunction, and dialogism, U.S. Latina authors theorize the processes into which postmodern subjectivity is often thrown in the course of formation. In this attempt, they emphasize that identity cannot be understood without understanding its constitution, which they present as traumatic, contradictory, ambiguous, and ongoing. The trauma of exilic separation and alienation, as some of these texts show, leaves an ever-lasting mark on one's identity, and hence its effects of psychic displacement need to be taken into account in the process of self-discovery and affirmation.

As they exploit textual dislocations to reflect social and political disjunctions of postmodernity, U.S. Latina narratives of displacement speak, not only of the hazards and challenges of survival under oppressive conditions, but also of the potentiality of new subject positions. They invest in a meaningful elaboration of empowering strategies of survival and emancipation that are located precisely in these disjointed locations of textual and material realities. Accepting the impossibility of homogeneity and stability, they search for agency and subjectivity in the creases of dominant social narratives, in the places of disjunction, or what Homi Bhabha calls a "split space of enunciation."[37] With their deterritorialized and hybrid narratives, they point at the "manuever in-between" that seeks to find resistance in the interstices between different discourses. Signifying one's refusal to be territorialized—that is, sanctioned and regulated—this movement leads to the positions of emancipated subjectivity by reacting against patterns of objectification.

In this manner, U.S. Latina literary texts not only propose new ways of representation and reading, but also construct a differential positioning and an empowering intellectual mobility. Engendered in differential and politicized hybrid subjectivity, this positioning is a critical and engaged response to the age of postmodernity through both the aesthetics and the thematics of postmodern literature.

Theoretical Approaches: Local/Global Connections

In order to provide an engaging and in-depth literary analysis, I employ some of the latest cultural and literary theory in my readings of the selected U.S. Latina narratives. Wanting to keep my argument accessible to those not very familiar with the complex theoretical discourse, I present and clarify the dense critical terminology and concepts where necessary. My intention has been to develop a stimulating dialogue between literature and theory in a clear and comprehensible way, while trying to avoid both oversimplifications and "overcomplications" of the argument.

In addition, I bring into my discussion a wide array of both Latino/ American theorists and international scholars in order to explore U.S. Latina literature through multiple lenses of leading literary and cultural theories. This allows me to examine modern U.S. Latina texts through local and global frames while drawing on contemporary feminist, postmodern, post-colonial, and psychoanalytic approaches.

In Chapter One, where I discuss the constitution and articulation of gen-dered identity in the context of U.S. Latina experiences, I engage the theory of U.S. third-world feminism, which bases its criticism on the experience of U.S. women of color.[38] I specifically use the work of Gloria Anzaldúa and Chela Sandoval, Chicana/Latina critics who identify themselves with this model of feminism and are prominent advocates of its theory and movement.

Formed in response to the U.S. feminist movement of the 1960s and 1970s, which mainly addressed issues of white middle-class women, U.S. third-world feminism calls attention to the multiple oppression experienced by women of color in the U.S., who, in addition to gender discrimination, suffer from racial and class marginalization. This insistence on the difference in female experience articulates the need to express criticism of the racial and economic oppression that intensifies gender inequality of minority women, the criticism that was unarticulated by the homogenous Anglo American feminism. Also, the shift from difference (male vs. female) to dif-ferences (among women) asserts, as many third-world feminists have ar-gued,[39] that gender is not a sufficient model of identification and commonal-ity. In order to distinguish themselves from the exclusive "first-world" feminist movement, women of color underscore the agenda of their specific lived experience and positioning, strategically adopting the economically marked term "third-world."[40]

U.S. Latina writers present the experience of multiple female oppression by developing in their narratives female characters who struggle with patri-archy, racism, homophobia, and poverty. Examining gender positioning spe-cifically in the context of biculturalism, they emphasize an intensification of gender objectification and victimization that women of bicultural origin often

encounter at the interstice of their native and Anglo cultures. Gloria Anzaldúa's theory on *mestiza* consciousness draws attention to this kind of oppression in a Chicana context by criticizing both Mexican and Anglo cultural
practices that place women in subjugated positions and deny them positive
self-definition and articulation. However, her theory also proposes strategies
of emancipation and transformation in conditions of oppression by redefining
mestizaje as a powerful source of female definition, a definition denied in the
masculinist *indigenista* movements.

Chela Sandoval's theory on methodology of the oppressed further elabo-
rates the notion of *mestiza* consciousness by investigating specific modes of
resistance based on constant, differential repositioning. Sandoval introduces
the concept of "differential consciousness," which emphasizes differentiating, self-representing, and oppositional social subjectivities emerging in the
conditions of postmodern forms of oppression. This form of consciousness
generates oppositional political positioning on the premise of affinity, rather
than difference and essence, recognizing the power of political insurgence in
strategic coalitional alignment of different subjects and groups. In my analysis, I engage Anzaldúa's and Sandoval's strategies of resistance in order to
identify different configurations of oppositional identities in several U.S.
Latina narratives, as well as to demonstrate how these narratives expand and
transform some of these theoretical paradigms.

In Chapter Two, I focus on trans-national, diasporic identities, utilizing
Homi Bhabha's post-colonial criticism. Although the majority of Bhabha's
critical analyses derives from his study of the Indian diasporic experience in
Great Britain, his work on identity in relation to nation and culture provides
some concepts that are not necessarily regionally bound and hence can be
translated and rearticulated in different postcolonial conditions.

The concept of the postcolonial condition has a significant resonance in
the U.S. Latino experience. The history of several Latino groups began in the
U.S. with their experience of annexation in the nineteenth century and the
subsequent loss of economic, cultural, and political autonomy (see endnote
3). A newly independent colony itself at the time, the U.S. asserted a position
of the imperial subject by exploiting simultaneously a nationalist discourse
of homogeneity and the colonial rationale of racial and cultural superiority
over the colonized people. In the twentieth century, the U.S. adopted neocolonial practices and imposed its political and military hegemony in Central
America and the Caribbean, initiating a widespread political instability and

violence in the region and forcing waves of political refugees into Mexico, the U.S., and Canada. Participating in the advanced, postmodern conditions of global capitalism and military industry, the U.S. has also significantly engaged in economic forms of neocolonial hegemony, which has impelled economic migration from many underdeveloped countries of Latin America into U.S. urban centers. Displaced and colonized internally and externally through multiple forms of colonial hegemony, Latino groups in the U.S. have become objectified by the "imperial history" and reduced to positions of "subalternity." In addition, their ethnic, racial, and class differences have constituted them as "the foreign Other" in the social space of the leading neocolonial power.

With this material history, which has often been denied them discursively, Latinos' experience in the U.S. can be read within and against some postcolonial concepts. I particularly employ Bhabha's concepts of "unhomliness," "migrant's narration," and "in-between passage" in order to examine the portrayal of diasporic, trans-national identities in U.S. Latina texts of displacement and exile. I explain and use these concepts in the chapter's analysis, emphasizing the ways in which the selected U.S. Latina narratives reconfigure these notions and complicate the current theories on postcoloniality.

In Chapter Three, I focus on exilic identities in three U.S. Latina texts, often referring to Amy Kaminsky's theory on exile. While Kaminsky's analysis in the third chapter of *Reading the Body Politic* (1993) expresses universal concepts of the problematics of exile, her specific examination of Latin American conditions of displacement provides an important point of entry for my investigation of exilic identities in U.S. Latina narratives. I structure my analysis around spatial and temporal negotiations of exile as a place of absence and loss, and Kaminsky's theoretical concept of "presence-in-absence" offers important insights into the condition of exilic existence. However, while she defines exile in spatial terms, I argue that the temporal aspects of exile, as shown in U.S. Latina literature, are of fundamental importance, too, because they condition imaginative recreations of home and the desire to return. Kaminsky's relation of exile to the conditions of female experience and feminization also contributes to my investigation of gendered positioning of the exiled as portrayed in U.S. Latina narratives of displacement.

The frequent theme of exile in U.S. Latina literature is framed within the social and geopolitical reality of Latin America. The texts that I analyze in this chapter specifically focus on the Central American/Caribbean experience determined by the conditions of authoritarianism and military regimes in the second half of the twentieth century. Forced to flee severe political oppression and state violence in their homelands, Central American and Caribbean civilians came to the U.S. as political refugees, participating in a massive population uprooting. In only three decades, from 1950–1983, close to two million people were forced to relocate: approximately 910,000 Cubans; 310,000 Dominicans; 200,000 Nicaraguans; 300,000 Salvadorans; and 200,000 Guatemalans came to the U.S. as documented and undocumented refugees (Pastor 300).

As many U.S. Latina texts demonstrate, the effects of such massive population displacements are experienced, not only as an individual "physical and psychic dislocation,"[41] but also as a communal and national dislocation that needs to be discussed and negotiated. Angelika Bammer points this out in her book *Displacements* (1994), stating that the separation of people from their native culture through physical dislocation or cultural displacement is one of the most formative experiences in the twentieth century.[42] Edward Said reinforces this statement by emphasizing the difference between earlier and more contemporary exiles: "The difference between earlier exiles and those of our time is, it bears stressing, scale: our age—with its modern warfare, imperialism, and the quasi-theological ambitions of totalitarian rulers—is indeed the age of the refugee, the displaced person, mass immigration" ("Reflections on Exile" 174).

The final chapter investigates the construction and positioning of geopolitical subjectivities in the space of authoritarianism and engages concepts from Latin American feminist theory and praxis. Since I particularly investigate the emergence of oppositional identities at the interstice of private and public spaces in the context of state authoritarianism, I find Jean Franco's work on Latin American feminist movements particularly helpful. Analyzing specifically the public protests of Argentine mothers during the "dirty war,"[43] Franco explains how the repressive state enforces a radical exile of women from the traditional family by violating the domestic space and attacking the traditional values of motherhood. As women become forced to leave the domestic sphere, traditionally assigned to them as the only location they can occupy, they seize the public space to expose the issue of political violence. In this process, Franco points out, women redefine their roles as mothers and emerge as agents of social change.[44]

U.S. Latina texts that dramatize effects of political violence on individual and communal self-definition express similar concerns, presenting the entry of the oppressed into the sanctioned public space as a politicization of marginalized identities and a reassertion of social agency. They suggest forms of resistance to authoritarian oppression by using private concepts, such as motherhood and romantic love, as political and public investments. Situating subject-constitution and subject-positioning in a geopolitical context, these texts emphasize the importance of recognizing geopolitical conditions as a category that significantly affects identity formation. Furthermore, they demonstrate that authoritarian practices permeate all social spaces and manifest themselves as a global phenomenon.

The inclusion of Central American experience in the narratives written for U.S. audiences brings to public attention the issues of U.S. involvement in the region and thus resists American political hegemony and military neo-colonialist practices. It demonstrates that this specific historical moment not only marks the lives of Central Americans but also implicates U.S. citizens. Exposing to visibility what has been erased in the hegemonic practice of media manipulation, Demetria Martínez writes in the introductory note to her novel *Mother Tongue* (1994):

> More than 75,000 citizens of El Salvador died during a twelve-year civil war, which officially ended in 1991. Most died at the hands of their own government. The United States supported this effort with more than $6 billion in military aid. Declassified State Department documents indicate that officials at the highest levels of the U.S. government knew of El Salvador's policy of targeting civilians, including Archbishop Oscar Romero, who was assassinated in 1980. Those in power chose to look the other way. (n. pag.)

Finally, recognizing that identity becomes formed, as Stuart Hall puts it, at the point of intersection between social and psychic reality,[45] I also integrate in my approach some psychonalytic concepts. In order to explain effects of social conditioning on identity formation, I frequently borrow terms from the Freudian theories on defense mechanisms and the Lacanian concepts of self-differentiation.

The interplay between the social and the psychological in the formation of identity is the main premise of psychonalytic theories. Both Freudian and Lacanian approaches indicate a profound impact of the social order in the formation of selfhood, seeing the process of self-differentiation in the symbolic order and during the Oedipal phase as one of the key moments in one's psychological development.[46] Abraham and Torok expand the theory of self-differentiation by arguing that formative influences do not cease after the early stage of self-differentiation, a stage defined by instinctual repression, since all life experiences affect one's identity development. In *The Shell and the Kernel* (1994), they state: "Even an ideally conflict-free childhood cannot escape crisis or catastrophes such as social humiliation, the desolation of war and bereavement, or racial persecution" (10). Abraham and Torok emphasize that repression resides in specific life situations and that major disturbances in self-fashioning may occur at any stage in life. This is an important point because it both recognizes self-formation as an ongoing process and integrates a broader historicizing dimension within a psychoanalytic inquiry. Conceiving of the social order in broader sociopolitical, sociocultural, and socioeconomic contexts, Abraham and Torok's theory expands the historicity of the familial order into the historicity of the public sphere, a social arena that shapes, regulates, and sanctions individual and communal identities.

The complex articulations of this ongoing and assimilating self-formation are the main focus of the selected U.S. Latina texts. Exploring identity constitution in relation to political and cultural oppression, they demonstrate that gender subjugation, racism, cultural dislocation, sexual abuse, exile, and political violence have a profound impact on one's self-formation and subject-positioning. As they place the self at the sites of cultural and geopolitical conflicts, U.S. Latina narratives urgently demand a rethinking of the psychoanalytic theory by emphasizing that formative experiences within the social order transcend the familial dynamics. Underscoring specific material conditions—the social forces of postmodernity—U.S. Latina narratives adamantly assert that discussions of identity must gain a historicized perspective; that is, the analysis of psychic reality must be grounded in a specific sociopolitical and historical context. Furthermore, these texts affirm the possibilities of survival and self-affirmation in conditions of social oppression by identifying specific ways of coping with and transforming oppressive and traumatic moments in the course of transition to empowerment. In this way, they theorize the emergence of subjectivity as a movement away from the objectified positions produced by social forces to the positions of enunciative agency gained in reaction to/against patterns of objectification.

Foregrounding these dialectical and ongoing links between the social and the psychic orders, U.S. Latina texts analyzed in this study force a rethinking of postmodern identities while comprising a rich source for the theorizing on and from U.S. Latina literature.

CHAPTER ONE

Gendered Hybrid Identities:
Maneuvering Between Two Cultures

> *Unlike a Western, postmodernist*
> *notion of agency and consciousness*
> *which often announces the splintering of*
> *the subject, and privileges multiplicity in*
> *the abstract, this is a notion of agency*
> *born of history and geography.*
> —Chandra Mohanty, "Cartographies of Struggle"

Focusing on the specificity of female experience in conditions of racism, colonialism, and patriarchy, Gloria Anzaldúa's *Borderlands/La Frontera: The New Mestiza* (1987) produces feminist theory on subject formation and positioning in a Chicana context. As it attempts to emphasize the difference of minority women's experience of oppression in the U.S., this creative /theoretical writing probes the problematics of female self-definition that is structured by contradicting and competing forces of bicultural conditioning. Using the sociopolitical geography of the U.S.-Mexican border-zone, *Borderlands* examines "living in and straddling of more than one culture" (20) as a conflict of plural identity in conditions of multiple oppression: "Alienated from her mother culture, 'alien' in the dominant culture, the woman of color does not feel safe within the inner life of her Self. Petrified, she can't respond, her face caught between *los intersticios*, the spaces between the different worlds she inhabits" (20).

Anzaldúa's placement of emphasis upon the psychic dislocation and entrapment in the space of cultural "in-betweenness" points at the painful experience of displacement and social marginalization embodied in the "border existence," where one is "caught in the crossfire between camps / [...] not knowing which side to turn to, run from" (194). The confusion of not knowing in which culture one will find acceptance and belonging is intensified with the awareness of the tension between different cultural orders. Furthermore, a *mestiza* subject may experience the hostility of both "camps" directed at her, finding herself doubly isolated and exiled into an unknown territory of non-belonging, and consequently feeling even more anxiety and self-doubt. Anzaldúa connects this sense of alienation and perplexity to the material conditions of racial oppression and gender/sexual objectification present in both Latino and Anglo cultures: "Woman does not feel safe when her own culture, and white culture, are critical of her; when the males of all races hunt her as prey" (20).

Many contemporary U.S. Latina writers engage in similar forms of criticism and investigation of the specifically female "border existence." In their literary works, they explore the problematics of multiple cultural identification by developing female characters who struggle to define themselves at the intersection of distinct cultures. In this chapter, I specifically focus on three U.S. Latina texts that examine the formation of female subjectivity in the polyvalent and ambiguous space of biculturalism. *The Mixquaihuala Letters* (1986) by Ana Castillo and *How The García Girls Lost Their Accents* (1992) by Julia Alvarez portray women characters who struggle to define themselves at the interstice between their Latin American heritage and the dominant U.S. culture. The main protagonists in *The Mixquaihuala Letters* strive to assert freedom and independence from patriarchal conventions that are present in both Mexican and U.S. cultures. Alvarez's characters encounter a discrepancy in gender roles that are constructed in the Dominican Republic and the U.S., and they learn to perform subversions of patriarchy in both cultural domains. Similarly, in their autobiographical work *Getting Home Alive* (1986), co-authors Rosario Morales and Aurora Levins Morales explore their own gender positioning at the crossroads of Puerto Rican and Anglo American cultures, resisting patriarchy in both cultural domains and yet finding inspiration and affirmation of womanhood across distinct and intimate cultures of their multiple identity (U.S., Puerto Rican, Jewish, and Eastern European).

These texts provide important insights into the postmodern border existence because they emphasize the complexity of female self-definition and positioning in the space of biculturalism while exposing different meanings of the bicultural experience. All three works portray biculturalism as a location of probable gender oppression and as a site of potential transformation and emancipation. Underscoring the double-encoded meaning of biculturalism, U.S. Latina authors depart from the unidimensional depiction of the borderlands condition as a state of one's confinement by invincible social forces. While they never lose sight of oppressive sociocultural patterns present in the border experience, as seen in the overt criticism they develop in their writings, their criticism does not end with the portrayal of victimization: U.S. Latina writers also seek modes of individual and communal empowerment by investigating the creative potentiality of the cultural crossroads. In this search, they are careful not to develop a celebratory image of the borderlands, an image that has become prevalent in the postmodern discourse. Often thought of in terms of cultural synthesis and postmodern exoticization of difference,[1] borderlands culture is not presented in U.S. Latina narratives in a fashion of uncritical and uninformed celebration of multiculturalism. U.S. Latina literature demonstrates that even though it seems to be legitimized in the mainstream ideology, the "exotic" difference of borderlands subjects is, in fact, manipulated by the dominant source of power in order to institute a marginalization, rather than a celebration and acceptance, of the "cultural Other." As Eliana Ortega and Nancy Saporta Sternbach emphasize, when diversity is approached without consideration of power relations, it "becomes a celebration of oppression and continues the marginalization of the 'diverse' people in question by assigning them a framed space and date in which to perform" (13).

Focusing on the workings of power used against marginal female subjects, Latina authors assert that women of color in the U.S. are exposed to different forms of marginalization not only in the dominant Anglo sphere but also in their Latino cultures. This is especially obvious in the female experience of oppression by gender ideology. Subjected to demands and expectations of two patriarchal orders, Teresa in *The Mixquiahuala Letters*, for example, is oppressed by patriarchy both at home, the location of her minority cultural heritage, and in the public sphere of Anglo culture. While she moves

between the two spheres, she encounters different and often opposing messages of two cultures and faces the uncertainty and contradictions of bicultural self-definition. In this way, gender positions become complicated by the
multiplicity of value systems and the tension of living "sandwiched between
two cultures" (Anzaldúa 78)that deny female agency and self-affirmation.

Finding themselves at the intersection of distinct cultural realities, minority women often experience the space of "in-betweenness" as a location of
entrapment, confinement, and isolation, where the pressure to perform gender roles in multiple cultural realms intensifies female objectification and
marginalization. However, the space of "in-betweenness" also carries a potential for transformation as it destabilizes the singularity and autonomy of
cultural authority and subsequently provides alternative forms of existence.
As the U.S. Latina texts in this chapter demonstrate, this in-between location
becomes a site of critical maneuver between essentialist and objectifying positions of womanhood. While they struggle to assert agency and freedom, the
women protagonists in these narratives learn to avoid subjugating social protocols and traditions by subverting patriarchy in both cultural domains
through an oppositional, differential positioning. Thus, as the resistance to
domination and oppression is forged in interstices of socio-cultural realities,
the paradigm of female entrapment between distinct cultures is transformed
and resignified into an oppositional movement. Rather than a trendy cultural
form, biculturalism is dramatized as a condition that generates everyday
struggles against cultural patriarchy and produces subjects who develop an
oppositional consciousness.

Strategies of Resistance

Calling attention to oppressive forces that determine constitution and positioning of Chicana subjects, Gloria Anzaldúa's *Borderlands/La Frontera*
also proposes strategies of women's emancipation and transformation. Redefining *mestizaje* as a powerful source of female definition, Anzaldúa develops the concept of "*mestiza* consciousness," a form of awareness and praxis
that entails an acceptance of hybrid racial and ethnic identities while generating positive modes of self-imagining and subject-positioning. This consciousness "comes from continual creative motion that keeps breaking down
the unitary aspect of each new paradigm" (80), validating multiple subjectivity as well as seeking to rupture patterns of oppression present across cultures and traditions. Reading postmodern reality through hybridity, Anzaldúa

urges a tolerance for ambiguity and contradiction as a skill of *mestiza* self-hood. In order to survive the crossroads, "the new *mestiza* copes by developing a tolerance for contradictions, a tolerance for ambiguity... Not only does she sustain contradictions, she turns the ambivalence into something else." (79)

This differential and politicized concept of *mestizaje* has a powerful presence in many U.S. Latina narratives. *The Mixquiahuala Letters* and *Getting Home Alive*, specifically, employ it in strategies of female self-definition as a transformational source of self-affirmation and emancipation. Teresa, a young Mexican-American in *The Mixquiahuala Letters*, embraces her double-voiced identity as she attempts "to find a place to satisfy [her] yearning spirit" (52) and declare independence from "society's tenets of heterosexist stereotypes" (45). In *Getting Home Alive*, Morales and Levins Morales mobilize their multiple cross-ethnic identities to assert affirmative forms of a hybrid being that resists social subjugation and exclusion. In their "Ending Poem" they weave their voices together to re-affirm their *mestiza* selfhood: "I am what I am./ A child of the Américas./ A light-skinned mestiza of the Caribbean./ A child of many diaspora, born into this continent at a crossroads" (212). The teenage sisters in *The García Girls* do not precisely claim this type of hybrid identity, but they engage in a negotiation of two cultural orders to secure liberating forms of self-definition and expression. In the conditions of gender oppression, they adopt the space of biculturalism to develop tactics of resistance and emancipation, and their strategic in-between positioning is transformed into a way of living, "a peculiar mix of Hispanic and American styles" (99) that stays with them throughout their adulthood.

In her elaboration of a "methodology of the oppressed,"[2] Chela Sandoval theorizes strategies of resistance that intervene in the postmodern patterns of objectification and oppression, advocating use of any tools at one's disposition in order to sustain survival and assert resistance. Appropriation of dominant ideological forms and their application in political struggle allows for subversion of oppressive protocols of subjugation and exploitation while ensuring social transformation. The significance of this political proposal lies in the possibility of transformation of the existing material conditions into sources of liberating strategies. Sandoval emphasizes that it is necessary "to comprehend, respond to, and act upon" economic, political, and cultural forces affecting consciousness and identity ("New Sciences" 408), understanding that these forces create "particular subject positions within which the subordinated can legitimately function" ("Feminist Forms of Agency" 57). As she recognizes cultural hybridity as an effect of postmodern conditions of cultural transnationalization, she theorizes it as a "differential postmodern form of oppositional consciousness" and a strategy of survival that has emerged out of postmodernity ("New Sciences" 409).

Relating her argument to Gloria Anzaldúa's concept of "*mestiza* consciousness" and Donna Haraway's "cyborg skills,"[3] Sandoval identifies hybridity's subversive political potential in its principles of mobility, partiality, non-essentialism, and cyborg forms. Undermining master narratives of sociopolitical forces—racism, colonialism, patriarchy, etc—and challenging the singularity of social reality, the positioning in hybridity generates an agency that counters objectification and oppression without reproducing hegemony that such positioning strives to overthrow. This is why Sandoval identifies hybrid positioning as the basis of "differential consciousness:" emerging out of "correlation, intensities, junctures, crises," hybridity initiates a continual movement between/among different oppositional ideological positionings ("Feminist Forms of Agency" 59).

In addition, validating the impossibility of wholeness and exposing the limitations of essentialism, the hybrid mode of being generates coalitional forms of social positioning, forms that insist on an alignment of different social subjects and theories around affinity rather than difference. Such lines of affinity, asserts Sandoval, occur through "attraction, combination, and relation carved out of and in spite of difference" ("New Sciences" 413). This is the political/critical stance articulated in both U.S. third-world feminism and Haraway's cyborg manifesto, political philosophies invested in "affinity-through-difference" for the sake of individual and social transformation. Sandoval sees the urgency of coalitional positioning precisely in the conditions of postmodern globalization that work across difference and essence in "techno-human" space.

Sandoval's theory advocates a flexibility of political praxis, asserting that polymorphous forces of oppression cannot be countered from a homogenous position and by a single strategy of resistance: "The differential mode of social movement and consciousness depends on the practitioner's ability to read the current situation of power and self-consciously choosing and adopting the ideological stand best suited to push against its configurations" (*Methodology of the Oppressed* 59). Sandoval demands a differential form of social movement that can challenge the spatially and temporally shifting forces of postmodernity, a political agency that operates differentially while enlisting horizontal and vertical alignments of oppositional praxis. As she is proposing new forms of social activism, Sandoval is also calling for new subjectivities, strategic and multiple, grounded in a differential oppositional movement. She emphasizes them as "tactical and performative" and with "the capacity to de- and re-center depending upon the kinds of oppression to be confronted, depending upon the history of the moment" ("Feminist Forms of Agency" 60).

The U.S. Latina texts studied in this chapter present "tactical and performative" subjectivities that appropriate different strategies of opposition not in organized social movements but in individual, everyday struggles. In order to ensure emancipation and transformation of individual realities, these differential subjects engage in oppositional forms of enunciation, contesting and deconstructing forces of subjugation that act upon them in their present moment. As Chandra Mohanty points out (see the epigraph to this chapter), this form of agency is generated out of the material conditions and the lived experience of women of color. It is formed at the level of everyday life, configuring one's self-identity and political consciousness within the context of specific socio-political and cultural forces—at the intersection of gender, race, class, sexuality, and geopolitics. Facing multiple forms and sites of oppression, the new subjectivities perform strategies of resistance that utilize their multiple identities in order to contest the hegemonic dualistic paradigms of "self vs. other." In this way, their agency is formed through a becoming that resists social forces and is directed toward a politicized mode of being that generates differential consciousness. In addition, although their agency is a response to specific social conditions, it also stems from their fluid positioning across cultural, generational, racial, and class boundaries.

The Mixquiahuala Letters: Postmodern Strategies of Female Resistance and Emancipation

Ana Castillo's *Mixquiahuala Letters* dramatizes a female quest for identity and self-affirmation through a number of lyrical and introspective letters that the main narrator, Teresa, writes to her friend, Alicia. The letters are centered on Teresa and Alicia's adventurous trips to Mexico and depict a development of the women's friendship as they fight for the same cause— independence from social limitations and freedom of self-definition. Castillo employs the first-person narrative voice in order to reflect female selfhood in an intimate and direct way, as well as to grant agency to woman's subjectivity and self-exploration. The self-reflexive style of the letters provides insights into the inner struggles of women caught between personal desires and repressive demands of the social order. In this way, the epistolary form of the novel allows the female subject to be the central consciousness in the textual narration as well as in the individual self-evolvement, connecting the discursive agency with the self-defined subjectivity.[4]

The main protagonists, Teresa and Alicia, engage in a cross-national movement between the U.S. and Mexico in search of a new cultural space that would allow them a liberating sexual agency instead of the objectified roles that they are assigned in both cultures. In this process of perpetual and subversive crossing, the women experience different forms of patriarchal abuse and objectification, but they also develop cross-cultural practices and alliances that help them ensure survival and resistance in the cultural domains governed by patriarchy and racism. As Roland Walter argues, the novel's politics of dislocation and relocation provides a mode of "counter-hegemony in the Chicano borderlands" (92).

In the opening letter, the patriarchal concept of *machismo*[5] is immediately exposed as Teresa humorously describes her relatives: her uncle Fermín, who likes to flirt with women although he is married; her aunt, who does not go anywhere without her husband; and another uncle, who "cannot see a woman driving for anything in the world" or "a woman gallivanting around without her man" (17–18). This humorous tone, however, is not for the sake of a light and charming ethnographic lesson: right away it rings a satiric note that will grow into a direct and sharp criticism as the letters begin describing Teresa's and Alicia's experiences of patriarchal oppression.

Mapping out the protagonists' back-and-forth trips between Mexico and the U.S., Ana Castillo discloses that the ways in which women are objectified are similar in both cultures. In Mexico, the two women are immediately categorized as "loose" because they travel alone, and in the U.S. their sexuality is labeled "homo" for they oppose marital conventions. Castillo goes on to assert that marriage stereotypes are strongly present in both cultures: "Stones of silent condemnation were thrown from every direction; relatives and friends who believed that 'bad wives' were bad people" (29). Subjected to patriarchal stereotypes in two cultures, Teresa and Alicia's quest for self-definition becomes further complicated as they experience a double weight of oppression and subjugation. Encountering the competing and contradictory forces of biculturalism, they experience an intensified form of patriarchal gender ideology and find themselves entrapped between two cultural domains. As Alvina Quintana notes, this text defines a woman's experience while she is maneuvering between opposing realities that fail to acknowledge her existence (*Home Girls* 83). This tactical maneuver reveals that although cultural realities in Mexico and the U.S. are distinct and often opposing, they have similar protocols and norms of female subjugation. Patriarchy is thus unmasked as a cross-cultural phenomenon: although its articulation may vary in specific socio-cultural conditions, its patterns of oppression invariably target women as the subordinate sex.

Criticizing patriarchy as a cross-national practice, *The Mixquiahuala Letters* also exposes institutionalized forms of gender oppression. Throughout the narrative, traditional Catholicism is portrayed as another system of patriarchal control, governed by limiting and contradictory norms that define women only in relation to men and condemn them as sinful for being in this relation. Being an integral part of the Latino experience, traditional Catholicism acts as an arbiter in social regulation of gender roles in Latino communities. The author unmasks the patriarchal logic of the Catholic church and its morals in Letter Four, where Teresa remembers her first confessional with a priest who did not trust her sexual innocence:

> He began to probe. When that got him no titillating results, he suggested, or more precisely, led an interrogation founded on Gestapo technique. When i didn't waver under the torment, although feeling my knees raw, air spare, he accused outright: *Are you going to tell me that you haven't wanted to be with a man? You must have let one do more than...than what?* (30)

The passage shows the religious myth of female purity colliding with the social stereotype of female sinfulness. Constituted by male desire, women are condemned as the sole guilt bearers, although men apparently participate in the same "sinful" act. The dichotomy of *la virgen/la puta* (virgin/whore) reveals its dynamic labeling of womanhood in relation to male expectations. While woman faces the impossible demands of the patriarchal order, requiring her to be saintly, she is at the same time morally accused for the impossibility of this task. Her very physicality and humanity become regarded as her failure, or, conversely, her lack of complicity with male sexual desire is seen as a frustration of man's libidinal energy.

Constructing Teresa and Alicia's trips as a search for emancipation and a process of self-exploration, the novel advocates a rebellion against female victimization. Experimenting with different sexual encounters in Mexico, Teresa and Alicia take control of their sexuality. They refuse male definitions of womanhood and assert agency and freedom of self-definition. Teresa clearly articulates this when a Mexican man mistakes woman's liberation for sexual promiscuity. She corrects him: "What you perceive as 'liberal' is my independence to choose what i do, with whom, and when. Moreover, it also means that i may choose not to do it, with anyone, ever" (79). When insisting on freedom from men's restrictive rules, woman becomes marked again as a transgressor—an immoral and worthless person: "Liberal: trash, whore, bitch" (79). Situating gender and sexuality in a cross-cultural context, this scene points out a clash of signification: woman's struggle for self-determination and sexuality receives a different signifying context in the two cultures. In Mexico, it still denotes a transgressive, non-permissible behavior that places woman in a stigmatized and outcast position: "In that country, the term 'liberated woman' meant something other than what we had strived for back in the United States. In this case it simply meant a woman who would sleep nondiscriminately with any man who came along" (79). Determined to continue their feminist struggle in Mexico too, Teresa and Alicia consciously assert their emancipated subjectivities against the patriarchal stereotype of a (married) woman that supposes her to be de-sexed, de-physicalized, and domesticated: they adopt a counter action, leaving the domestic space and openly asserting their sexuality and physicality in the public domain.

However, Ana Castillo is careful to warn that a rebellion against patriarchal oppression is not an easy and safe task. As the novel traces the women's oppositional movement in the public space, it also demonstrates that female positioning in the social arena poses a threat to women's physical safety. Teresa and Alicia's cause becomes imperiled when they are physically threatened by sexual abuse and manipulation. Not skilled to resist violence and not possessing a comparable physical strength, they remain vulnerable and defenseless before the physical dominance of men. In addition, they know that they are not protected by society: patriarchal abuse is justified by the traditional social concept of woman's submissiveness and man's sexual need. Letter 23 dramatizes the female vulnerability and lack of protection before male aggressiveness. Teresa remembers a party where Alicia almost got raped:

                        [a]n invitation to dance
    in the auditorium
                with bored men fed up with poker
                who should have had to coerce you
    twist your arm threaten your life
    lead you bodily in had only to *ask* you to dance...
                        Again, the self appointed
    guardian, i follow
                knowing there is little in the end i can do. i have a vagina too. With
    all the tender fat which makes me soft like veal there are no muscles developed to
    protect you no black belt with reflex of a paralyzing kick in the neck or groin no
    hidden blade in my hair no pistol in my bag to surprise them when they attack and
    they will attack because they are bored and they've been *waiting* for you. (84)

The physical abuse of women is presented via the traditional perception of woman as a submissive object of male desire: "The legend that you were for taking ... sentenced you that night" (84). This episode points out that transgression of social codes causes not only social scorn but also a physical threat: "[w]omen traveling alone were vulnerable to harassment from all sorts" (91). Castillo utilizes the image of female vulnerability to reinforce the concept of patriarchal oppression. Treated only as objects of men's needs, women are denied agency and 'integrity,'[6] and when they rebel against the mute, passive roles assigned to them, they face violent abuse.

In her article "The Politics of Rape" (1996), María Herrera-Sobek claims that textual utilization of sexual assault scenes encodes a political metaphor for society's marginalization of women. She analyzes several Chicana texts that incorporate the theme of rape,[7] viewing the literary topic of sexual assault as a motif that engages the reader in a reconstruction of the female experience from the victim's perspective. *The Mixquiahuala Letters* offers this reconstruction, too: although Teresa and Alicia act as free agents in search of their self-affirmation, their quest is marked by numerous experiences of victimization and maltreatment by men. Many of Teresa's letters express the victim's experiences and painful recollections of abuse, revealing violations of Teresa's selfhood and her feelings of alienation and loss. Herrera-Sobek observes that sexual violation symbolizes the final act that obliterates women from the social system. The process of raping transforms women into "silent, invisible, non-existent entities" (249). The victim loses her identity as a human being and is transformed into a formless object. In *The Mixquiahuala*

Letters, Ana Castillo describes this psychological loss of form and subjectivity as a physical obliteration: "It happened quickly. They were anxious to have you, chew you up, one would have the legs, the other a breast, devour and throw your bones into the ocean, never to be heard of again" (84). The encoded threat of sexual assault in this scene points toward the male perception of women as non-identities, as objects to be thrown away after being used up. Teresa is immediately aware of this danger when Alicia joins several drunken men in a dance, and she dares to interfere. Impulsively, she shatters the mute passivity by cursing and shouting at the men: "Leave her be! Son of a bitch! Leave her alone or..." (84). Teresa's voice becomes the only means of resistance and refusal, the only way to assert woman's existence against sexual appropriation. The men leave, looking surprised that somebody dared to interrupt their "game." The women remain scared: they have escaped physical violence in this instance but are aware of its permanent threat. As Carl Gutiérrez-Jones argues in his analysis of the novel, the process of patriarchal gender construction continues "after an only momentary challenge" as it keeps on undermining the women's attempts at liberal self-definition (*Rethinking the Borderlands* 117).

The structural power of patriarchy—often exercised through physical violence, as shown in the previous scene—is indubitably strong enough to subdue female opposition. Teresa is unable to finish her "threat"—"leave her alone *or*..." (84, emphasis mine)—understanding that she cannot do anything to counter the violent force. However, the attempt to challenge it, and not give up challenging it, demonstrates a subjectivity that is oppositional and resistant. Renouncing limiting and objectifying roles designed for women in the patriarchal order, the female protagonists refuse to be passive victims of patriarchy. They adopt Chela Sandoval's concept of "oppositional consciousness" by evolving into differentiating, self-representing, and oppositional subjectivities, who are, first, able to recognize patterns of subjugation and, then, ready to resist them. Teresa conveys this in one of her letters:

> It was apparent i was no longer prepared to face a mundane life of need and resentment, accept monogamous commitments and honor patriarchal traditions, and wanted to be rid of the husband's guiding hand, holidays with family and in-laws, led by a contradicting God, society, road and street signs, and, most of all, my poverty. Its drabness. (28)

This argument disagrees with Norma Alarcón's understanding of female agency in *The Mixquiahuala Letters*. In Alarcón's discussion of this narrative,[8] the critic regards Teresa and Alicia's opposition as unsuccessful, claiming that although they act as free agents in their expression and practice of sexuality they still remain imprisoned by heterosexist ideology. It is true that Teresa and Alicia often adopt heterosexist ideology as they explore different sexual experiences. Even when they face male manipulation and humiliation, they are sometimes unable to break away. Many times, Teresa goes back to her husband when she feels lonely, and Alicia looks for comfort in other men when her boyfriend leaves her. Also, when the novel is read, as Carl Gutiérrez-Jones suggests, through a lesbian erotic register, Teresa and Alicia's relationship and positioning are undoubtedly frustrated by heterosexuality. Gutiérrez-Jones, too, sees their transgression undercut by the persistent desire to connect with men; but, as he points out, this "failure" is critically connected to larger forces that determine social interrelations (*Rethinking Borderlands* 117). Teresa herself begins to understand this connection, becoming aware of the patriarchal manipulation via heterosexual norms. Therefore, what distinguishes these women as oppositional, instead of simply "imprisoned" by heterosexuality, is their awareness of being entrapped:

> We were not free of society's tenets of heterosexist stereotypes to be convinced we could exist indefinitely without the demands and complications one aggregated with the supreme commitment to a man.
>
> Even greater than these factors was that of an ever present need, emotional, psychological, physical...it provoked us nonetheless to seek approval from man through sexual meetings...(45)

As Roland Walter asserts, the significance of Castillo's narrative lies in its emphasis upon the necessity of a female liberatory struggle. However, while he states that the novel's importance "does not so much reside in the ways and outcome of the liberatory struggle" (85), I find the methodology of female resistance considerably significant for the meaning of this feminist text.

By illustrating the women's need for social integration, Castillo exposes the power of patriarchal ideology to persistently deny female agency and self-determination. In fact, this need for man's approval points to the "larger forces," the social order that exploits and solidifies the social marginalization of women. In addition, these very moments of subjugation and objectification act as transformative forces in their continual struggle, for an impetus for resistance arises in the moment of oppression. Teresa's and Alicia's experiences of marginalization and confinement by patriarchy initiate their quest for liberation, and as they actively and often effectively employ some forms of resistance and subversion, they demonstrate agency and differential consciousness in their quest for self-determination. Their strategies parallel what Chela Sandoval defines as the "methodology of the oppressed," methods of survival and resistance in conditions of objectification and subjugation.

In her article, "New Sciences: Cyborg Feminism and the Methodology of the Oppressed" (1995), Sandoval identifies specific methods of resistance: 1) semiology, or sign-reading; 2) deconstruction; 3) meta-ideologizing; 4) democratics; and 5) differential movement. These five technologies together comprise a "methodology of the oppressed" that leads to "differential mode of oppositional social movement" (410). Sandoval emphasizes that these forms directly emerge from conditions of domination and are developed by the oppressed to secure survival under hegemony. The oppressed are not only women but also all disenfranchised/colonized people. This is an important claim for it generates grounds for alliance and coalition and thus advocates a joined struggle against all forms of oppression. The major strengths of this coalitional practice are the multiplicity of positions, the movement across boundaries, and "affinity-through-difference" (413). In addition, this oppositional praxis can be applied in any condition and site of disempowerment since its technologies are translatable and adaptable across specific contexts. Sandoval adds that the methodology of the oppressed is, in fact, a methodology of emancipation as the end goal of these resistant practices is not only a survival but also a complete liberation of the subjugated.[9]

Sandoval identifies U.S. third world feminism as a specific form of oppositional consciousness that is generated through the methodology of the oppressed. Employing hybrid differential forms of resistance and opposition, U.S. third world feminism has developed its particular subaltern politics that recognizes difference but allows a community across difference, across racial, ethnic, gender, sex, and class specificities. In this practice, U.S. third world feminism advocates a non-essentialist, hybrid, and mutable form of being that emerges in contradictory moments and in conditions of hegemony and subjugation.

The Mixquiahuala Letters, as a literary practice of U.S. third world feminism, promotes a methodology of resistance based on critical opposition and differential positioning. The novel emphasizes that such resistance is not just an active participation but, above all, a form of consciousness. Teresa and Alicia's ideological positioning against patriarchy is fundamental in their struggle against female subjugation. Even though they are not always able to resist their oppression effectively, they are able to recognize and challenge their victimization. In addition, their awareness and conscious resistance allow them to use empowering strategies against what Norma Alarcón calls "imprisonment." Based on oppositional differential consciousness, Teresa and Alicia's "acting as free agents" is a much more self-conscious activity than Alarcón has suggested.

Castillo's narrative protagonists consciously confront stereotypical concepts of womanhood in both cultures through deconstruction and critical opposition: they de-mythologize *marianismo* and *machismo*, traditional concepts of gender roles in Latino cultures, by exposing these social norms as culturally encoded concepts of female inferiority and submission and thus oppressive protocols of male control. Teresa's introspective letters disclose distinct norms of conduct for men and women, condemning a double standard that allows all freedom to men while denying it to women. Also, they illustrate that *machismo* exists across cultures as a patriarchal system that assigns woman a role of a sacrificing and submissive caregiver without granting her individual freedom:

> A woman takes care of the man she has made her life with, cleans, cooks, washes his underwear, does as if he were her only child, as if he had come out of her womb. In exchange, he may pay her bills, he may not. He may give her acceptance into society by replacing her father's name with his, or he may choose to not. He may make her feel like a woman, or rather, how she has been told a woman feels with a man—or he may not. (118)

By emphasizing the women's awareness of these patriarchal codes and their refusal to conform to them, Ana Castillo demonstrates their capacity to read cultural signs below the surface and assert an agentic subversion of male ideology. In order to convey the characters' subversion of feminine gender roles, the author allows them to borrow from masculine ideology. To reclaim their own freedom, Teresa and Alicia exploit the "male code" of behavior—sexual freedom, personal independence, decision to travel alone, drink, smoke, etc. This practice of meta-ideologizing, of using the very tools that confine women, de-essentializes gender[10] and allows an appropriation of patriarchal practices as tools for transformation and emancipation. Castillo affirms Sandoval's claim that a strategic appropriation of dominant ideological forms may engender some form of liberation. It is important to emphasize that this is a temporary solution, but it, nevertheless, serves as a potent criticism of the dominant social structure.

By engaging her protagonists in a feminist resistance through practices of critical opposition, deconstruction, semiology, and meta-ideologizing, the author criticizes and rejects cultural/sexual stereotypes created in both Mexican and Anglo American cultures. However, she does not completely discard and break away from these cultures. By allowing her narrative protagonists to find liberating concepts in the available cultural material, Castillo advocates a new hybrid consciousness, an awareness of multiple cultural self-definition and inclusiveness of different cultural traditions. As they adopt a critical stance toward Anglo-American and Mexican cultural traditions, Teresa and Alicia embrace both cultures through a strategic hybridity. They enjoy the greater agency that women have in the U.S., but they also need the close connection with family and community experienced in the Mexican tradition. They choose to define themselves at the crossroads of two cultures, resisting cultural hegemony and patriarchy while, at the same time, synthesizing different emancipatory positions. As Gloria Anzaldúa asserts, "in attempting to work out a synthesis, the self has added a third element, [...] a new consciousness—a *mestiza* consciousness..." (79–80). Born out of a struggle for self-survival, the new consciousness brings about a divergent thinking while breaking down oppositional binarisms and inflexible boundaries; it engages multiple self-definition and positioning in order to ensure existence at the crossroads.

As a Mexican-American, Teresa experiences Mexican culture as an intimate part of her identity. For her, the journey to Mexico becomes a way of reconnecting with her primordial being: "There was a definite call to find a place to satisfy my yearning spirit, the Indian in me that had begun to cure the ails of humble folk distrustful of modern medicine; a need for the sapling woman for the fertile earth that nurtured her growth. [i] searched for my home... [i] chose Mexico" (52). Castillo posits that the reconnection with Mexican culture and people gives Teresa a sense of belonging to the originary place while affirming her double-voiced self: "i too was of that small corner of the world. i was of that mixed blood, of fire and stone, timber and vine, a history passed down from mouth to mouth, since the beginning of time..." (101). Teresa needs this affirmation of belonging and origins as an antidote to patriarchal and racial discrimination that she encounters as a woman of color. Paradoxically, she seeks affirmation in the culture that provides her with a source of desired self-identification and simultaneously denies her agency of free female identification by its patriarchal protocols. This tension points back toward her ambivalent need to be accepted back into society and yet be independent of its patriarchal tenets, a condition that is frequently denied to her but that she nevertheless struggles to accomplish.

Alicia is a white American of Spanish/European descent, but her racial identification is presented throughout the narrative in ambiguous and shifting terms. Although she has darker skin (her grandmother supposedly was a Spanish Roma) and can pass in Latin America as a non-gringa—"couldn't they see by our coloring that we were not gringas" (69)—Teresa identifies her as a "priviledged white girl of the suburbs" (48) and a "WASP chick or JAP from Manhattan's west side" (50), seeing Alicia's upper-class and European origin as "white, privileged, and unjust" (50). Initially thinking that they "could not possibly relate" (50), Teresa changes her perception after they become friends. "You were partially white," (50) Teresa concludes, realizing that they share, in spite of differences, a common experience of patriarchal oppression and female solidarity.[11]

Sharing with Teresa the same quest for an emancipated selfhood, Alicia, too, experiences Mexican culture as a catalyst for her self-definition. As she gets to know intimately Mexican people, customs, places, and history, she finds a source of affirmation and inspiration. By fusing different cultural experiences, she finds a source for her greater personal freedom and creativity. "The idea of the journey that would lead from ruin to ruin offered your creativity new dimensions..." (52), writes Teresa to Alicia in one of the letters. Castillo shows that cultural hybridity may be used as a strategy that allows one to make connections to his/her deepest feelings and sense of self. At the same time, this self-knowledge may offer an entry into the knowledge of the Other, transcending difference and creating cross-connections.

Both female protagonists challenge paradigms of unicultural and national self-definition by fusing different cultural horizons and grounding their identities in the polyvalent space of cultural hybridity. Castillo demonstrates that this synthesis of different cultural aspects does not present a mere assembly but a creative selection and combination that is used as a strategy of resistance and critical positioning. Questioning of tradition does not signify a complete refusal of the traditional, she conveys in her narrative, but rather a critical contestation and deconstruction of the systems of control and power. Teresa and Alicia break paradigms of patriarchal regulation and cultural prejudices but also explore new ways by being hybrid and mobile. Their perspective is oppositional and yet synthesizing: they develop new strategies of self-creation through a constant movement between essentialist definitions of gender and ethnic identity. This movement is symbolized in their geographical border-crossings, through which they develop and affirm their fluid and multiple subjectivities.

In addition, Ana Castillo underscores that women's alliances do not have to base their strategy and unity on the premise of essentialism; rather, their coalition and methodology should be based on political affinities and common agendas. Teresa and Alicia unite not only because they are women, but also because they share the experience of oppression and are determined to transform their objectification. As postmodern subjects, they embrace their particularized conditions but sustain the possibility of shared knowledge and experience through which they can initiate a joined transformation of individual and social identities. This is a political action that takes difference into account but departs from essentialist confines in order to generate a radical sociopolitical change.

It has to be emphasized that even though *The Mixquiahuala Letters* portrays a female experience of patriarchy in sometimes different racial and ethnic terms, it underscores that feminist alliances and methods of resistance are grounded in solidarity and unity. This is why it cannot be said that this text addresses the concerns of only Chicanas and other women of color. What is crucial here is the experience of oppression that is not exclusively racialized or ethnicized. The narrative shows that Alicia is abused and threatened by patriarchy although she is not a "woman of color," according to Teresa. Even though they are not related through ethnic or racial "essence," Ana Castillo unites these women in a struggle for the same cause—the resistance to patriarchal oppression and the "New Woman's Emergence" (35)—foregrounding the shared ideological positioning and what Chandra Mohanty emphasizes as the "common context of struggle rather than color or racial identifications"(7).

How The García Girls Lost Their Accents: Claiming Alternative Gender Positioning

How The García Girls Lost Their Accents by Julia Alvarez depicts gender struggles in a context of the immigrant experience by tracing the growth of feminist consciousness as an effect of acculturation and new ethnic identification. The Garcías are an upper-class family that immigrates to the U.S., escaping political violence in their native Dominican Republic. As they struggle to adjust to their new life in New York City, the four teenage daughters quickly learn from their bicultural experience. The discrepancy between the gender politics in the native and immigrant locations allows the sisters to recognize the patriarchal order of their family and native culture, as well as to perceive positive alternatives to subjugated gender positions. Although their subsequent assimilation results in a loss of their original cultural identity, it also provides them with a more liberating self-image and gender consciousness.

In the opening part of the novel, Julia Alvarez introduces the patriarchal order of an upper-class Dominican family. Although it seems that Yolanda García's rich aunts and cousins do not lack socioeconomic power and independence—"women with households and authority in their voices" (11)—patriarchal ideology is strongly present in their lives. Upper class women have access to privileges of education and social influence, but these privileges are owned and controlled by men: "Carmencita's quip in English is the product of her two or three years away in boarding school in the States. Only the boys stay for college" (6), Yolanda comments on her Dominican cousin's education, noticing the difference between male and female access to higher education. Also, even though they are not forced to do housework, wealthy Dominican women uphold typical gender roles by governing their households and satisfying the ideal of devoted mothers and wives: they "supervise their cooks in preparing supper for their husbands who will troop home after Happy Hour" (7). The deceptiveness of female authority is revealed as the men follow a hypocritical macho conduct: "this is the hour during which a Dominican male of a certain class stops in on his mistress on his way home to his wife" (7), learns Yolanda from one of her male cousins who "bragged that the pre-dinner hour should be called Whore Hour" (7).

Focusing on the question of social class in the opening scene, the novel sets out to demystify the patriarchal logic of social hierarchy. The social category of class inevitably intersects with gender dynamics, conditioning the articulation of patriarchal dominance. The author asserts that even though women with a certain amount of economic power may not experience acute oppression in patriarchal society, they still remain victims of male ideology. In fact, their economic and social distinction usually comes from their wealthy fathers or husbands and is given to them as an affirmation of male authority and prestige. Even though the upper-class women enjoy this limited and relative power, other women become subjugated by it: the maids in the de la Torre family clearly have a subordinate status and are treated as inferior and ignorant by their doñas. In this context, the wealthy women's complicity with patriarchy functions to ensure a continuation of female subjugation and thus affirm male power in the domestic space. Instead of wives, maids carry the weight of all housework duties and are often sexually exploited by their male employers.[12] In this way, the presence of housemaids, who act as recipients of double oppression, preserves the patriarchal order and provides an illusion of the upper-class women's emancipation.

The novel emphasizes that the patriarchal order seeks to uphold this false consciousness in order to maintain its own power and authority. Manipulating prerogatives of the upper-class, patriarchy provides the illusion of female power in the domestic space while preserving male domination in the sociopolitical sphere, and, by extension, in the private domain. Alvarez reveals the limitedness and deceptiveness of the Dominican concept of social class by exposing the lack of female freedom even within the domestic space of wealthy housewives: Yolanda's mother comes to understand that her position is of "a high-class house slave" (143). This consciousness is granted to the female protagonist only after she arrives in the U.S. and experiences possibilities that extend beyond the domestic setting, allowing her to be more than "just a wife and a mother" (143). Her desire to come up with a successful invention for the consumerist U.S. market reflects her need to take an active part in the public sphere and earn her own economic power and social reputation. Her teenage daughters ridicule her ambitions, expecting her to be a devoted mother and a dedicated care-taker of her family: "[t]hey needed help figuring out who they were... and here was their own mother, who didn't have a second to help them puzzle any of this out, inventing gadgets to make life easier for the American moms" (138). This scene shows that the girls uphold the patriarchal gender dynamic in their mother's case, although they themselves are eager to transgress the traditional female roles. In fact, they realize that it is better to have their mother distracted with her inventions than "on [their] cases all the time" (139). Discouraged by her family, Laura García gives up inventing but still insists on doing work outside the house. By cleaning and organizing her husband's medical office she deploys the role of "a devoted wife" to obtain more self-affirmation and independence. She also takes evening classes in economics and business, seeing education as a way to social empowerment and gender emancipation in the new, immigrant location: "Recently she had begun spreading her wings, taking adult courses in real estate and international economics and business management, dreaming of a bigger-than-family-size life for herself" (116). Of course, the need for intellectual participation in society points toward the feminist struggle of middle/upper-class women, and while this feminist concern alienates economically disadvantaged women, it reaffirms the pervasiveness of patriarchy across class boundaries: the division between the domestic and public spheres is maintained in all social strata to reinforce female subjugation and thus facilitate male dominance in the social order.

Unmasking the patriarchal logic in the division of social space, Alvarez's novel also exposes a double standard in the regulation of gender roles. Focusing on a female experience of immigration, *The García Girls* exploits the inconsistency of socially regulated gender positions to suggest a subversive potential of the spatial division "private vs. public," which the text also translates into the binarism of "home(land) vs. exile(land)." Laura's daughters' coming of age takes place in the U.S. and is troubled by the discrepancy between the gender politics of their home and of the public sphere. Their gender consciousness is shaped in the domestic space by the typical patriarchal ideology, represented in the authority figure of their father. "'I don't want loose women in my family,' he had cautioned all his daughters. Warnings were delivered communally, for even though there was usually the offending daughter of the moment, every woman's character could use extra scolding" (28). In the social sphere, on the other hand, the García girls learn that being "loose" signifies a free, uninhibited womanhood that allows them power and personal autonomy. As in *The Mixquiahuala Letters*, the negative connotation of emancipated womanhood in the Dominican Republic reveals its positive signification in the U.S. as "loose" in the context of female experience translates into "free." The conflict arises when the girls try to negotiate these opposing messages that remain with them even in adulthood, internalized as a "peculiar mix of Catholicism and agnosticism, Hispanic and American styles" (99).

However, this opposition between "Hispanic and American styles" opens up a space for critical consciousness. Focusing on the conflictual processes of multiple cultural self-definition, Alvarez underscores the subversiveness encoded in a bicultural upbringing. Perceiving alternatives to subjugated female selfhood, the girls begin to question the traditional gender ideology and challenge their father's authority. The first sister to openly rebel against his repressive control is the youngest one. When he invades her privacy and accuses her of "unchaste" behavior, Sofía leaves home and marries without her father's consent. Years later, she tries to reconcile with him, but when he does not recognize her effort, she challenges him again—this time by embarrassing him in public. During their favorite family game, Sofía gives an erotic kiss to her blindfolded father and exposes his pleasure. She seizes his accusation of her sexual transgression and hurls it back on him, revealing the hypocrisy of the double standard. As Ellen McCracken points out, the tactic of subversion in this scene remains at the level of protofeminism, directed to the symptoms rather than the patriarchal repression (*New Latina Narrative* 160). However, as in *The Mixquiahuala Letters*, this practice of "meta-ideologizing" projects an oppositional consciousness, for the very norms of patriarchal control are temporarily appropriated as a mechanism of subversion. Even though it is a momentary intervention within the oppressive structure, the appropriation of dominant tools requires an understanding of the workings of power and thus promises a further advancement of oppositional movement.

This clash between father and daughter projects the conflictual processes of the Garcías' immigrant experience, where traditional gender roles collide with the liberated gender consciousness. At the site of this conflicting encounter, the girls begin to form a critical consciousness that contests the tradition of female subjugation and privileges liberating cultural attempts at gender equality. Alvarez asserts that the girls' acculturation in the immigrant space of the U.S. proceeds not only from their desire to fit in their peers' world but also from their need to ensure more independence and affirmation for their evolving selves. Their struggle to "figure out who they were" (138) is primarily based on their need for positive self-images in both cultural and gender terms. Finding tools of emancipation available in the 1960s U.S. social arena, the García sisters readily engage in subversions of sociocultural traditions present in both Anglo and Dominican society. Similar to *The Mixquiahuala Letters*, Alvarez's novel presents the immigrant, or "border," experience as a condition that generates critical consciousness. Defined by contradictory and ambiguous processes of cultural adjustment, immigrant biculturalism destabilizes authority of both original and adopted cultural traditions, bringing about a critical examination and contestation of what has been projected as essential and natural. This new way of perceiving the order of sociocultural values and norms engenders, as the novel shows, a set of different subversive practices that can be adopted interchangeably, depending on specific circumstances.

The girls perform subversions of patriarchy not only in their U.S. household but also in the traditional environment of the Dominican Republic, where gender roles are stricter and machismo more pervasive. As they deploy the same strategy of importing the gender politics of the public sphere into the domestic, their subversion is again directed against the patriarchy of the home(land). They educate their young Dominican cousins about women's emancipation, they argue with men about gender equality, and they talk to their aunts about women's rights. This consciousness-raising could be interpreted as a colonizing attitude of the first-world feminism in a third-world country; however, the environment where it is undertaken is more than privileged, as the opening scene of the book reminds us. Rather, the girls' feminist mission is governed again by their immigrant/bicultural experience that has provided them with alternative ways of seeing and being, with the ability to perceive from both the inside and the outside. When their youngest sister falls in love with a controlling and chauvinistic Dominican boyfriend, they manipulate the Dominican social code of female chaperoning to break up the ongoing love affair: they stage a scene to reveal that Fifi is seeing her boyfriend without any supervision, which spurs their mother to immediately take Fifi back to the U.S. They also challenge their cousin Mundín, who upholds the patriarchal norm of female chastity before marriage as he assumes that his younger sister must be a "virgin." While the girls challenge him, facing him as "a line-up of feminists" (125), the double standard is questioned: "For all his liberal education in the States, and all his sleeping around there and here, and all his eager laughter when his Americanized cousins recount their misadventures, his own sister has to be pure" (125). Mundín's patriarchal logic follows the distinction between the private and the public as he also perceives the opposition between the Dominican Republic as a space of the intimate, personal realm—the home(land)—and the U.S. as an outside, public location—the space of exile/immigration. Because of his schooling in the U.S., Mundín himself has some bicultural experience that allows him to recognize the discrepancy between gender norms in the more protected and regulated "home(land)" and out in "the world," where female transgression is allowed. But, upholding the male order, he knows that the boundaries between the two social spheres should not be erased.

Dramatizing the García girls' continual rebellion against social norms, the novel affirms the significance of female agency and feminist consciousness. Its espousal of female subversiveness constitutes a departure from the traditional *Bildungsroman* plot.[13] As Annie Eysturoy argues, traditional female *Bildungs* stories trace the development of the female protagonist through her acceptance of and adjustment to traditional social expectations, while her identity formation reaches its completion by the affirmation of her social role. In *The García Girls*, however, the female protagonists affirm their selfhood through a refusal of predetermined social roles and conducts. The sisters struggle to define their emerging identities in the context of the communal sphere, both Anglo American and Dominican, but they do not accept its restricting norms. They strive to create their own non-confining creative spaces within the social arena, while learning to appropriate social norms as strategies of subversion and emancipation.

Using the space of biculturalism to detect contradictions and defects of patriarchal repression, Alvarez's narrative protagonists perform a maneuver between two cultures and gender ideologies. The García girls' subversive in-between movement allows them to assert self-affirmation and independence. Similarly, their mother claims an emancipated gender positioning by strategically using her access to both cultures: "She still did the lip service to the old ways, while herself nibbling away at forbidden fruit" (116). While her daughters have an easier access to mainstream culture and its liberating practices—the college years provide not only a quick acculturation but also a time away from "the traditional ways" of their home—Laura cannot leave the domestic space that easily. Struggling with a new language and still upholding the authority of her husband, Laura is forced to employ less direct strategies of female subversion of patriarchy. In addition, her experiences of exilic uprooting and social marginalization in the new location complicate her transition to new cultural practices and her acceptance of the new social environment, which I discuss in my analysis of exile in Chapter Three.

Engaging the female protagonists in a creative negotiation of two cultures, *The García Girls* suggests tactics of resistance and emancipation encoded in the space of biculturalism. The novel maps out the emergence of a consciousness that is differential and oppositional, being directed toward self-affirmation and emancipation. As the García women enter the public sphere and subversively adopt an alternative gender positioning, they develop identities that are, as Chela Sandoval states, "tactical and performative" and capable of repositioning depending on specific circumstances. This strategic in-between positioning allows them to attain a positive self-imagining and critical subject consciousness.

Alvarez's novel provides an unconventional study of assimilation by investigating it not only as a cultural process but also as a politicized subject positioning. While it portrays the process of losing one's original cultural identity, symbolized by the loss of accents, the narrative underscores that the change in identity is based not only on an imposed acculturation but also on a conscious resistance to the original culture. Redefined as a tactic of resistant female positioning, assimilation is presented in this novel as a necessary skill for the strategic maneuver between patriarchal cultures and ideologies. In addition, even though it signifies a movement toward the new culture, acculturation does not have to imply a complete abandonment of the original one. In the process of adopting a different culture, the native cultural identity still remains a point of reference, an original referent in relation to which one acquires the sense of a new, different identity. As I demonstrate in my analysis of *The García Girls* in the second chapter, the original cultural identity does not have to completely disappear even after many years of a successful assimilation. Its sources of self-identification may be reclaimed and used as a strategy of self-reinvention when acculturation turns out to be a limiting and reductive position of self-definition.

Getting Home Alive: Asserting a Cross-National Feminist Consciousness

Getting Home Alive, co-authored by Rosario Morales and Aurora Levins Morales, is an autobiographical work of mother and daughter, who lyrically explore their identity defined by a multiple and heterogeneous ethnic heritage. While they claim a belonging to "many diaspora" (50), they also delve into the meaning of gender, class, age, and ideology in the context of their cross-ethnic consciousness. The narrative itself is a collage of poems, journal entries, vignettes, stories, and photographs, depicting multiple definitions and articulations of the women's cross-national identity, which embraces Afro Caribbean, Anglo American, East European, and Jewish traditions.

EDINBURGH UNIVERSITY LIBRARY
WITHDRAWN

Although an autobiographical piece, *Getting Home Alive* transcends individual self-definition to speak of the potentiality and the problematics of *mestiza* selfhood in any multiply defined self-construction. As its representation of individual positioning translates into a portrayal of collective existence, it can be argued that the particularized self of the poet ("I") translates into a collective voice of her community ("we") even though this is not a conventional *testimonio*. On the other hand, any claim of the universality of *mestiza* experience is immediately undermined as both Morales and Levins Morales choose to map out hybrid identity in distinct and sometimes conflicting voices. Their polyphonic narration, however, seeks to uphold an oppositional consciousness that leads to coalitional positioning across difference, as Chela Sandoval proposes, while allowing a continual movement between different self-representations and positions.

The struggle to define the self within multiple cultural streams is articulated in the need to identify where one belongs. Rosario Morales' piece titled "Puerto Rico Journal" begins with Rosario's journal entries on her flight to Puerto Rico: "Home. I'm going home, I thought, and the happiness bubbled in me and spilled over" (76). The next entry already states a negation of the long-awaited experience—"But this was never home!" (76)—as she realizes that the noisy and crowded urban setting of the Caribbean island does not quite feel like a familiar and intimate environment. She concludes that she is more at home with the vegetation of the countryside. However, even after several visits to the interior, Rosario repeats: "This is not home" (79), adding that the eleven years of her stay in Puerto Rico could not make her parents' native place her "home." The significance of this temporal insufficiency is identified primarily in the different gender positioning that Rosario claims in the North American culture: "Maybe it has to do with not having been a little girl in this place. I was shaped on Manhattan island," asserting that "it has to do with the kind of woman I am. Nothing so crude as docile, catholic womanhood..." (79). Similar to Ana Castillo's construction of female agency in *The Mixquiahuala Letters*, Morales employs bicultural experience as a critical position towards the patriarchal ideology of Puerto Rican culture, juxtaposing the island's traditional concept of womanhood to the more liberal female positioning in the U.S. She identifies a Catholic influence in the construction of womanhood, perceiving the traditional norm of female submissiveness and docility in connection to the patriarchal authority of the church and its religious doctrine of hierarchy and male superiority. By distancing herself from such definitions—"nothing so crude as docile, catholic womanhood"—Rosario not only prefers the womanhood she inhabits, the one that is more emancipated and U.S. based, but also denounces the patriarchal authority in any cultural context.

Morales's narrative highlights the discrepancy between the gender norms in the private sphere and the ones in the public sphere. While she emphasizes that in her parents' household in the U.S. the patriarchal conduct has been always prevalent, Rosario understands that the more liberal gender culture of the public space has allowed her to rebel against her parents' pressure. Now, as an adult woman revisiting the island, she recognizes the similarity between her family and the people on the island "nagging, harping, pushing you into line, into feminine behavior..." (79). She is annoyed not only with the communal expectations of proper geder conduct but also with the lack of individualism and privacy, of one's independence from intrusive and demanding community. As she juxtaposes this lack to U.S. ideals of privacy and individualism, the ambivalence and contradiction of her identification with the island is reflected in her need to keep her privacy and at the same time reconnect with the community. However, this ambivalent identification reveals her positioning in strategic hybridity, allowing her to refuse or accept particular cultural practices depending on their nature. Resisting patriarchal practices while embracing communal support, Rosario exhibits a "*mestiza* consciousness," a differential positioning that validates her multiple subjectivity while rejecting oppressive forms of self-definition.

Continuing to examine the problematics of finding a place of belonging, Morales problematizes the traditional sense of selfhood that is conceived in terms of territorial identifications, principally in terms of one's native place. Initially enthusiastic about the countryside, Rosario comes to realize that "only the landscape is home" (80), making a clear distinction between nature and culture of the interior. The diary records a strong presence of patriarchal conduct in the rural environment, where women define lack of their freedom by the law of the husband—"*Mi marido no me deja*" (79)[14]—and accept this regulation as the absolute authority in women's lives. Rosario learns to redeploy this law when she wants to justify her voluntary decline of something and assert her own choice: "And when somebody nagged at me and wouldn't take no for an answer, I'd say it too. It was unanswerable, everyone understood that '*El no me deja*'" (79).[15] Ironically, she adopts the prerogative of male decision-making to grant autonomy to her own decisions. Although she understands the pervasiveness and the logic of patriarchal ideology, Rosario also criticizes the women's obedient compliance and their lack of resistance, commenting that female passivity further perpetuates gender oppression: "¡*Pero tu lo dejas que no te deje!*" (79).[16] Taking on this critical posture, she reasserts her oppositional gender positioning and at the same time demands such consciousness of her female friends.

As in *The Mixquiahula Letters*, the cross-ethnic positioning of the female protagonist initiates the emergence of a differential gender consciousness that advocates female emancipation. Morales states that Puerto Rican culture provides "little freedom of thought and action, freedom to expand, grow, dare to do something different, to change" and is full of "predatory males who punish you for being female" (80). It is precisely this lack of freedom that constructs the absence of her home-like experience of the Caribbean island: "The U.S. is home now. None of this is home" (80). Clearly, in this scene home is identified as a place where one has a greater freedom of thought and action as a woman, and this meaning determines which country or culture is home to her. In this way, Morales challenges the notion of home if one is confined in its space, insisting not on the romanticized or privileged conception of home as a place of domesticity but on the notion of freedom in the space that one inhabits, whether that be the private or the public sphere. Unlike Ana Castillo's protagonist Teresa in *The Mixquiahuala Letters*, who needs to feel and experience Mexico as her home, Rosario cannot claim a belonging in the culture that denies this freedom.

While she attempts to demystify gender positioning in the domestic space, Morales emphasizes that hybrid identity is an ambiguous and contradictory condition. In spite of her initial disappointment, at the end of her stay in Puerto Rico Rosario feels sad about leaving, realizing the ambivalence of her emotions and the fact that Puerto Rican culture carries multiple meanings in relation to her sense of self. In this instance, her feelings are closer to Teresa's: while she questions and refuses its patriarchal tradition, Rosario still feels connected to the island. Although she did not grow up there, she associates it with her childhood defined by her mother's and her grandparents' stories about "the old country." The idealized imagining of the primordial home during her childhood reveals its residue in her descriptions of the perpetual nostalgia: "Nostalgia for Puerto Rico. I grew up with it, felt it even before I first visited there the summer I turned ten" (87). However, reflecting the ambivalence of her emotions, the opening sentence of her first entry in the Puerto Rican journal replicates itself: she is writing it again on the plane, but this time heading to the U.S.: "I'm going home" (83).

Rosario's journal entries challenge the traditional meaning of home, and, by extension, a territorially defined sense of self. Using her female experience to construct the meaning of where she belongs, Rosario's self-reflexive exploration asserts women's refusal of the domestic confinement and, at the same time, one's resistance to singular cultural definitions. Rosario does not negate Puerto Rico as her home or deny its cultural and social influence on her self-definition. However, as an emancipated woman, she refuses to accept its patriarchal oppression, and as a cultural "border-crosser," she cannot define herself only within its boundaries.

In Aurora Levins Morales' vignette "Puertoricanness," the Caribbean island carries a different signification. Primarily defined by Aurora's nostalgia and romanticized memories,[17] Puerto Rico is experienced as her internalized being "waking up inside her" and exposing the duality of her womanhood. "There was a woman in her who had never had a chance to move through this house the way she wanted to, a woman raised to be like those women of her childhood, hardworking and humorous and clear" (86). This memory of Puerto Rican women on the island is present in Morales' journal piece, too, as she writes: "Lots of women here are strong and independent" (79); but she immediately adds, "And yet…" (79), questioning their acceptance of patriarchal patterns of oppression. Levins Morales focuses more on what she sees as the positive element of the womanhood in Puerto Rico, perceiving the domestic chores of cooking and grocery shopping as meaningful rituals of "clockless" and "uncluttered" life, as opposed to her daily routine in the U.S. which is based on "appointment books" and "digital clocks" (85–86). Although this is a romanticized perception of gender positioning in the domestic sphere, it nevertheless validates the traditionally unrecognized female labor. Juxtaposed to the entrance of women into the professional public sphere, it seeks to recuperate the meaning of womanhood that has been not only exploited by patriarchy but also suppressed by (post)modern capitalist society and its oppressive work ethic.

While Rosario Morales writes about her preference of the island's nature over its culture, Aurora Levins Morales reveals that she identifies with both aspects. She remembers "the perpetual food pots of her childhood" and "the overwhelming profusion of green life that was the home of her comfort and nest of her dreams" (84). Her nostalgic memory identifies Puerto Rico as home—"yes, this is still home" (79)—through images of food and nature, symbols of physical and mental nourishment. And although Aurora's image of the kitchen invokes gender positioning in the domestic space, it does not convey Rosario's criticism of the island's patriarchal culture. Instead, it provides again a romanticized idea of the domestic, which in her childhood years was not perceived as oppressive. Later, in her adult years, Aurora recognizes the confining and suffocating meaning of the domestic space as she reimagines her grandmother's life and her longing "for New York or some other U.S. city where a woman can go out and about on her own, live among many voices speaking different languages, out of the stifling air of that house, that community, that family" (23). Aurora's conceptions of home project her own struggle for an affirmative and inclusive sense of self. Dissatisfied with the meaning of modern womanhood, she longs for the simplicity of a more archaic domestic lifestyle. However, she realizes that such life does not entail less female confinement.

In her piece on "kitchens," Levins Morales reasserts the notion of the domestic as the workspace of women: "[...] when I lift the lid from that big black pot, my kitchen fills with the hands of women who came before me, washing rice, washing beans, picking through them so deftly..." (37). The kitchen also becomes a space where she connects not only with her idyllic childhood but also with the island women: "It's a magic, a power, a ritual of love and work that rises up in my kitchen, thousands of miles from those women in cotton dresses who twenty years ago taught the rules of its observance to me, the prentice, the novice, the girl-child..." (38). This affirmative image of women's work marks Aurora's initiation into womanhood and celebrates female community as the source of knowledge and empowerment. It also defines her feminist solidarity across cultures and generations, providing her with a consciousness of female selfhood that embodies creativity and power in spite of marginalization and objectification.

Even though Rosario and Aurora approach the gender construction in Puerto Rican culture quite differently and come from different generations, they both arrive at the point of feminist consciousness through their cross-national passage, a perpetual movement between/among different cultures. As Jacqueline Stefanko argues, both Morales and Levins Morales affirm the power of *mestizaje* through their polyphonic writing/speaking and through their subjectivity that emerges in the process of their fluid and heterogeneous positioning, their "shifting among many worlds [they] inhabit and altering them in the process" (58). Recognizing her multiple identity, Rosario insists on its hybridity and the impossibility of suppressing any part of it: "I am what I am I am Puerto Rican I am U.S. American I am New York Manhattan and the Bronx... I am what I am I am Boricua as Boricuas come from the isle of Manhattan and I croon sentimental tangos in my sleep and afro-Cuban beats in my blood..." (138). Aurora, too, claims her hybridity as an internalized history of several generations of immigration and as a memory of the primordial places and cultures that converge in her body: "I am not african. Africa is in me, but I cannot return. / I am not taína. Taíno is in me, but there is no way back. / I am not european. Europe lives in me, but I have no home there" (50). Both poets seek self-meaning and completion in the recognition of their multiple identities, rooted in the history of the Americas and in a continual process of reinvention.

Inspired by Gloria Anzaldúa's *Borderlands/La frontera*,[18] Morales and Levins Morales use Anzaldúa's "To live in the borderlands" at the beginning of their autobiography. This poem-epigraph functions as an introduction to their own work and philosophy of multiple and hybrid positioning. For them, like for Anzaldúa, "living in the borderlands" signifies both multiple oppression and potential transformation. Anzaldúa's description of survival under oppression—"you are wounded, lost in action / fighting back, a survivor" (14)—is articulated in Rosario Morales' powerful poetic account of "living in ghettos" and surviving to "get home alive." Hybridity in their narration and subject-formation is developed as a strategy of individual positioning and communal existence, with the border-zone as a physical and psychological terrain that must be claimed and explored as "the meeting of so many roads."[19]

Gendered Hybrid Identities

As they reveal manifold aspects and meanings of bicultural conditioning, the U.S. Latina texts in this chapter expose not only the multiplicity and intensification of female oppression in the site of biculturalism but also different possibilities of self-transformation and emancipation. Placing selfhood at the interstices of distinct cultures and traditions, they present, in Donna Haraway's words, "transgressed boundaries, potent fusions, and dangerous possibilities" (154) of an in-between positioning as a strategy of survival and liberation. The authors of these texts engage their female protagonists in a tactical differential movement between divergent cultures and traditions in order to demand an oppositional agency against patriarchal subjugation and against unitary paradigms of self-definition. They advocate feminist struggles against abuse and objectification by mapping out their protagonists' critical maneuver between essentialist and confining sociocultural positions through strategic positioning in cultural hybridity.

Ana Castillo traces an evolvement of self-enunciative and differential subjects who assert their agency against patriarchy of Mexican and Anglo American cultures in their struggle for liberal self-definition. She demonstrates that in conditions of oppression and subjugation hybrid identity becomes a politicized mode of existence at the intersection of distinct cultures and values. Julia Alvarez, too, portrays female characters that consciously situate themselves at the crossroads of their native Dominican tradition and the adopted Anglo culture in order to seize the freedom of self-definition and affirmation in both the private and public spaces. Basing their differential consciousness in the hybridity of their ethnic origins, Rosario Morales and Aurora Levins Morales seek self-realization through the recognition of multiple and inclusive identities. While they advocate a female resistance to patriarchy in multiple cultural domains, they also recognize the inspiration and affirmation of womanhood that is defined across distinct cultures.

Becoming, as Homi Bhabha puts it, a "terrain for elaboration of new strategies of selfhood" (*The Location of Culture* 1) in the context of female experience, the ambiguous and polyvalent space of biculturalism is transformed in these texts from an initial condition of entrapment into a site of emancipation and self-affirmation. It is constituted as a locus where one culture contests the other and thus reveals alternative and critical modes of cultural practice and subject positioning. As they situate their female protagonists in this shifting and unstable terrain, all three texts demonstrate that an effective subversion of oppressive and subjugating aspects may be forged through a creative synthesis of empowering possibilities and a critical opposition to patterns of subjugation. In addition, they reaffirm that the survival in the space of biculturalism may engender hybrid, fluid, and multiple subjectivities that engage in the transformation of postmodern social reality through the "unity-across-difference."

This new form of subjectivity epitomizes postmodern dialectics of identity. Materialized through the interplay of different social categories—race, ethnicity, class, gender, sexuality etc.—the postmodern *mestiza* self incorporates the political investment of identity determinants in the struggle for emancipation. At the same time, the hybrid self refuses to be subjected to these categories, understanding that they threaten to claim control over one's body and arrest one's agency. Even though the new *mestiza* identity cannot escape the sociopolitical factors that shape its formation, its fragmentary and fluid form makes it possible to transcend the territorializing nature of these factors, which aim to restrict the boundaries of self within fixed markers of identification. The methodology of this resistance to essentialist categories is grounded in the translation of *mestizaje* into a form of consciousness rather than identity politics. In other words, the original racial denotation of *mestizaje* is transfigured to signify a condition that challenges the purist notion of identity and being, a condition that generates an awareness of differential being and knowing. Referring back to the act of miscegenation, the *mestiza* ontology breaks down oppositional binarisms of self-representation and identification, allowing one to accept the otherness of oneself and of another. Thus, this new consciousness becomes attainable not through a certain racial, ethnic, or sexual subject-position but via what Chela Sandoval terms a "differential subjectivity," the self free to engage not only in a movement across borders of self-identification but also across different political tactics of self-emancipation. Therefore, the categories of *mestiza* and *mestizo* become concepts of differential self-identification, grounded on the premise of a consciousness-based identity rather than biological dispositions.

Furthermore, one's "assent to identity" is attained via a differential movement rather than a socioculturally-based self-identification. While it could be argued that this political practice goes against the notion of identity, I suggest that the primacy of political identification in one's subject-positioning is still a form of identity; but this is an identity that allows more diverse and politically effective forms of agency for it is geared toward affinity-based coalitions rather than exclusive self-differentiations.

In the 1960s Chicano and Puerto Rican movements, *mestizaje* was deployed as a means of self-defined and resistant subject formation with an emphasis on racial dynamics. In the 1980s and '90s, U.S. Latina writers redeployed *mestizaje* in feminist terms and expanded its racial/ethnic signification through the concept of *concientización* (political consciousness-raising). In her 1987 *Borderlands/La Frontera*, Gloria Anzaldúa theorized it as a unique political consciousness developed and embraced by Chicanas, women of color, and queers. Since then, *mestizaje* has been employed and reconfigured by numerous Latina and other writers as a powerful concept of female identification and reinvention under conditions of social subjection and oppression. In her theoretical writing throughout the 1990s, Chela Sandoval redefined *mestizaje* as a moving force behind methodologies of the oppressed, tying its political signification to differential tactics of populist resistance and liberation in the postmodern world.

The U.S. Latina writers discussed in this study conceive of new forms of subjectivity and positioning in response not only to sociopolitical and cultural marginalization by the dominant cultural center but also to the new social organization reconfigured by postmodern displacement and globalization. As they recognize the complexity of identity formed at the intersection of race, class, sexuality, and geopolitics, they also recognize the complexity of material reality, with its forces of subjection in a continual temporal and spatial shift. This is why they begin to be concerned with oppositional struggles on an individual level and in particularized contexts while advocating an awareness of global geopolitical conditions. In the face of polymorphous and ubiquitous social forces, they promote strategies of resistance across divisive sociopolitical and cultural boundaries while adapting to new cultural and national topographies.

Thus, even though the new concept of *mestizaje* employed in contemporary U.S. Latina writing transcends the racial/ethnic signification, it does not obfuscate the history of colonization that has produced racial and cultural hybridization: the new *mestizaje* points at the continuation between former imperial forms of colonialism and new forms of colonial hegemony—capitalist and militarist neo-colonialism of postmodernity—advocating new subject-positions in conditions of economic, geopolitical, and cultural globalization.

Although hybrid identity is inevitably racialized, gendered, and sexualized, its postmodern dialectics allows for an oppositional differential movement against specific and varied forces of social subjection. In addition, its resistance to singularity and closure validates the state of multiple being and knowing while integrating the alterity of the Other. This intervention extends as well into the psychic realm, mediating the unconscious opposition between the 'I' and the 'other.' Generating the awareness that self-meaning cannot be attained without this duality, without multiple reference and varied signifying systems, the differential *mestizaje* intervenes in the state of psychic conflict—what Gloria Anzaldúa poetically calls an "inner war"—

reconfiguring the modern crisis of identity into a postmodern reinvention of the self.

CHAPTER TWO

Diasporic Identities: At the Frontiers of Nations and Cultures

> *I am a child of the Americas,*
> *a light-skinned mestiza of the Caribbean*
> *a child of many diaspora,*
> *born into this continent at a crossroads.*
> —Aurora Levins Morales, "Child of the Americas "

The "in-between movement" that often constitutes gendered subject construction in the space of biculturalism is employed in U.S. Latina literature not only as a maneuver between essentialist definitions of womanhood but also as a passage between fixed national and ethnic identifications. This passage is created in conditions of individual and communal dislocation as a new site of self-affirmation and self-reimagining and as a mode of subversion of the hegemonic national moment. The young protagonists in Judith Ortiz Cofer's *Silent Dancing: A Partial Remembrance of a Puerto Rican Childhood* (1990), Cristina García's *Dreaming in Cuban* (1992), and Julia Alvarez's *How the García Girls Lost Their Accents* (1992) and *¡Yo!* (1997) engage in fluid cross-cultural passages in order to negotiate their identity between two conflicting national narratives and two distinct cultural realities. Marked by the experience of exile and cultural displacement, their existence becomes defined by multiple locations and "shifting boundaries between the home and the world."[1]

The young protagonist in *Silent Dancing* comes of age in the process of constant "shuttling between New Jersey and the pueblo" (17). After her family's relocation in the U.S. out of economic necessity, she learns to live a bicultural and bilingual childhood as she attempts to find a place of belonging in two cultural and sociopolitical realities. During her father's long navy trips to Europe every year, her mother relocates the whole family back to Puerto Rico, and in this erratic pattern of living she develops "a habit of movement" (131) that stays with her even after her father retires and she gets married. Pilar in *Dreaming in Cuban* grows up in New York City but feels a perpetual longing to visit Cuba, the place of her birth. As she questions where her home really is, her thoughts cross the city boundaries and follow the ships that head out to the Atlantic: "When I hear those whistles, I want to go with them" (31). Finding herself dislocated between two places, Pilar feels an urge to know the space beyond and, as Jacqueline Stefanko argues, she engages in a quest to resolve this displacement.[2] Yolanda and her sisters in *How the García Girls Lost Their Accents* grow up going back and forth between New York and the Dominican Republic as their family tries to negotiate the condition of exilic displacement and decide where to settle down. Although the girls acculturate in the U.S.—"We began to develop a taste for the American teenage good life, and soon, Island was old hat, man" (108)— they remain caught between the internalized Dominican tradition and the adopted liberal practices of a U.S. lifestyle. The ambiguity of their ethnic/cultural identification in the U.S. impels Yolanda's return to the island and her search for affirmation of a double-voiced identity.

These U.S. Latina texts provide a significant cultural criticism by addressing the problematics of diasporic conditioning and self-positioning in a distinctive mode. Understanding the importance of diasporic memory and recreation of home for the self-definition marked by cultural and territorial displacement, these narratives approach new ways of coping with the spatial/temporal deferral of the past and the originary location. As I will illustrate in the succeeding analysis, the selected texts engage their protagonists in a differential subject-positioning by allowing them to physically reconnect with the originary location. This intervention is significant because it demonstrates that the return to the site of displacement and loss—the return traditionally seen as fruitless—may provide new meanings and resolutions for the fragmented self. In this way, the narratives redefine post-colonial migrancy as a movement that involves a constant process of self-repositioning and self-displacement, a movement generated in response to one's need to resolve the psychological dislocation.

De-territorialized, Postmodern Identities

The condition of dislocation, induced by the process of (im)migration, disrupts the possibility of a singular, stable place of belonging and confuses the boundaries between the local and the global. The immigrants from Latin America and the Caribbean coming to the U.S. in search of a better life often find themselves living simultaneously in two locations. This transnational and bi-directional existence has been asserted and affirmed by postmodern conditions of technological advancement and globalization of capital. As Roger Rouse demonstrates in his anthropological study of migrations from Mexico,[3] migrant movement ceases to represent a process in which people remain nostalgically tied to the places of their origin while maintaining an involvement in only one location. With means of modern transportation and telecommunication, it is possible to keep up spatially extended relationships and be involved in life of distinct and remote environments. Consequently, migrants develop an identity that is double-voiced and fluid: bicultural, bi-lingual, and cross-national, shifting among multiple locations and engaging in cross-connections. This type of identity transcends territorial boundaries and identifications and becomes what Nestor García-Canclini terms "deterritorialized."[4]

While postmodern conditions encourage this type of subjectivity, it is important to recognize the psychological basis of this process. The condition of displacement is always defined by the negotiation of multiple locations: uprootedness from one place inevitably troubles settlement in another place, and the self constituted in this process always seeks to remedy the dislocation. The often forgotten fact that territorial displacement dominantly signifies a forced departure[5]—in the context of migrations from Latin America and other underdeveloped regions—intensifies the problematic of spatial detachment. Infused with feelings of loss and absence, diasporic dislocation becomes informed, consciously or subconsciously, with a perpetual desire to return to the originary place, whether the return is possible or not. This desire is effectively played out in postmodernity through the active trans-border connections, described by Rouse, that migrants keep with their native environments.

In Cristina García's *Dreaming in Cuban*, Pilar, a young Cuban American, does not have access to modern means of communication with her native island, but she, nevertheless, develops the necessary connection: she engages in telepathic conversations with her grandmother who "speaks to [her] at night just before [Pilar] falls asleep" (29), telling her stories about Cuba and her life. Pilar's mental cross-border migrancy proves effective only temporarily since the images of the past home become deferred with her temporal and spatial removal. Unlike Pilar, Yolanda and her sisters in Julia Alvarez's *The García Girls* and *¡Yo!* are able to physically and frequently visit their Dominican homeland, engaging in the circular process of migration typical of postmodernity. However, the need to return stays with Yolanda throughout her adulthood as a residue of the never-resolved psychological displacement that her whole family undergoes. Described in her diary as "a hole opening wide inside" that would never be filled (*García Girls* 215), her experience of departure will propel a search for the missing home. Experiencing a similar void—"there is only my imagination where our history should be" (138)—Pilar, too, will engage in a quest for self-knowledge. The young protagonist in Judith Ortiz Cofer's *Silent Dancing* participates in the back-and-forth travel too, and while she initially feels resentment for being "yanked from her environment in Paterson, New Jersey" (132) every time her mother takes the family back to Puerto Rico, she continues to return to the island during her adulthood in order to learn about her past and reconnect with the basis of her imaginative being.

The need to be in touch with the other aspect of selfhood, spatially and temporally deferred, becomes a significant factor in subject-constitution under (post)modern conditions of displacement.[6] Always referring back to the event and condition of displacement, desire for the other place constructs territorially de/constructed subjectivities. I argue that postmodern identities are still spatially constructed, but it is different categories of space that actuate them. As Rouse explains, the traditional organization of space shifts and expands beyond the socially drawn boundaries (of nation, culture, and ethnicity), producing new spatial images. The multiply and diversely articulated conceptions of borders—Rouse's 'border-zone,' Saldívar's 'border contact-zone,'[7] Anzaldúa's '*la frontera*,' Bhabha's 'in-betweenness,' third world feminists' 'third space,' etc.—all point toward a new location of identity construction, a location that becomes a space in itself since it contests previous spatial categories while providing, in Homi Bhabha's words, a "new terrain for elaborating selfhood" (*The Location of Culture* 1).

Judith Ortiz Cofer, Cristina García, and Julia Alvarez explore the new spatial construction of self as they create narrative protagonists who learn to negotiate the problematic dislocation between two places by reclaiming a bicultural identity on the premise of cross-connections rather than roots. All three authors utilize the concept of differential hybrid subjectivity, accentuating its signification of a self-positioning that transcends territorial boundaries and shifts among multiple configurations of the home and the world. This cross-cultural and cross-national constitution of the self challenges the singularity and homogeneity of cultural and national paradigms, redefining social space as transnational and contiguous while foregrounding synthetic and oppositional cultural practices. With its resistance to cultural insularism and national enclosure, the diasporic notion of self blurs the boundaries between home and world, here and there, outside and inside, questioning the otherness of the other, as voiced in Pilar's need to know "what's really there" on the other side (176). Aurora Levins Morales defines it in *Getting Home Alive* as a self "belonging to many diaspora" (50), as inheriting "all the cities through which my people passed, and their dust has sifted and settled onto the black soil of my heart" (90).

Homi Bhabha examines this re-imagining of social space in a postcolonial context. In his study *The Location of Culture* (1994), he describes the migrant experience as a condition of "extra-territorial and cross-cultural initiations" marked by the "unhomely" moment of displacement (9). Bhabha defines the unhomely as a connection between "the traumatic ambivalences of a personal, psychic history" and "the wider disjunctions of political existence" (11). This moment manifests itself, he argues, when the borders between home and world become confused and redrawn in the process of dislocation. One's existence in this condition is still spatially bound, but the space is frightfully mutable as it first shrinks and then enormously expands. The private and the public become part of each other while the domestic space becomes a site for "history's most intricate invasions" (9).

While Homi Bhabha uses spatial configurations of the domestic found in the texts by Henry James, Toni Morrison, and Nadine Gordimer to illustrate the unhomely moment of displacements, [8] I find the reverberations of "unhomeliness" also in U.S. Latina narratives of displacement and exile, where the realities of the displaced are strikingly unhomely.

In *Silent Dancing*, Judith Ortiz Cofer relates the immigrant experience of dislocation to a frightening dream that Virginia Woolf describes in her memoirs. Remembering the confusion and pain of female adolescence, Woolf tells of a nightmare in which, as she looked at herself in the mirror, she saw "a horrible face—the face of an animal" looking at her over her shoulder (Ortiz Cofer 118). She describes this unhomely split from one's body as a "looking-glass shame," a female condition of insecurity and alienation enforced by patriarchal objectification. Ortiz Cofer comments that this disconnection from the self is intensified in conditions of biculturalism and exilic displacement, noting that both she and her parents feel out of place in the new land, always confronted by "another face in the mirror" that reminds them of their difference and displacement. Similarly, in *Dreaming in Cuban*, Pilar's uncanny memory of her departure from Cuba resonates with the turbulent history of her homeland:

> I was only two years old when I left Cuba but I remember everything that's happened to me since I was a baby, even word-for-word conversations. I was sitting in my grandmother's lap, playing with her drop pearl earrings, when my mother told her we were leaving the country. Abuela Celia called her a traitor to the revolution. Mom tried to pull me away but I clung to Abuela and screamed at the top of my lungs. (26)

Finally, in *The García Girls*, Yolanda's adolescent writing becomes transformed into her family's history, profoundly informed by the violation of home that originated in her childhood under a military dictatorship. Yolanda remembers her girlhood interrupted by an enforced exilic departure and associates this displacement, as Jacqueline Stefanko points out, with the kitten separated from its mother: "There are still times when I wake up at three o'clock in the morning and peer into the darkness. At that hour and in that loneliness, I hear her, a black furred thing lurking in the corners of my life, her magenta mouth opening, wailing over some violation that lies at the center of my art" (290).

As each unhomely reality of these narratives stirs with a deeper historical and sociopolitical displacement, the individual and the social "develop an interstetial intimacy" and the private space becomes rearranged as "the world-*in*-home" (*The Location of Culture* 11, Bhabha's emphasis). Focusing on trans-national spatial configurations, the selected Latina texts emphasize that the 'world' is not a wider sociopolitical realm confined only to a singular national territory but rather a private sphere extended into a globalized space.

Disrupting and Rearticulating the Nation

With the boundaries between home and world becoming confused and redrawn in the process of postmodern displacements, a tension arises between the need to know the home and the desire to leave its boundaries. This ambivalence can be related to Homi Bhabha's postcolonial analysis of culture and nationhood in "DissemiNation" (1992), where Bhabha identifies a tension between the national desire for homogeneity and the postcolonial process of cultural hybridization. He theorizes this conflict as a critical moment that pushes for a redefinition of nation and its history, noting that cultural difference disrupts the notion of the national as it undermines the possibility of commonality and subverts the fantasy of "many as one." The presence of cultural otherness counters the process that seeks to establish a homogenous group identity and national organicism through neutralization of difference. However, this decentering creates new, hybrid sites of cultural negotiation and seeks to establish an alternative narrative of national history from an experience of cultural displacement. This is where Bhabha takes a postcolonial approach by seeing the migrant as an embodiment of the alternative narration. The migrant "alienates the frontiers of the nation" (315) and forces the national history to account for the Other, and this recognition of difference destabilizes homogenous national identity and the master narrative of historiography. Although the migrant narration ruptures hegemonic notions of nationhood, it is still integral to national narrative because it multiplies and diversifies its meaning. Articulating difference and discontinuity, this hybrid type of narration challenges "harmonious totalities of Culture" (312) while it suggests a cultural meaning that is disjunctive and informed by displacement and deferral.

Bhabha's paradigm of the migrant, diasporic intervention in national discourse translates in the context of U.S. Latina narratives as a motif of perpetual border-crossings that disrupt the national and cultural narratives of singularity and homogeneity. The subjects in several Latina texts are constituted through the movement between and across cultures and nations, a movement that becomes an act of survival and the necessary affirmation of plural aspects of individual selfhood. The narratives discussed in this chapter depict the emergence of new emancipated subjectivities as the protagonists embrace cross-cultural and diasporic identities as strategies for a dialogic and liberating self-creation. This new positioning allows the postcolonial subjects to confront the unhomely element of their physical and psychic dislocation and claim a place of belonging in multiple locations. In addition, performing a passage between fixed territorial identifications, the narrative characters contest national organicism while redefining identity as de/re-territorialized, transnational and mobile. In this process, not only do the migrants reconceptualize social space, but they also subvert the myth of national uniformity and totality by recovering the history of displacement.

Silent Dancing: Confronting the Unhomely

In *Silent Dancing: A Partial Remembrance of a Puerto Rican Childhood*, Judith Ortiz Cofer combines poetry and personal essays to tell a story of her growing up bilingual and bicultural. Ortiz Cofer left Puerto Rico at the age of two, when her father joined the Navy and was transferred to the U.S. The whole family made a new home in Paterson, New Jersey, but whenever the father left for long trips overseas, the children and the mother returned to the island to stay at their grandmother's house. While the mother never "got over yearning for *la isla*" (86) and the father "had no yearning to return to the Island" (122), Judith and her brother learned to juggle and live in two cultures at the same time: "Cold/hot, English/Spanish; that was our life" (123).

As she draws on her childhood experiences, Ortiz Cofer fuses autobiography and fiction to provide a visual description of her coming of age in an artistically, rather than factually, truthful way. She names this hybrid genre a "creative non-fiction," explaining that the events described in the essays actually happened but that "the way [she is] transmitting them to the reader may be a recreation" (Ocasio 745). Understanding that memory is unavoidably infused with fiction, she declares that her recollection of the past has to rely on a "combination of memory, imagination and strong emotion" (Ortiz Cofer 11). Her concern is to make her past meaningful and worth telling, believing that if her writing is evocative and precise in its portrayal of "moments of being,"[9] her recreation of the past will result in truth. This truth is poetic, rather than historical, and as such it gives her freedom to explore the origins of her being and her creative imagination by providing an immediate connection to strong emotions that mark "the winding path of memory" (Ortiz Cofer 13).

Like Rosario Morales and Aurora Levins Morales' *Getting Home Alive*, Ortiz Cofer's *Silent Dancing* explores the meaning of female selfhood in both the U.S. and Puerto Rico. In an intimate and lyrical way, it tells a story of a young girl's coming of age as she traverses the border between two cultures; daily, between the public domain of mainstream America and the privacy of her Puerto Rican household in New Jersey, and, every year, between the mainland and the Island. In this process of perpetual border-crossing, her female consciousness forms as she searches for an affirmative gender and ethnic self-definition in two cultural/national realities. The narrative illustrates that her adolescent quest for self-meaning is complicated not only by the "trauma of leaving childhood" (118) but also by the complexity of diasporic conditions.

In one of the essays in the collection, "The Looking-Glass Shame," the author relates the confusion and loneliness of female adolescence to the alienation and pain of immigrant displacement by identifying the element of the "unhomely" in both conditions. The feelings of personal disconnection and isolation symptomatic of both states are related to a wider sociopolitical disjunction. Experienced as "both alien and familiar" (118), the face of the "looking-glass monster"[10] that appears to one in a moment of self-reflection comes to symbolize the otherness of the self. The face that terrifies and shames one's self is an exposed internalized reality of personal incongruity with society. It signifies the dislocation that one consequently suffers and represses in an act of psychological "defense,"[11] leading to another level of disconnection. In the case of female adolescent development, Ortiz Cofer identifies the psychic dislocation as a result of the lack of social support for a young woman's transition into adulthood: "Society gives clues and provides rituals for the adolescent but withholds support" (118). Not knowing how to deal with emotional and physical aspects of this crucial life stage, a female adolescent may become "a stranger to herself and her new developing needs" (118). She may experience an alienation from the self and society and develop a "looking glass shame" (118), a concept that the author borrows from Virgina Woolf's description of female self-doubt and insecurity in a patriarchal society. Ortiz Cofer remarks that this disconnection is intensified in the condition of bicultural existence because the splitting of identity that is typical of diasporic existence carries the same unhomely reverberations. Often exposed to cultural and political marginalization by the dominant culture, the diasporic self, too, may encounter the terrifying looking-glass face, the signifier of the feelings of self-doubt and shame that one undergoes in the condition of exile. While Ortiz Cofer sees the looking-glass shame as a widespread condition in her Puerto Rican community in New Jersey—"I saw that 'cultural schizophrenia' was undoing many others around me at different stages of their lives" (118)—she specifically identifies it in her own family.

Judith's own trauma of entering adolescence and experiencing love for the first time is further complicated by her shame of her ethnic and class background. Having fallen in love with "a boy who was out of [her] reach" (123), she experiences adolescence as a condition of invisibility: "He could not see me because I was a skinny Puerto Rican girl, a freshman who did not belong to any group he associated with" (125). Even though most of her mates at her Catholic school are ethnic minorities too—Irish and Italian—she still feels excluded because of her ethnic and class difference: "I felt lost in the sea of bright white faces and teased blond hair of the girls who were not unkind to me, but did not, at least that crucial first year, include me in their groups [...]" (119). Experiencing a sense of incongruity with her environment, she internalizes the feelings of lack and shame, typical of female adolescent development but deepened by her marginal socioeconomic status. Years later, Judith gains enough confidence to free herself from the "looking-glass shame" by learning to make herself visible. Discovering self-affirmation and independence in her writing and storytelling, she gains more understanding of her bicultural selfhood. As I argue in the final part of this analysis, this helps her deal successfully with the complexity of gender and ethnic self-definition in diaspora.

While Judith successfully emerges out of silence and invisibility by finding her voice, her parents experience the migrant dislocation as a permanent condition of silence. Her mother's perpetual nostalgia for Puerto Rico is played out in her adamant resistance to assimilation in the U.S. While her husband strives to move the family out of the barrio and disallows them "to form bonds with the place or with the people who lived there" (86), the mother finds comfort in the familiar sounds and smells of her ethnic community. When they move out of the barrio, she lapses into silence and loneliness as her displacement becomes even more pronounced: "My mother carried the island of Puerto Rico over her head like the mantilla she wore to church on Sunday. She was 'doing time' in the U.S. She did not know how long her sentence would last, or why she was being punished with exile, but she was only doing it for her children" (121). The mother's "sentence" is made easier by the promise of not only her children's better future but also her eventual return home: "[...] perpetual nostalgia, constant talk of return, that was my mother's method of survival" (121). Grounding her self-definition only in her native Puerto Rican culture, she fears diasporic hybridization as a threat to her "pure" identity, tied to a singular national territory. Ortiz Cofer captures the depth of her mother's dislocation by describing it as the other face in the mirror: "When she looked in the looking-glass, what did she see? Another face, and old woman nagging, nagging, at her—*Don't bury me in foreign soil...*" (121). A constant reminder of displacement, of her removal from the originary place and her detachment from the new environment, the voice of the Other defines the mother's experience of exile by symbolizing her fear of having to live disconnected from her native place. For her, this disjunction signifies a personal dislocation, a disconnection from her "authentic" self.

The father's experience of displacement, on the other hand, is described as his fear of looking into the mirror because it might reveal "his lost potential" (123), the part of himself that had to be sacrificed for a survival in diaspora. Having suppressed his sensitive and intellectual side, he never talks about the past and has no nostalgia for the island. He embraces silence as a protective barrier against the pain of departure from the homeland and the harshness of immigrant struggle in the new land. Continually confronting the racial prejudice against minorities in the U.S., he instructs his whole family to practice silence: "We were going to prove how respectable we were by being the opposite of what our ethnic group was known to be—we would be quiet and inconspicuous" (61). Silence signifies here a suppression of ethnic/cultural difference for the sake of acceptance in an environment that does not accommodate otherness. While the father uses it as a defense mechanism against prejudice and exclusion, he in fact replicates the process of social suppression of difference by silencing his own and his family's otherness. Symbolizing his experience of exile, the monstrous face in the mirror signifies the father's internalization of self-doubt and shame. As he continues to be separated from his family during his frequent and long trips overseas, he lapses into a deeper silence, this time because of his repression of the pain of continued dislocation: "His absences from home seemed to be harder on him than on us. Whatever happened to him during those years, most of it I will never know. Each time he came home he was a quiet man. It was as if he were drowning in silence and no one could save him" (122). Although the father's trips allow the family to go back to Puerto Rico and stay there while he is gone, the continuity of family separation and personal isolation reiterates the painful aspect of economic migration. Referring back to the state of loss and fragmentation, the unhomely face in the mirror connects the father's and his family's individual anguish to a wider sociopolitical disjunction, the economic instability of his native country. His enlisting into the U.S. Military service at eighteen was "the only promise of a future away from the cane fields of the island or the factories of New York City" (122), the only option for "the young men of Puerto Rico who did not have money in 1951" (122).

Investigating different psychological reactions to the experience of displacement, Ortiz Cofer goes on to explore the unhomely reverberations of the immigrant condition as she describes Puerto Rican migration to the U.S. as a communal escape from poverty. Throughout *Silent Dancing*, she consistently refers to Puerto Rican women waiting for their men to return from "Los Nueva Yores" (16). Separated from one another by economic necessity, those left behind on the island and the ones faraway on the mainland experience the family dispersal as a condition of perpetual nostalgia and suspension. The poignant reminder of this separation in many island homes is a collection of the souvenirs sent from the U.S. In Judith's grandmother's house, for example, "each year more items were added [on the wall] as the family grew and dispersed [...]" (24). Displaying them on her bedroom walls together with important religious symbols, the grandmother treats the souvenirs as a spiritual medium that connects her with her far-off family. She attaches a story to each object, and as she sees pictures of the distant places where her family resides and travels, she imagines their lives in homes away from their *casa* in Puerto Rico. In this way she, too, crosses the borders of home and world and imaginatively lives in multiple locations. However, the fact that the souvenirs signify her family's absence from the original home, and that their growing number suggests the continuation of family dispersal, exposes her family's history as profoundly marked by personal and social disjunction. In her case, the entrance of the world into the home, as Bhabha argues, becomes an unhomely moment that resonates with absence and silence.

While the unhomeliness of diasporic conditions may produce a state of permanent silence and isolation, it can also foster a process of polyphonic speaking and hybrid self-formation. *Silent Dancing* demonstrates that younger generations of (im)migrants tend to cope better with the merging of the world and the home. The author indicates that even though she and her brother have lived in a "twilight zone of sights and smells" (121), a household that their mother has made into a "facsimile of a Puerto Rican home" (144), they have inevitably become hybridized: "I had spent my early childhood in the U.S. where I lived in a bubble created by my Puerto Rican parents in a home where two cultures and languages became one. I learned to listen to the English from the television with one ear while I heard my mother and father speaking in Spanish with the other" (49). The children's ability to keep up with two languages and cultures has been further developed in their daily passages from the private into the public sphere: "[…] we led a dual existence: speaking Spanish with her [the mother], acting out our parts in her traditional play, while also daily pretending assimilation in the classroom […]" (144). While dealing with divergent cultural norms, the younger generation adopts the *mestiza* consciousness, juggling different cultures and engaging in a perpetual movement between different subject positions: "Being the outsiders had already turned my brother and me into cultural chameleons, developing early the ability to blend into a crowd…" (17). Even though they have to suppress the "otherness" of a specific cultural group, the ease with which the children perform a culturally "pure" identity in multiple environments speaks of their actual hybrid identity. In its constant negotiation of displacement and difference, the hybrid generation develops a cross-cultural subjectivity and a diasporic affirmation of plural selfhood. In addition, their chameleon-like transformations testify to their early developed ability to use the fluid and multiple self-positioning as a strategy of survival and resistance. Paralleling Chela Sandoval's description of hybrid positioning, the children exhibit the "tactical and performative" identity, which allows them to de- and re-center depending upon the specific context and regulations that they confront.

With her childhood spent "shuttling between New Jersey and the pueblo" (17), the young female protagonist in *Silent Dancing* experiences a constant relocation and dislocation, a process that complicates her sense of belonging but ultimately affirms her diasporic being. In one of the poems in the collection, "The Habit of Movement," the author describes this process of continual uprooting: "We bore the idea of home on our backs / from house to house, never staying / long enough to learn the secret ways of wood / and stone […] / In time we grew rich in dispossession / and fat with experience" (lines 11–14). Speaking of her family, and by extension of the Puerto Rican condition of migrancy, she notes that while in the beginning the nomadic life may feel awkward, it gradually becomes familiar and comfortable. Its perpetual movement across the boundaries of different cultures and nations engenders a fluid, transnational identity that gains a greater freedom of multiple subject positioning and self-definition. The poet suggests that there is a certain safety in this type of mobility: "As we approached but did not touch others, / our habit of movement kept us safe / like a train in motion— / nothing could touch us" (lines 19–22). Born out of displacement and repositioning, the diasporic self engages in a continual passage between multiple locations in an attempt to avoid further dislocation. Participating in a constant re/deterritorialization, it paradoxically becomes protected from loss and fragmentation, knowing that a position of stasis inevitably carries a possibility of uprooting. However, Ortiz Cofer is careful not to romanticize the nomadic lifestyle, being aware of its less pleasant cause. The ambiguity of the poem's images—"balloons set adrift," "home on our backs," "the eyes of the unmourned dead," and "rich[ness] in dispossession"—implies the unhomely element of the migrant condition. Even as the nomad's ability to appreciate "dispossession" may sound liberating, it also carries a connotation of perpetual loss and displacement.

While those left behind may encounter "the world-in-the-home" as an unhomely reminder of the diasporic separation, the ones who leave often experience it as a synchronized living in multiple locations. Ortiz Cofer identifies it as a "dual existence" that often entails contradicting standards. She explains that at her home in the U.S. she was exposed to conflictive expectations, "the pressures from my father to become very well versed in the English language and the Anglo customs, and from my mother not to forget where we came from" (Acosta-Belen 92). However, rather than disorienting and debilitating, these expectations turn out to be empowering. Judith learns that her knowledge of both cultures makes her and her family's survival easier. While her father is away, she acts as her mother's "interpreter and buffer to the world" (98), realizing that she cannot afford to resist an immersion into the dominant culture: "English was my weapon and my power" (98). She also understands that she cannot forget her place of origin—"*el olvido* is a dangerous thing" (65), her mother warns her—and she goes on "yearly pilgrimages to my mother's town where I had been born also" (143). She cultivates "the habit of movement" because it allows her self to evolve and live on the boundaries of two cultures that have shaped her identity. Her positioning in cultural hybridity is an act of survival as well as an affirmation of her female and artistic self.

The fulfillment of the conflicting expectations materializes in Judith's writing as she uses her mastery of English to write about her Puerto Rican heritage. Her creative self-expression allows her to recover her personal and communal history by reimagining her past in both cultural locations. Recognizing that her childhood recollection is a creation of not only her own imagination but also her family's storytelling, she draws on the collective memory and experience: [...] I wanted to try to connect myself to the threads of lives that have touched mine and at some point converged into the tapestry that is my memory of childhood" (13). She traces the origins of her writerly and female consciousness to the adult women of her island family, especially her grandmother, who used oral tradition to "teach each other and my cousin and me what it was like to be a woman, more specifically, a Puerto Rican woman" (14). Told during female gatherings at her grandmother's house in Puerto Rico, the stories provide not only an invaluable instruction to female community but also an exclusively female space and support network that foster a free expression of women's voice and autonomy: "Then Mamá's house belonged only to us women" (19). Similar to Aurora Levins Morales', Judith's re-inhabiting of her grandmother's and mother's domestic space during her adult "pilgrimages" to the island connects her with not only her idyllic childhood but also the strength and solidarity of the island women. Providing her with knowledge of female creativity and power, "*la casa de Mamá*" (22) is also a source of her artistic inspiration and imagination that has defined her female self-development in both Puerto Rico and the U.S. Ortiz Cofer acknowledges its influence by remembering it as place of female storytelling "that became part of my subconscious as I grew up in two worlds, the tropical island and the cold city, and which would later resurface in my dreams and in my poetry" (15). Guided by the voices of her grandmother and the women of her family, she herself has become a storyteller: "[...] the voice telling the story became my own" (81).

The storytelling skill passed to her by female members of her island family constitutes the foundation of Judith Ortiz Cofer's writing. In *Silent Dancing*, as she recreates the *cuentos* heard during her childhood, Ortiz Cofer creates her own stories and translates them into a written medium. While she acknowledges the presence of other female voices in her self-expression, she also develops an independent voice and mode of expression. The fact that her own version of a childhood event may conflict with her mother's story of it, as conveyed in the closing essay of the collection, affirms not only the distinctness of her memory but also the confidence and individuality of her artistic and gendered self. When the mother finishes her account of the event by saying, "*Es la pura verdad.* [...] Nothing but the truth,'" the daughter questions it by commenting to herself, "But that is not how *I* remember it" (156). This is the concluding line of the final essay in the collection and, when related back to the essay's title ("The Last Word"), it grants authority to Ortiz Cofer's project of writerly storytelling and thus affirms her narrative agency. In addition, it validates her emancipated female selfhood since her own capacity of storytelling confirms her successful transition into adulthood. Like the female storytellers of her family, she herself can teach "the lessons of the past" (157) from her own experience and from the tradition of her community.

Ortiz Cofer states in her preface to *Silent Dancing* that she writes about her past in order to understand her self-formation. Inspired by Virgina Woolf's memoir *Moments of Being*, she understands that one meditates on past events "to study ourselves and our lives in retrospect, to understand what people and events formed us" (11). The need to know the self is articulated and fulfilled in the process of creative self-expression, an enunciative process that confronts the exilic condition of silence and invisibility lived through by earlier generations of (im)migrants. As described in the title essay of the collection, "The Silent Dancing," the distant past is reinterpreted and infused with the voice of the new diasporic generation that listens to its predecessors, "like Odysseus in the Hades" (93), before it can ask questions and learn from their experience. Lending her voice to the dancing characters of a silent family movie made right after her family's move to the U.S., Ortiz Cofer recreates a part of her Puerto Rican childhood in an effort to explain and understand her diasporic selfhood. Similarly, she returns to the island during her adulthood to reconnect with her place of birth and motivate her further recollection and storytelling.

Through an imaginative and physical connection with the place and time of origin, Ortiz Cofer traces a becoming informed by a continual uprooting and rerooting. This return serves to resist the loss of personal and collective memory by recovering the past that has been mediated not only by a temporal and spatial deferral but also by wider sociopolitical disjunctions. As she imaginatively reinterprets the past through her storytelling/writing, the author gains an understanding of her present moment and confronts the unhomely effects of the past displacement.

Dreaming in Cuban: A Migrant Narration of the Home and the World

In Cristina García's *Dreaming in Cuban*, characters struggle to define themselves at the interstice of two antagonistic national identities, Cuban and U.S. American. The revolutionary upheavals of the 1950s cause a geographical and political fragmentation of the del Pino family: one part immigrates to the U.S., shunning the revolution, while the other stays on the island, supporting the new social order. Reflecting the conflict between the two geopolitical domains, the del Pinos develop conflictual relationships among themselves while struggling to define their experiences. The older generation remains entrapped in nationally defined stereotypes and political dogmas, while the younger generation declares its independence by challenging essentialist positions.

In order to problematize the relation between nationhood and individual selfhood, Cristina García develops multiple narrative voices and multidirectional time shifts. Her characters articulate mutually opposing views as they respond differently to the national discourse: while Celia is a passionate supporter of *El Líder* and his social policy, her daughter Lourdes becomes a fervent opponent of the Revolution. Felicia, on the other hand, does not dismiss the new social organization in Cuba, but she remains resistant to its militancy and propaganda. As these protagonists present different political positions by defining themselves through singular national identifications, their individual experiences reveal the multiplicity and contradictoriness of national reality. Struggling with conditions of displacement and fragmentation, members of older generations construct their present reality either on the nostalgic reminiscence or through the "defensive repression" of the past:[12] Celia's present is infused with a nostalgic memory of the past familial unity, ruptured in the turbulent revolutionary days; on the other hand, Lourdes' projection of the future is frequently interrupted by a haunting memory of the traumatic experience of political violence. Revealing contradictions and conflicts between individual realities, these multiple shifts in narrative perspectives destabilize monologic, concurring, and linear constructions of personal and national narratives and, consequently, disrupt the organicism and homogeneity of national discourse and identity.

Cristina García explains the multiplicity of experience and the slippage in reality by foregrounding the interplay between social forces and the psychological structure. She attributes her characters' views and positions not solely to ideological conditioning but also to material and psychic reality. The narrative suggests that these views reflect the psychological processes of the characters, processes that relate to specific sociopolitical and economic conditions. Although Lourdes sees everything through "her distorting lenses" (176) and appears to be a grotesque and bizarre character, her limitations and obsessions are connected to a very complex psychic reality. Her insatiable cravings for food and sex manifest the repressed traumatic experience that she has suffered in Cuba (rape, miscarriage, and loss of family estate). Her eating disorder points specifically toward the sexual abuse, reflecting the victim's belief that food will fill up the "inner emptiness" and block the pain. Sexual satisfaction, in the same way, offers Lourdes a temporary fulfillment and gratification that she is unable to get from anything else. As Mary Vásquez puts it, "Lourdes is reaching for something beyond him [her husband], something he cannot give her" ("Cuba as Text" 23). Her hatred of Communism, *El Líder*, and Cuba in general is a projection of the pain and anguish of her violated self. In a similar fashion, Celia's devotion to the national cause is psychologically induced and based on her past experiences. Like Lourdes' overeating, her commitment to the revolution is compulsive. Her social activism is her effort to insert herself into history and regain the agency that she has lost in her unhappy marriage. As she puts national integrity before the people—"Cuba is still developing…[a]nd cannot afford the luxury of dissent" (235), she explains to Pilar—Celia symbolically fights to protect her own personal wholeness and dignity. As the psychological rupture connects to the sociopolitical disjunction, the nation becomes a space where the tension between the individual and the social is played out as an act of difference neutralization.

Presenting different and conflictual voices defined by the discourse of the nation, Cristina García attempts to address historical and sociopolitical representations in a deconstructive and interrogative mode. The multiple positions of her narrative characters challenge dominant social narratives about the Cuban and the American experiences, subverting the hegemonic project that strives to establish and maintain a monologic discourse. This polyphonous narrative technique follows the dialogic essence of the novel theorized by Mikhail Bakhtin in many of his writings.[13]

Bakhtin posits that the novel is governed by "heteroglossia," a plurality of social conditions that produce meaning and allow for a multiplicity of independent speech types and voices to coexist in social and literary discourses. Heteroglossia deepens the dialogic essence of the novel by fostering links and interrelationships between/among distinct and often conflictual narrative voices. This dialogic multivocality allows for the voice of the Other to be heard and refuses to privilege any specific enunciative position. Thus, it displaces a determinate, monologic meaning with ambiguity and polyphony. This decentralization and dispersal of meaning, Bakhtin argues, intensifies the stylistic and thematic unity of the novel. More importantly, the polyphonic form also intensifies the novel's multiple layers of signification and representation of reality, allowing for a coexistence of different epistemologies of experience and, ultimately, revealing the complexity and heterogeneity of social meaning.

Bakhtin's model of dialogic narration is crucial to Homi Bhabha's concept of subaltern narration since its polyphonic form allows for an inclusion and recognition of difference. Rather than neutralizing the voice of the Other, a narrative governed by heteroglossia accentuates otherness and its effect of displacement, deferral, and disjunction. Governed by "centrifugal force,"[14] it is instrumental in the migrant project of rewriting the national history from the experience of sociopolitical and cultural displacement. As it moves discourse away from a single, unified center of enunciation, a dialogic narration integrates the "speaking" from the margins and thus acknowledges what is removed from the center.

In an interview given to Iraida H. López, García reinforces the necessity of a decentralizing approach to both social and literary reality by stating that the dominant voices in the debate on Cuba "are not speaking for as many people as they think" (608). As she recognizes the existence of many other voices, García also emphasizes the repressive and hegemonic nature of the dominant ideology by pointing out that "they tend to dominate the airwaves and the news and they have a stranglehold on the debate about Cuba. A lot of people and opinions are muted and shouted down" (608). Seeking to recuperate the silenced voices, García's novel shatters dominant social narratives that centralize and monopolize representation and reduce material reality to exclusive and limited constructs. *Dreaming in Cuban* challenges both the demonization and the idealization of ideological narratives of nation-states, refusing to present Cuba and the U.S. in singular terms. Written in English and primarily addressed to U.S. audiences, the novel contests the stereotypes of the demonized Cuba/Communism and the celebrated U.S./capitalism, cliched in dominant social narratives. As William Luis points out, the Cuban question is discussed in both positive and negative terms, presenting both sides without appearing to privilege one point of view over the other (216). Similarly, the U.S. experience is approached critically and through multiple positions that reveal contradictions and disjunctions in U.S. sociocultural and political reality.

García's contestation of one-sided, monologic, and isolated perspectives achieves a transformational political dimension with the novel's emphasis upon the concept of cross-border mobility and differential hybrid consciousness. The young characters in the novel, Pilar and Ivanito, represent, as David Mitchell puts it, "a hybrid generation" (53), a new generation that reaches both sides of the dividing lines and creates a space for their encounter. Expressing "a disregard for boundaries" (García 176) and fusing different cultural horizons, they transcend the ideological conflict between the U.S. and Cuba and challenge fixed national paradigms. Engaging her young protagonists in a search for a space where they can claim independence from confining national and nationalistic identifications, the author traces an evolvement of cross-national identity and hybrid consciousness. To nationally defined characters, Celia and Lourdes, she juxtaposes Pilar and Ivanito, characters who break away from national definitions and claim their freedom by crossing geographical and psychological boundaries of cultures and nations. She grants agency to the younger generation by insisting on an epistemology of their own experience. Pilar, for example, is determined to see "what's really there" (176) on the other side while refusing ideological constructions of knowledge: "Who chooses what we should know or what's important. I know I have to decide these things for myself" (28). Challenging the authority of a single source of knowledge/utterance through her young protagonists, Cristina García underscores the Bakhtinian concepts of social heteroglossia and dialogism in the acts of individual and collective self-formation and expression.

Telling a story of political exile, the novel foregrounds the psychological effects of physical dislocation in an attempt to investigate how these effects configure one's self-definition and positioning. The author explains that physical uprooting translates into a fragmentation of self since one's identity has been traditionally closely tied to spatial definitions. In the case of exile, specifically, the severing of self from the home/nation-land destabilizes the projected fantasy of an equivalency between individual and national self-hood. While this rupture has more severe effects on those who leave at a later age, it nevertheless affects younger exiles too. Although she was only two when her family left Cuba, Pilar's coming of age in the U.S. is troubled by the feeling of exilic dislocation: "Even though I've been living in Brooklyn all my life, it doesn't feel like home to me. I'm not sure Cuba is, but I want to find out. If I could only see Abuela Celia again, I'd know where I belonged" (58). Because of her younger age and more removed experience of departure, Pilar's reaction to displacement is less defined by an exclusive national identification: she is ready to engage in a cross-national movement and self-definition. In addition, as she questions her belonging to a singular place, Pilar also understands that she cannot identify with the other location without knowing it. This is why she is determined to visit Cuba in spite of her mother's categorical disapproval, understanding that self-knowledge is gained by the return to the originary place and the recognition of the Other (the process that her mother is unable to perform for many years).

Conveying Pilar's frustration through the impossibility of knowledge, Cristina García points out one's loss of individual agency and one's objecti-fication by sociohistorical forces: "[I] felt like my destiny was not my own, that men who had nothing to do with me had the power to rupture my dreams, to separate me from my grandmother" (199). Pilar rebels against her lack of agency by refusing to accept monologic national narratives that cor-roborate objectification and compliance. The novel suggests that her decision to go to Cuba signifies her counter-positioning toward hegemony and reflects her determination to assert free will, take control of her future, and create her own history. As she states, "there is only my imagination where our history should be" (138), Pilar asks for a "hybrid narration" that would reproduce the missing meaning, informed by displacement and repression, and recuperate the lost agency.

In order to seize agency and enunciative subjectivity, Pilar develops a hybrid self by mediating two different cultures and resisting their limitations. Like Teresa and Alicia's positioning in *The Mixquiahuala Letters*, her differ-ential consciousness develops through both synthesis and resistance. The narrative portrayal of Pilar illustrates that she rejects hypocritical ideals of Anglo American culture (she paints a punk version of the Statue of Liberty), and that she also condemns the political violence in Cuba (she supports

Ivanito's decision to escape the island). With this critical posture, she declares her freedom from loyalty to any ideology or nation. Rupturing patriotic myths and symbols, she contests monologic national definitions and subverts the hegemonic moment. However, this is not a complete dismissal: Pilar grounds her identity in both cultures, being aware that she belongs to both places. After visiting Cuba, she learns to accept New York as her home but also experiences Cuba as an integral part of her being. As she reconnects with her primordial being, symbolized by her "dreaming in Cuban," Pilar succeeds in bridging the distance between the two locations.[15] Adopting a fluid, migrant positioning, she reconstructs the missing history and heals the fracture of displacement and exile: "I've started dreaming in Spanish, which has never happened before. I wake up feeling different, like something inside me is changing, something chemical and irreversible. There's magic here working through my veins" (235).[16]

The novel suggests that the young generation's desire for identification and sense of belonging drives their urge to construct home as a site where both cultures meet and generate multiple locations of being. Similar to Aurora Levins Morales' articulation of her yearning for "the meeting of so many roads,"[17] Cristina García constructs Pilar's longing for a converging location of the U.S. and Cuba. This simultaneous inhabiting of different locations becomes what Homi Bhabha calls an "extra-territorial existence," or what García-Canclini names a "deterritorialized identity," an identity that eludes socio-territorial regulations of the self. Renouncing a hegemonically delineated space of belonging, Pilar's positioning alienates national boundaries and merges the topoi of home and world. In this way, social space is reimagined as contiguous and heterogeneous while identity is configured into a hybrid diasporic selfhood defined by a perpetual negotiation of displacement and difference. The reorganization of social space is presented as a projection of the desire to negotiate the spatial and temporal deferral of the past and the originary location.

García shows that the reorganization of social space often emerges out of violent circumstances. Pilar's cousin Ivanito, too, decides to inhabit multiple locations. Yet his disavowal of the imposed national topicality is enforced by a serious threat of physical annihilation. Ivanito's physical transgression of national borders becomes a passage to freedom as he leaves Cuba in an escape from political violence. Here I question William Luis's claim that Ivanito and Pilar betray their grandmother by arranging Ivanito's departure.[18]

I argue that their action signifies their rejection of Celia's political devotion
to the revolution rather than of Celia as a person. Ivanito takes a position
against the regime and for his own future by refusing to subordinate himself
to ideological hegemony. Both he and Pilar question Cuban ideals without
any favoritism of American ones, and this questioning does not signify a betrayal but a rejection of coercion. Cristina García develops the story of
Ivanito's exile in order to point up the continuum of family fragmentation.
Throughout the novel, the dispersal of the del Pinos is attributed to historical
forces rather than to individual will. The opening section of *Dreaming in
Cuban* introduces Celia's grieving over the scattering of her family across
the world as she is questioning its cause:

> She considers the vagaries of sports, the happenstance of El Líder, a star
> pitcher in his youth, narrowly missing a baseball career in America. His wicked
> curveball attracted the major-league scouts, and the Washington Senators were in-
> terested in signing him but changed their minds. Frustrated, El Líder went home,
> rested his pitching arm, and started revolution in the mountains.
> Because of this, thinks Celia, her husband will be buried in stiff, foreign earth.
> Because of this, their children and their grandchildren are nomads. (6)

The personal cost that Cuban families and people had to pay for the sake
of the revolution becomes a thematic thread through the novel: it opens the
novel with the scene of Celia's learning of Jorge's death in the U.S., and it
also closes this story with Celia's discovering of Ivanito's departure from the
island. In both scenes, the protagonist is posed to question history and its
development at the personal expense of people, which allows the author to
expose the fallacy of national unity and security. As Celia's story focuses on
her realization of her family's entrapment within historical unfolding, the
promise of individual participation in history is translated into a loss of individual agency. Celia's present frustration echoes with the past indignation:
"Don't you see how they are carving up the world, Gustavo? How they're
stealing our geography? Our fates? The arbitrary is no longer in our hands.
To survive is an act of hope" (99), reads one of Celia's letters from 1945,
reflecting the post-war disenchantment and dejection. Utilizing a temporal
analepsis, García reveals the continuum of historical objectification across
time and in spite of historical change. This allows her to present the process
of modern nation building as an ultimate loss of individual agency.

In the novel's narrative, the story of Celia's life functions as a poignant criticism of postmodern geopolitical conditions that invade the private sphere and enforce a reorganization of social space. Celia is aware that the dispersal of her family is not voluntary: "the happenstance of El Líder's career" turns her family into "nomads" (6), and the ocean cannot represent comfort any longer as it is converted into a potential source of aggression and a constant reminder of exilic departures. "It exists now so we can call and wave from opposite shores" (240), complains Celia to Pilar. The meaning of the nation-space becomes altered from the promise of unity to the act of disintegration, based in both cases on the exclusion of difference. The merging between the home and the world, symptomatic of postmodernity and postcoloniality, becomes invasive rather than liberating: while Celia cannot inhabit the world, her children and grandchildren cannot remain at home.

At the same time, the national and ideological antagonism between Cuba and the U.S. complicates the diasporic condition by obstructing active connections between the diaspora and the homeland. In the case of Lourdes and Celia, as I have shown, the antagonism exploits personal traumas and translates into hegemonic national discourses. Even when she goes back to Cuba after many years of resistance to the return, Lourdes maintains her national antagonism and profusely criticizes the new social order and its ideology: "Look at those old American cars. They're held together with rubber bands and paper clips and *still* work better than the new Russian ones" (221). Similarly, Celia never decides to visit her family in New York, since the trip would mean a "betrayal to the revolution" (26) and a "reminder of the ongoing shortages in Cuba" (117). The mocking tone conveyed in these passages is used to reflect the extremity of self-identification with the nation and the subsequent lack of one's individuality and autonomy.

As the novel shows geopolitical and national hegemony colonizing Celia's life, it becomes evident that Celia is betrayed by historical and political objectification rather than by her grandchildren. This awareness of individual and collective delusion is tied to the protagonist's final and fatal disappointment. Celia commits suicide in the way she has foreseen upon receiving the news of her husband's death: she walks into the ocean and floats away "with wide-open eyes" (45). She is not buried in a foreign land, like her husband, but instead occupies the fluid border zone between the two countries. This end juxtaposes the opening scene of the novel, where Celia guards the coast of Cuba from the *gusano* traitors and regards the ocean as a protecting border-zone and a symbol of national integrity. While in the initial scene the self merges with the nation and is subjected to the sociopolitical sphere, in the final scene the self ceases to exist; and yet, in this termination, it is liberated, it can be argued, from objectification and social appropriation. As Ivanito decides to leave the national space of Cuba, Celia in a similar way, leaves the bordered space, realizing that "she has never been farther than a hundred yards off the coast of Cuba" (243). She ventures into the space that she used to regard as a source of danger for the "nation-family." Rather than a capitulation before larger sociopolitical forces, Celia's suicide can be interpreted as a rebellious act declared against territorializing forces of the nation.

As David Mitchell posits in his reading of *Dreaming in Cuban*, family and nation coexist in this narrative as parallel structures sharing a desire for unity that proves to be illusory and contradictory (52). Paradoxically, while the nation-state foregrounds family as its micro unit and a "guardian" of its autonomy (Celia's guarding of the coast), the very construction of nationhood ruptures the structure of family (the dispersal of the del Pinos). Following Mitchell's argument, this impossibility of familial unity projects the nation's inability to assert unity, proving its imaginary space of individual and collective belonging to be contradictory and antagonistic. However, while Mitchell points out that neither grouping succeeds in sustaining the singularity to which each necessarily aspires, I emphasize that familial unity in *Dreaming in Cuban* fails precisely because of the national project of homogeneity, in both Cuban and U.S. contexts.

Intertwining the narratives of personal and national history, the novel insists on the importance of memory for the continuity and heterogeneity of historical narration. Celia's 25-year-long writing to her former lover, Gustavo, represents her resistance to amnesia after her jealous husband puts her in an asylum and asks doctors to give her a shock treatment. This authoritarian attempt to erase memory of the past reveals the fear of "otherness," the presence of difference that disrupts the desired unity and singularity. In this instance, the "other" is not only Gustavo but also Celia, because she preserves the memory of the otherness and is able to perceive the multiplicity of meaning and reality. Celia strives to recuperate her lost agency discursively and preserve her memory in writing. The amnesia she fears is both personal and communal, and in her letters she records not only her inner turmoil but also social upheavals, understanding their mutual connection. Similarly, Pilar keeps a diary and seeks to preserve her memory when she begins to experience the loss: "Every day Cuba fades a little more inside me, my grandmother fades a little more inside me" (138). She decides to recreate her memory by visiting Celia and reconnecting with the place of her birth. When Celia gives her a box of letters, letters that she wrote but never mailed to Gustavo, Pilar symbolically takes on the task of narration that her grandmother began as a practice of self-affirmation and historical enunciation. As Katherine B. Payant claims, this act allows Pilar to preserve family history and "in the process know her identity and place" (172). Furthermore, Pilar becomes the migrant and diasporic narrator who creates historical meaning through her "disregard for boundaries" (García 176) and multiple, hybrid positioning in Cuba and the U.S. Celia herself gives validity to this hybrid narration of the self and the world when she sees Pilar's birth as the beginning, and at the same time a continuation, of personal and collective narration. In this way, the re-writing of familial and national history emerges from, what Bhabha calls, "the hybrid sites of meaning" ("DissemiNation" 312) created in the course of displacement and articulation of difference, while developing as a project that resists the loss of memory and the occlusion of meaning.

Exploring the trauma of displacement across different generations, *Dreaming in Cuban* presents experiences on both sides of the dividing lines while creating a hybrid migrant narration. Emphasizing a diasporic and cross-national movement in the process of writing a personal history, it engages the migrant project of rewriting the historical text in order to articulate repressed voices, histories, and subjectivities. While it problematizes homogenous conceptions of nation and culture, it also strives to introduce a contact-zone between two antagonistic national narratives as well as to propose a healing of the trauma of dislocation. As Rocío Davis asserts, Pilar's narrative functions as "the vehicle through which the wounds are healed and the pain of exile overcome" (64). In *Dreaming in Cuban*, the conjunction between nation and narration becomes a site where narration as a process of remembering simultaneously recreates and ruptures the idea of nationhood. The power of narrational agency is presented both through the criticism of social discourse of the nation-state and via the portrayal of narration as a process of individual and collective healing.

The García Girls and *Yo*: **The Return of the Migrant**

How the García Girls Lost Their Accents (*The García Girls*) by Julia Alvarez presents dilemmas of bicultural identity through a *bildungs* story of four sisters born in the Dominican Republic and relocated in the U.S. After they experience the usual culture shock, the girls gradually enter mainstream Anglo culture and distance themselves from the Dominican tradition. Nevertheless, they become caught between their parents' old-world views and liberal cultural practices in the U.S. Their coming of age becomes even more complex as they immerse themselves in the lifestyle of the 1960s and openly rebel against their parents' controlling influence and cultural traditionalism. However, twenty years later, they recognize their bicultural identity and yearn to reclaim the repressed past.

Like Cristina García, Julia Alvarez applies a polyphonous narrative structure: she articulates the voices of all four sisters and arranges them in fifteen stories told in reverse chronological order. However, while García develops multidirectional time shifts, Alvarez sticks to retrospective and linear narration. The novel is divided into three parts that correspond to different time periods of the Garcías' life. The first relates to the present moment and introduces the sisters as adult women. The second goes back to the time of their adolescence and depicts their psychological and cultural conflicts that they encounter after moving to the U.S. The final part narrates the story of their childhood in the Dominican Republic and explains the reasons for their emigration.

Alvarez employs this retrospective line of narration in order to reflect the journey back to "the origin" that one of the sisters undertakes in 1989. The narrative reconstruction of the return depicts an attempt to reclaim the past and reconnect with the Dominican identity. Yolanda's return to the island symbolizes, as William Luis observes, a spiritual journey in search of communion with a mythical past associated with her childhood (216). However, while he claims that Yolanda does not look for communion with contemporary Dominican culture, I argue that she immerses herself in the present moment in an attempt to reconstruct the past through the present. The narrative illustrates that Yolanda goes to the island in order to find in its culture what she could not find in the American, seeking to affirm her hybrid and multiple subjectivity. Like Teresa and Alicia in *The Mixquiahuala Letters*, she performs a creative cultural synthesis in her search for self-definition and a place of belonging. This is re-affirmed in the follow-up novel *¡Yo!* (1997), where Julia Alvarez describes Yolanda's repeated returns to the island and her integration in contemporary Dominican culture.

In *The García Girls*, identity is explored at the interstice between U.S. and Dominican cultures. The young generation engages in a quest for ethnic definition and gendered subjectivity while dealing with the complexity of exilic and bicultural conditions. The *bildungs* story conveys that the condition of biculturalism, defined by multiple referentiality, comes to represent for the García girls a profound cultural dislocation and entrapment between two distinct cultures. In addition, their experience of exilic absence and marginality in the new location is portrayed as an intensification of their feelings of uncertainty and displacement. The girls' initial reaction is to embrace only one culture, to adopt assimilation in order to block the feelings of loss and confusion. However, when they become part of mainstream U.S. culture, they reencounter the feelings of lack and alienation. Their monologic self-definition proves to be limiting and unfulfilling, but it is at this contradictory moment that the sisters begin to explore different possibilities of being.

The novel opens with a scene that describes the third sister's arrival in the Dominican Republic after five years of absence. Yolanda is back on the island to reclaim her Dominican identity and thus her bicultural self. This time, her stay on the island is different from the summer visits during her teenage years. Before, the four sisters "used to shock their Island cousins with stories of their escapades in the States" (7), but now Yolanda returns in order to embrace the values that she could not find in her Anglo culture: "She and her sisters have led such turbulent lives—so many husbands, homes, jobs, wrong turns among them. But look at her cousins, women with households and authority in their voices. Let this turn out to be my home, Yolanda wishes" (11). The opening section of the narrative articulates Yolanda's desire to find home, reflecting one's need to identify a place of belonging and resolve exilic displacement. One's removal from home, even at a young age, is experienced as an event of personal fragmentation and uprootedness. Suggesting that the rupture must be negotiated with a return to the place of traumatic experience, the author presents Yolanda's stay on the island as a search for the other, repressed part of the young woman's self-hood, for everything that "has been missing all those years" (215). As in *Dreaming in Cuban*, the importance of displacement in the constitution of subjectivity propels the young generation's return to the site of loss.

In the exile's experience, the return is performed as a physical reconnection with the originary place of loss. The urge to find the missing home translates into the need to explain and understand the self. A symbol of Yolanda's missing home is a *guayaba*, a tropical fruit she craves and goes to pick in the Dominican hills. While her idea of traveling alone through the interior horrifies her aunts—"'By yourself? [T]his is not the States. [A] woman just does not travel alone in this country. Especially these days,'" (9)—Yolanda is ready to assert not only her female independence but also her will to encounter the deferred and unhomely presence of "danger," of the past violation that has defined her exilic identity. The author projects the unhomely onto the innocent landscape, where Yolanda senses a lurking presence of violence: "The rustling leaves of the guava trees echo the warnings of her old aunts: you will get lost, you will get kidnapped, you will get raped, you will get killed" (17). In this scene, the safe and idyllic place of childhood translates into a site of turbulent sociopolitical reality, connecting the source of personal displacement to the continuing instability and disjunction of the social realm. Yolanda's realization that the serene and rustic interior is "what she has been missing all those years" (12) is immediately undermined by the appearance of two soldiers, and it is her American identity and the mention of her rich island relatives that protect Yolanda in the end. However, Yolanda's venturing into the unknown and forbidden is narrativized to invoke the hazardous border-crossing between the private and the public space in search of the home that has been invaded and displaced by sociopolitical reality. The scene in the backwoods interrelates with the scenes from Yolanda's childhood, narrated in the last part of the book, where the safety and stability of home are ruptured by state violence.

As I have mentioned at the beginning of the chapter, this violation leaves its persistent mark on Yolanda's identity and asserts its unhomely presence in her development as a writer. However, the process of writing becomes a creative negotiation of the unhomely when the young protagonist begins to write about her family and her childhood experiences—"I began to write, the story of Pila, the story of my grandmother..." (289)—in order to bring to light the deferred past and thus understand her self-becoming. Modifying the tradition of *Kunstlerroman*,[19] Yolanda's (and Alvarez's) writing becomes a quest for not only a creative voice and individual autonomy but also for personal and collective histories that have been fragmented and displaced from memory. This allows for the discursive subject formation to expand into a historiographic project, recuperating the lost memory and history. It also represents an imaginative recreation of the originary place, deferred and displaced through sociopolitical disjunction.

Yolanda is identified as the writer of the Garcias' history in the final part of the book, and this merging of the novel's author and the main protagonist constructs the novel as a literary recreation of the memory and past of a displaced family. The reverse chronological narration traces Yolanda's trip back to the originary place and reproduces a process of becoming defined by displacement and disjunction. Like *Silent Dancing*, this narrative suggests that the protagonist's return to the island does not represent a search for her ethnic roots but for a knowledge of becoming that would elucidate the presence of the unhomely in her life. Recalling Lacan's argument, the process of becoming differs from and counters the process that attempts to establish what one is. The process of becoming provides knowledge of one's formative experiences and interprets the present moment through the past. Its return to the place of the Other is not for the sake of arriving there, emphasizes Lacan, but for the sake of tracing and thus understanding and "restoring" one's identity ("The Agency" 173). This new self-knowledge is gained by recognizing the other, repressed part of the self and thus accepting—rather than building a defense against—one's selfhood as partial, multiple, and dynamic. This is why I argue that Yolanda's trip back to the Dominican homeland receives an "archeological" purpose: it signifies one's attempt to recreate the past in order to gain understanding of one's present positioning rather than to reinhabit the lost time and place. The past is approached and reconstructed through the present moment, unraveling the occlusion and disjunction of the immediate enunciation in order to reconstruct the lost meaning and, subsequently, interpret one's present condition. In addition, the narrative reveals that the discovery of the past does not occur in an attempt to recreate and exclusively claim the original selfhood: Yolanda searches for the Dominican part of her self in order to satisfy the need for a double-voiced individuality rather than for a homogenous identity. Her willingness to reoccupy the middle territory between the two cultures that define her is generated after Yolanda realizes that the repression of the other self must be remedied via differential diasporic positioning, even though this liminal form of existence may invoke isolation and confusion: "I saw what a cold, lonely life awaited me in this country. I would never find someone who would understand my peculiar mix of Catholicism and agnosticism, Hispanic and American styles" (99).

The lack of understanding for the multiplicity of one's self-definition and positioning projects the failure of mainstream culture, or national culture, to recognize and include difference. The novel demonstrates that monolithic conceptions of culture exist not only in the U.S.: Yolanda's aunts and cousins in the Dominican Republic joke about her Americanized ways, complaining that she has lost her Dominican identity. By depicting Yolanda's determination to find a middle-ground, the author reaffirms that only multiple perspectives can explain the complexity of the exile's being and identity. In order to develop this multiplicity, it is necessary to adopt diasporic border-crossings and a commitment to explore the space of in-betweenness, a mediating and shifting terrain between two "intimate" cultures. Inhabiting an interstitial location that contains both contradictions and correlations, one develops a hybrid identity, or what Donna Haraway calls a "multiple subject with at least double vision" (195), an identity that resists cultural singularity and its fixed codes of one's cultural self-definition. Shifting among multiple positions, the diasporic self situates itself at the boundaries between the home and the world to resolve and avoid further dislocation.

The movement between different positions and the simultaneous belonging to multiple locations are further emphasized in the novel *¡Yo!*, which Julia Alvarez writes as a continuum of *The García Girls*. In this narrative, Yolanda is in the central focus as a published writer of her family history, the project that very much upsets her family members, who do not like their fictional representations and insist on their versions of the stories. Their own accounts comprise the narrative of *¡Yo!*, in which Yolanda—Yo for short—becomes a narrative character herself while her life history enfolds through different narrative points of view.

Forming the narrative around the need to seize agency in storytelling, both novels reflect the necessity of an imaginative recreation of the past and the importance of stories in personal and collective (re)imagining. The creative process of storytelling/writing becomes a site of the agentic enunciation and the resolution of displacement and amnesia, as asserted in Cristina García's *Dreaming in Cuban*. However, the vividness of imaginative narration is presented as confusing for the García family. The sisters grow up listening to their parents' stories of life in the Dominican Republic, and this passed-on history comes to substitute their "actual" memory. Internalizing and retelling each other's story, the family creates a collective and multiply revised history, a postmodern narrative that decentralizes the singularity of reality and truth. This is why, when Yolanda writes her interpretation of their family history, nobody is sure any longer which is truth and which is fiction. Confronted with multiple versions of one family episode, the oldest sister, Carla, voices her frustration: "And I am shaking my head, no, no, because I don't know what to believe anymore except that everyone in our family is lying" (*¡Yo!*, 13). Although Yolanda's narration displaces previous versions, the novel shows that the process of re-telling and re-creating allows her to assert her own agency in the reconstruction of memory and self-imagining. Analogously, it generates further storytelling and self-imagining as her family takes on the task of additional narration and reinterpretation.

Chronologically, *¡Yo!* continues the story of Yolanda's return to the Dominican Republic and describes her subsequent summer visits as a quest for artistic inspiration and a double-voiced identity. As she learns more about her family history and her native place, Yolanda reconnects with the originary locus. "This is my home" (192), she tells her Anglo lover when he calls her during her stay in the Dominican Republic and asks her to return home to the U.S. Making a clear distinction between the two locations, he questions her belonging "there" instead of "here:" "She hasn't lived there for a quarter of a century. She works here, pays taxes here, will probably die here" (193). The quote reflects the tendency to localize one's subjectivity in a singular place, defining the more immediate dwelling as the location of 'home.' However, Yolanda's identification of the local questions the conventional conception of and distinction between 'home' and 'world:' to her the global, too, is the home.

The blurring of boundaries between two distinct spatial positions destabilizes not only the traditional organization of space but also one's sense of self. Alvarez points out that shifting from one place to another is hard even when there is a strong determination to maintain a fluid, diasporic positioning. After each of Yolanda's visits to the island, "there's bound to be some homesickness... the first few days of reentry are the hardest. You are neither here nor there" (263). In this constant relocation, one goes through a repeated process of uprooting, re-experiencing cultural dislocation in a temporarily defamiliarized location of home. To convey the anxiety that arises after one's experience of uprootedness, the author describes Yolanda's creation of symbolic modes of dealing with the perpetual relocation. Yolanda uses the Dominican practice of spiritualism to protect places that she inhabits: when she rents a room in a New Hampshire house, she makes sure that she sprinkles the spirit powder around the yard, and in her own house on a U.S. farm "all the spirit waters have to be changed before she can relax or even unpack" (258). Ironically, these rituals fail to offer the desired protection, reminding Yolanda of the impossibility of an absolute rootedness and security.

Transitioning from one home locale to the other, the novel's protagonist travels through the in-between passage, where one reality displaces the other. This shift, as a result, creates the feelings of non-belonging and decentered-ness, "neither here nor there" (263). However, this "deterritorialization" (in García-Canclini's sense of the term) does not elude spatial definition. Yolanda is aware that her place of belonging is defined by multiple locations and that the space she inhabits cannot be defined in singular terms. Her desire to physically belong to both places at the same time is manifested in her symbolic synthesis of American and Dominican soil: after a summer visit to the Dominican Republic, Yolanda brings a bag of Dominican soil and her husband buries it in their garden, performing Yolanda's ritual of "protection." However, this Santería-like act brings the "unhomely" moment to their American home, putting her husband "under a spell" and disrupting the peace of their domestic space. This is also a symbolic act of the post-colonial migrant, who brings the colony to the metropolis, recreating the marginal location in the imperial center. Aurora Levins Morales talks about it from her own diasporic Puerto Rican experience as a process of recreation of the is-land life in the U.S.: "She would live as a Puerto Rican lives en la isla, right here in north Oakland, plant the bananales and cafetales of her heart around her bedroom door, sleep under the shadow of their bloom and the carving hoarseness of the roosters, wake to blue-rimmed white enamel cups of jugo de piña..." (85). The action of fertilizing, planting, and hybridizing in the new location represents an attempt to physically recreate the lost or aban-doned space and reestablish the spatial image of the always deferred "ideal self."[20] It also symbolizes a process of re-rooting, an effort to resolve the past rupture and displacement. The ambiguity remains whether this act of trans-planting signifies recreating of the home in the global or bringing the world to the local, since the cross-national self-positioning often confuses the two locations.

However, as shown in this narrative part, the process of transplantation may reveal the "unhomeliness" of the other location, which is perplexing especially to those who experience its difference as apprehensively foreign and invasive. To Yolanda's husband, the bag of Dominican soil "has come to represent all his troubles these last two weeks, [...] all his anger at the country that keeps claiming her and taking her away from him..." (273). Like the perturbing voice of the Other, the unknown and removed location of "world" invades Doug's location of "home," disrupting its autonomy and spatial integrity. The disturbance is manifested through continuous telephone calls of a poor Dominican peasant asking for Yolanda's assistance. As the whole family tries to figure out how to help him, the peaceful domestic space becomes transformed, in Bhabha's words, into a site "for history's most intricate invasions," while Yolanda's displacement begins to reveal a deeper historical and sociopolitical meaning. Responding to this spatial confusion and reconfiguration of "the world-in-home," Yolanda's husband is eager to remove the soil even though he dismisses the power of "Dominican spells." However, this symbolic act of drawing a line between "here" and "there" is impossible, for even "he knows damn well that [the] soil is plowed throughout the garden" (273). The presence of the unhomely remains, and the initially frightful confusion of spatial boundaries translates into an "interstetial intimacy" as Doug himself gradually begins to experience a belonging to both places: "This year, he daydreams, a kind of mind travel, as if he has another simultaneous life going on long distance" (276). In his essay on exile, Edward Said calls this awareness of simultaneous dimensions "contrapuntal" (186). Generated out of the plurality of vision that is typical in the experience of exile, the contrapuntal awareness challenges the notion of homogenous and singular locations of home and culture. Clearly, the presence of Dominican reality is inevitable in Doug's life since he intimately relates to its difference and foreignness through Yolanda, who herself embodies otherness. His intimate knowledge of the Other expands boundaries of his sense of self, initiating cross-connections between the spatial and temporal positioning of the 'self' and the 'other.'

Yolanda's strong reconnection with the Dominican Republic reflects her need to retrieve the repressed past and lost memory, the symptoms of her forced departure from the island and her subsequent assimilation. Like Pilar in *Dreaming in Cuban*, Yolanda struggles with the never resolved exilic displacement and with what Marianne Hirsch calls "postmemory," a form of memory that is characteristic for second generation exiles and distinct from memory of their parents.[21] Diasporic and removed from direct experience, second generation exiles deal with an imaginary past. The lost world of their parents survives only in stories and memories as an idealized place and time that cannot be retrieved. Becoming an object of perpetual yearning and desire, the originary location forever remains elusive and imaginary. Hirsch draws attention to the power of postmemory because "its connection to its object or source is mediated not through recollection but through an imaginative investment and creation," which provides a more direct connection to the past (420). Moreover, the importance of this form of memory lies in an active effort to negotiate exilic disconnectedness and absence: "[...] postmemory seeks connection. It creates where it cannot recover. It imagines where it cannot recall. It mourns a loss that cannot be repaired" (422).

The García children are not second generation exiles, but—having left the island at a young age—their memory of their childhood in the Dominican Republic, as I have argued earlier, is constructed through the internalization of their parents' narratives, which themselves are mediated and idealized in exile. This is why the young exiles face a double removal from the originary locus: they are forced to reimagine an imaginary space. Even though the García girls visit the island many times—which is their parents' effort to preserve memory—they never reconnect with the past because they go there with no awareness of the loss. Their desire to reclaim the past resurfaces only when Yolanda realizes the absence. Like Judith and Pilar, she feels that her distance from her Dominican origins allows her only a partial remembrance. When she reaches for the memory of her childhood, the past comes to her only as a mediated and incomplete memory that is partially recreated through her parents' stories. As depicted in *The García Girls*, this is the moment when her decision to go back takes place. Even though postmemory represents an imaginative attempt at the negotiation of displacement, being a creative form of mourning, it never transcends the state of perpetual exile, as Hirsch points out. Mourning in exile/diaspora can never be overcome because "the lost object can never be incorporated," prolonging the feeling of exile, displacement, and nostalgia (422). For this reason, diasporic generations may be stimulated to look for more direct ways of negotiating their displacement.

Seeking to negotiate their temporal and spatial removal from the originary place, young generations attempt to recreate memory by connecting physically with the distant location. Their desire to "witness" the imaginary space reflects the need to remember and create at the site of loss and retrace the process of becoming. It has to be emphasized that this strategy becomes attainable to the García girls only after the fall of the regime, when the family's return to the Dominican Republic becomes safe and physically possible. Furthermore, their recreation of memory is facilitated by the affirmative conditions they find upon their return: their home and relatives have been spared the violation. The novel shows that Yolanda's physical presence at the site of memory and loss reveals the illusion of a return to the site of innocence. As the past becomes de-idealized through the present moment, the originary place receives new meanings, and this process of memory recovery becomes defined by multiple temporal frames. The possibility of new creations and connections drives Yolanda's repeated returns to the island, described in *¡Yo!*, allowing her to recreate the past through the present moment.

In this way, postmemory is mediated not only mentally but also corporeally, through a physical return and insertion of the body into the site of symbolic dismemberment. The connection between memory and the body is suggested in Yolanda's process of remembering: "Still, when she talks about the D.R., she gets all dewy-eyed as if she were crocheting a little sweater and booties for that island, as if she had given birth to it herself out of the womb of her memory" (193). The novel depicts Yolanda's reconnection with her native place not as a return to the "motherland" but, in reverse, a mother-like creation of a new being. This symbolic act of giving birth to the lost place of origin is also expressed in the older sister's decision to be artificially inseminated by sperm brought from the Dominican Republic. Although she spent many summers on the island as a teenager, Sandi does not return afterwards, like Yolanda, to deliberately reconnect with her native place. Instead, she searches for other ways to establish a connection, making an attempt to recreate the desired space in the new location. Sandi decides to reproduce a corporeal image of the lost land by transporting and physically internalizing the Dominican seed, which becomes the master signifier for the ideal and intimate connection with the lost origin.

While Sandi symbolically reproduces the lost place through a "genetic project," Yolanda does it through a discursive creation. Her physical reconnection with the place of her childhood allows her to create her own stories, stories that her family questions as exaggerated and fictitious when she attempts to "mirror life in art" (*¡Yo!*, 9). However, she claims them as her modes of dealing with displacement and loss, creating her own historical and de-colonized voice. Like García's *Dreaming in Cuban*, Alvarez's *¡Yo!* presents the project of hybrid, diasporic narration as an act that seeks to reinterpret sociopolitical disjunction and recuperate individual agency.

Focusing primarily on the character of Yolanda in her stories on the García family, Julia Alvarez attempts to explore ways of resolving exilic displacement. The story of Yolanda's arrival in her native Dominican Republic is a postcolonial narrative of a migrant in search of home in the imagined space of belonging. Yolanda's diasporic positioning in the present moment, while reclaiming the deferred past, depicts an emergence of her double-voiced, hybrid identity in the process of continual shifting between multiple locations of home, the process where one re-experiences uprooting and rooting of the self every time one leaves and arrives at a new location.

Portraying cross-national and diasporic subjectivities, Alvarez's novels of displacement reveal alternative paradigms for imagining the space, where the home and the world converge and the self becomes redefined as multiple, fluid, and continuously re/deterritorialized. Diasporic border-crossings are rendered as a project of enlightenment: providing a multiple being and vision, the diasporic positioning brings about a new identity and agency of the postmodern subject.

Cross-National Subjectivities

Foregrounding cross-national and multiple identities, the Latina texts analyzed in this chapter present new strategies of self-definition and self-positioning in conditions of displacement and re/de-territorialization. By engaging in oppositional forms of enunciation, identities constituted under the forces of sociopolitical disjunction become transformed into differential and politicized modes of being. The new subjectivities challenge the notions of self-definition based on the rootedness in a singular place and on the compliance with monolithic national identifications. In the selected texts, members of younger generations adopt a fluid cross-national positioning and a hybrid differential consciousness, refusing loyalty to singular national narratives and exclusive cultural practices.

In Judith Ortiz Cofer's *Silent Dancing*, hybrid consciousness develops in a quest for a creative voice and affirmative gender/ethnic self-definition that takes the main protagonist across the borders between the home and the world. The young Puerto Rican girl confronts the adolescent and immigrant conditions of silence and invisibility through her hybrid story-telling/writing. As she reconnects with the community and events that have formed her selfhood, she retraces the process of becoming and learns to live and survive, in Aurora Levins Morales' words, in many diasporas. In Cristina García's

Dreaming in Cuban, the affirmation of hybrid identity occurs in the context of political definition. Dislocated between two opposing sociopolitical realities and ideologies, the young protagonists search for a space where they can assert freedom from hegemonic national identifications. They contest and refuse the essentialist and dogmatic positions of their parents and grandparents by engaging in alternative and conscious modes of self-definition and positioning. In Julia Alvarez's novels, *The García Girls* and *¡Yo!*, younger generations initially cope with their cultural and exilic displacement by adopting assimilation and distancing themselves from the Dominican tradition. However, as their displacement continues to assert its "uhomely" mark, the need to reclaim the repressed past resurfaces as the desire to claim a hybrid identity and recreate the originary place. All four texts demonstrate that diasporic identity does not transcend the need to belong to a particular location, emphasizing that the belonging desired by a displaced subject is defined my multiple locations rather than a singular one.

The young protagonists' search for self-definition and a place of belonging is formed as an attempt to negotiate the existence defined by displacement and exilic departure. Their physical return to the imagined place of belonging emerges as a signifier of not only their postmodern and postcolonial migrancy but also of their psychic negotiations. Their journeys back point toward their psychological need to heal the rupture at the site of the original loss and thus regain agency in the process of self-definition. Hence, this psychologically motivated return of the diaspora is not a terminal arrival or a part of the circular process of postmodern migrancy; rather, it is a project of coming to terms with the trauma of displacement, an act of tracing back one's becoming in order to understand and liberate the present self. The possibility of new meanings and resolutions in this act of recuperation calls attention to the necessity of migrancy in identity negotiation, a negotiation established not only in cultural but also in psychological terms.

The migrant's return as an act of healing allows for an encounter with the "unhomely" that has been repressed in the course of physical and psychic displacement. This project is based on a conscious decision to return to the site of the unhomely, as opposed to the non-premeditated "return of the repressed," which reveals the unhomely but does not necessarily initiate its acceptance. The psychological negotiation that takes place in a conscious act is based on the recognition of the Other through a topographical movement, providing a remedial physical/psychic relocation that heals the traumatic disjunction of selfhood. This is where the process of an archeological recovery of self-becoming exhibits the interplay between spatial and temporal constructions of identity, leading toward a subjectivity that experiences and integrates the otherness of self.

As the "curative return" of the diaspora establishes a state of multiple belonging, of a simultaneous existing in different locations, the boundaries between the topoi of the local and of the global become blurred. The final destination of the return renders itself ambiguous as the direction of diasporic movement may be both toward the home or the world. In other words, a clear identification of the points of departure and arrival is complicated, confused in the process of re- and de-territorialization of the self. As the subject transforms itself in the act of migrancy, social space shifts its delineations and changes its meaning. This process of decentering is also evident in the hybridizing acts of the diaspora, in the symbolic recreation of other locations in the present space. Whether the local is recreated in the global or, in reverse, the world is brought home remains a postmodern dilemma of the diasporic subject.

To present a transnational hybridization of identity, U.S. Latina literature connects postmodern subjectivity to a becoming that encompasses different topographies of the self. Expanding identity in relation to territorial, national, and geopolitical definitions, the narratives analyzed in this chapter deterritorialize and empower the self through fluid, syncretic, and diasporic positionings. They assert that an understanding of self is gained in migrancy and displacement, in a circular local/global relocation that renegotiates spatial and temporal constructions of identity. In this way, these texts also provide alternative paradigms for imagining the space of the individual and the social. Employing the motif of perpetual border-crossing, they contest individual subjection to nation-space and simultanously demonstrate the impossibility of nation-space to contain difference and unhomely otherness.

However, U.S. Latina narratives of displacement do not present the possibility of physical migrancy as always easy and attainable. Psychological factors may be an obstacle as much as a motivation to return to the place of departure, as I will explain in the following chapter. Furthermore, the four texts emphasize that, in addition to individual motivation, geopolitical factors always play a crucial role in the cross-border movement since they regulate and sanction the physical passage.

CHAPTER THREE

Exilic Identities: The Interplay
Between Time and Space

*The sudden violent dispossession accompa-
nying a refugee flight is much more than the
loss of a permanent home and a traditional
occupation, or than the parting from close
friends and familiar places. It is also the death
of the person one has become in a particular
context, and every refugee must be his or her
own midwife at the painful process of rebirth.*
—Dervla Murphy, *Tibetan Foothold*

As U.S. Latina authors explore the problematics of hybrid identity, they insert in their texts the complications of geopolitics: narratives that deal with
the themes of exile and political immigration bring Latin American history
and politics into a U.S. context. The upheavals in El Salvador, the Dominican Republic, and Cuba[1] are depicted as traveling across international borders in the form of internalized, psychological realities of main protagonists.
In many of these texts, the experience of political violence in the homeland is
translated into a haunting presence in the space of exile. Fear of persecution,
for example, is shown as a constant in spite of spatial deferral, being internalized in the victim's psyche and projected onto the new location. Portraying
the loss of distinct boundaries between danger and safety, U.S. Latina writers

set out to demonstrate the presupposed safety of exile as a relative and easily disrupted condition, a condition greatly dependent on and connected to the space beyond its territorial boundaries.

The inclusion of the Central American/Caribbean experience in U.S. Latina literature focuses attention on the lasting effects of political violence in the process of individual self-development. This international connection foregrounds the investigation of identity construction not only in relation to the interplay between psychological and cultural processes but also in the context of specific historical and political conditioning. As U.S. Latina narratives of displacement demonstrate, the upsurge of violence and political instability in Central America and the Caribbean initiates multiple waves of immigrations into the U.S.,[2] and the effects of physical displacement become manifested as crucial formative factors in an individual and, by extension, a socio-cultural development. Political immigrants' positioning in the new location is continuously disrupted by an unhealed trauma, which becomes intensified when political victimization intertwines with cultural repression and this trauma is passed on to new generations.

Articulating the geopolitical concern across national borders, U.S. Latina literature illustrates that geopolitical conditions—in addition to those of race, ethnicity, gender, and class—are fundamentally important in the formation of individual identity and therefore need to be included in the discussion of identity politics. The short story "The Cariboo Café" (1985) and the novels *Dreaming in Cuban* (1992) and *How the García Girls Lost Their Accents* (1992) dramatize a fragmentation of personal 'integrity'[3] through the complications of exile. As the protagonists in these narratives struggle to negotiate their cultural displacement, they also have to face the effects of geopolitical factors. Fleeing political violence and oppression, they suffer from, in Amy Kaminsky's terms, "a physical and a psychic dislocation." Removed from their native countries and thrown into a foreign land, the narrative exiles initially belong to neither place and consequently internalize this emptiness.

As Edward Said notes, a rift between a human being and native place often results in an alienation from the self ("Reflections on Exile" 173). This absence of a strong grounding provokes feelings of uprootedness and nonbelonging, endangering one's personal sense of being and propelling one into perpetual solitude and nostalgia. The inability to find a stable and complete meaning provokes a crisis of self, a fragmented subjectivity placed in a continuous state of lack. This condition parallels the feelings of disorienting loss and anxiety that the self may experience in the conflictual space of biculturalism, the problematics I have explored in the first chapter. However, while the feeling of loss emerges in the bicultural self through a repression of the other culture, in the condition of exile it proceeds from a complete erasure. Denied home and integrity in both the homeland and the immigrant location, exiles become confined to the space of absence and loss, or what Said calls "a perilous territory of not-belonging" (177).

In her analysis of Latin American women's writing in exile, *Reading the Body Politic* (1993), Amy Kaminsky theorizes exile as a particular form of "presence-in absence." She emphasizes its spatial configuration, pointing out that exile is primarily "from, and not to, a place" (30). As a physical topicality constituted by departure, exile is defined by "what is missing, not by what it contains," and its conditions of loss and emptiness foster "a will to return into presence" (32). Desire to reclaim presence is manifested, Kaminsky states, in perpetual longing, nostalgia, a wish to return, and a fear of return to the place where one can no longer be. Consequently, exile is experienced as dislocation, both physical and psychic. The exiled person is "the stranger, not seen, misperceived," and as such he/she projects this internal emptiness onto the surroundings (32). In addition, being "no longer present in the place departed, but not part of the new location," the exiled person is in a "perpetual state of suspension" (30). As a condition of displacement, exile is constructed as "presence-in-absence," a topos defined by lack and erasure.

On the other hand, exile also offers liberating possibilities. Kaminsky notes that the experience of physical and emotional rupture can lead to personal growth and transformation. Through the discovery of an inner capacity "to survive and grow in the new environment" (37) one may find a greater independence and confidence and thus gain a more fulfilling self-affirmation and realization. Kaminsky compares this act of self-discovery to rebirth, an emergence of new personhood and subjectivity. As Dervla Murphy states (see the chapter's epigraph), the exilic rebirth is inevitably connected to death, "the death of the person one has become in a particular context." Evidently, this individual liberation—or, in Murphy's words, the painful process of rebirth—is attained in traumatic circumstances, but this is precisely why its meaning is so powerful and valuable.

U.S. Latina literature offers similar insights into exilic experiences. Most of the exiled characters in the narratives discussed in this chapter are portrayed as experiencing exile in terms of loss and erasure: they perceive the U.S. in terms of their missing home, limited agency, and fragmented identity. However, many of them are depicted transcending this absence by transforming it into a form of presence and a site of self-affirmation. They are allowed to gain confidence and affirmation not only through the "capacity to survive and grow in the new environment" but also by seizing opportunities for self-transformation that are found in the new location. Yet, some protagonists are shown experiencing exilic absence in a different way: they embrace it as a comforting distance from the source of pain and trauma. As its complexity and ambiguity become revealed through diverse and distinct personal experiences, exile in these texts ceases to be a homogenous and immutable condition: while its state is demonstrated to be debilitating, it is presented as also potentially liberating. By emphasizing this multifold nature, U.S. Latina literature investigates exile as a complicated and complex condition that evades generalization and consistency.

Exile is so often thought of in terms of loss and nostalgia for place—Kaminsky's theory, for example—but U.S. Latina narratives demonstrate that temporal dimensions of exile are fundamentally important, too, as they condition imaginative recreation of home and desire to return. To depict how exilic experience becomes negotiated in both spatial and temporal variables, U.S. Latina writers portray main protagonists conceiving of home either through a construction of memory or through a form of self-imposed forgetting. Also, the traditional notion of exile as a space of safety is destabilized through the representation of violence and oppression as a continuum across national borders. Narrative protagonists often experience in the new location similar protocols of dehumanization and regulation from which they have initially escaped. In addition, they often struggle with an internalized trauma that does not diminish with physical distance but, in fact, manifests itself in an imagined temporal synchronicity. Lastly, although often rendered in terms of disempowerment and terminal loss, exilic absence in these texts also exhibits a creative and transformative potential. As the absent home in the space of exile acquires a non-traditional signification—absence of absolute male dominance and power—the absence becomes redefined into a form of female presence and self-reinvention. Kaminsky argues that exile may offer to women self-transcendence by freeing them from the patriarchal culture of homeland. In the female experience of exile, the rupture from home comes to signify an emergence of another self that can engender self-transformation, "a split not from but within the self, into two distinct beings—the self and the double—that can enable transcendence" (39). Engaging varied perspectives on exile and exposing different meanings of exilic absence, U.S. Latina writers redefine exilic existence as a meaningful effort to survive, an effort based on the renegotiation of time, space, absence, and power.

In order to emphasize the importance of temporal dimensions in negotiation of exile, authors discussed in this chapter build narrative structures that go against the traditional temporal conventions of the plot line. The nonlinear retrospective line of narration in their novels functions as a reflection of the exilic desire to return, which arises as a reaction to marginalization and alienation experienced in exile. This narrative structure also reconstructs the process of returning to the originary place, a process that offers the possibility of self-knowledge and reveals the illusions of innocence and completion. The frequent use of narrative silences, too, conveys the idea of loss— the impossibility of a return to the site of innocence and of a recuperation of the lost object. The absence of closure and the state of perpetual lack in exile resonate in these texts as mute or missing passages of the narration. The series of analepses, or flashbacks that retrieve the past experience, reveal the return of the repressed, demonstrating the failure to completely repress the painful experience of political violence and the forced departure from home. The continuation of the traumatic experience in the presumed safety of exile further problematizes the traditional understanding of exilic condition and its spatial and temporal constructions. The multivoiced narrative structure employed in U.S. Latina narratives exposes a multiplicity of reality and the complexity of exilic circumstances. Articulating different experiences of displacement and different responses to exilic conditions, the polyphonic structure exposes the complications and dialectics of exile, where exilic absence and loss acquire multiple, shifting, and contradictory meanings.

The Interplay Between Time and Space

In his rendering of exilic existence, Edward Said captures the interplay between time and space: "For an exile, habits of life, expression, or activity in the new environment inevitably occur against the memory of these things in another environment. Thus, both the new and the old environments are vivid, actual, occurring together contrapuntally" ("Reflections on Exile" 186). This experience is typical of exilic existence, but it takes place when exilic memory is based on a profound nostalgia for the place and time left behind. An exile, in that case, fights to preserve his/her connections with the removed location of home. Home, in this process, receives a signification of the cultural matrix that informs and affects one's identity—the familiar social milieu of family, friends, community, and cultural practices—and is associated with the feelings of rootedness, belonging, and security. The rupture of an individual from this matrix induces the exilic nostalgia for home and is projected as the absence and loss of home.

U.S. Latina literature further complicates subject-positioning in the space of exile by foregrounding different constructions of exilic memory, primarily defined by variable temporal and spatial discontinuities. The selected texts show that an exile may be detached from the present and completely immersed in the past, or distanced from the past and turned towards the future. In these instances, the old and the new environments do not occur contrapuntally and cannot be experienced as vivid and actual. The Central American mother in the story "The Cariboo Café" is so traumatized by the murder of her son that she is unable to situate herself in the present; her living in exile is infused only with the memory of her past reality. On the other hand, Lourdes Puente in *Dreaming in Cuban* completely represses the traumatic past and inserts herself in an escapist construction of the present; her exilic existence is based on a persistent "denial"[4] of memory, rather than a vivid remembrance of the past.

These narratives demonstrate that while the geographic displacement of exiles is a forced physical movement, their temporal dislocation is psychologically induced. The protagonists' minds function in a singular time frame, repressing other temporal dimensions and thus avoiding conflicting realities. In Lourdes' case, the past time frame is associated with her traumatic experience, and the present is constructed as an escape from that past. In the case of the Central American mother, the past time is associated with happiness and home, and the present—as a negation of the past—is consequently experienced as depressing and traumatic. The repression of one temporal dimension takes place in order to evade a disruption of one's positioning in a fixed time frame. This time frame is usually an escapist one, functioning as a defense mechanism. To alleviate her pain, the Central American refugee derealizes and displaces the present moment by building her immediate reality on the memory of time spent with her son. Lourdes, on the other hand, obsessively invests herself in the plans for present and future business enterprises in order to forget the traumas of the past.

It is important to note that exilic repression and absence occur in both involuntary and "voluntary" exile since departure from home is experienced as a traumatic moment in both cases. As U.S Latina authors assert, the trauma of departure problematizes the voluntariness of exile: none of the Latina/o protagonists is portrayed deciding to leave her/his homeland and become an exile with complete ease and consent. All characters in the selected texts are introduced as having a painful remembrance of the separation, and their efforts to survive in exile are presented as a persistent confrontation with the distressing memory through either a persistent repression or mourning of the past.

Their pressure to leave, whether direct or indirect, is always connected to an external force: although not expelled, voluntary exiles do not leave by their own choice; their decision is always enforced by the outer, sociopolitical reality. Unstable economic and political situations in their homelands induce fear of persisting violence, political oppression, poverty, corruption, and psychic depression. Thus, their willingness to leave is never arbitrary, and their exile is never completely voluntary.

Resettlement in a foreign land implies another common trauma that all exiles face—the struggle for identity and presence in an alien environment that enforces either their assimilation or marginalization. While the Puentes family faces a loss of the original culture because of the mother's pressure to assimilate, the Garcías encounter a lack of recognition in the public space as the parents struggle to retain the original cultural identity. However, both families gradually learn to cope with the absence, finding out that the gain and loss are dialectically connected in the space of exile. On the other hand, the exiled mother from Central America meets a tragic end as she struggles to recuperate her obliterated presence. Carrying the meaning of loss of connections with the home left behind, exilic relocation adds new discontinuities to the subjectivity placed in an unfamiliar location.

The selected Latina narratives make it evident that exile is not only a spatial location but also a temporal projection: it is the present time frame, associated with either a negative or a positive experience. In the same way, home is a symbol of the past, carrying positive or negative connotations. The fluidity of these configurations—exile and home—and their different articulation in time and space reveal the complexity and ambiguity of the exilic experience. The exiled in the narratives discussed in this chapter struggle with the complexity of exile while they try to negotiate their displacement, both spatial and temporal, both physical and mental.

"The Cariboo Café:" A Deterritorialization of Violence

The threat of erasure experienced in political displacements begets a desire to recuperate the loss, to regain presence and visibility, and to reclaim the originary place. This desire to restore emerges as a vision of a return, embodying possibility and hope. As Amy Kaminsky points out, exile's desire to repair and return into presence rests on "a project of transformation" (33). In Helena María Viramontes's story "The Cariboo Café," an exiled woman leaves her country in order to construct a return and recuperate the loss. After losing her five-year-old son in the Central American civil war, she goes to the U.S. in search of a better future, which she defines as a reunion with her son. With the loss of her child, her homeland loses its meaning of home and is projected as a land of absence and erasure: "Without Geraldo," she realizes upon her loss, "this is not my home; the earth beneath it, not my country" (75). The haunting memory of the loss follows her across multiple national borders to the U.S., where a desperate desire for recuperation leads her to vicariously recreate her son through an unknown Latino boy. The scene describing their encounter suggests that the woman's relationship with the boy has cathectic dynamics.[5] Detached from reality, the mother clings to her "newly found child" because he completes her fantasy of the reunion and thus displaces her anxiety and trauma. The depth of her delusion is conveyed in the moment when she plans an immediate return to Central America, her country regaining its meaning of home as the loss appears to be recuperated: "Tomorrow she will make arrangements to go home. María will be the same, the mango stand on the corner next to the church plaza will be the same. It will all be the way it was before" (76). The "way it was before" does not denote here the time before the war; rather, it signifies a condition of the familial unity and grounding that existed even during the political upheavals. However, when the destructiveness of the outer, sociopolitical reality invades the domestic space, this condition becomes ruptured. The wholeness of motherhood and family is violated by the separation and dehumanization enforced from the outside, the sphere of the repressive military apparatus of a Central American government.

Loss and erasure, or in Kaminsky's terms "departure into exilic absence" (32), occur in this story even before the exilic border crossing. This is illustrated in the first part, where the author describes denial of individual identity in the public sphere. After her child "disappears," the mother is not allowed to search for him in the "detention centers"; a government official simply ignores her presence and dismisses her pleas. As the woman feels too paralyzed to fight for presence in the public space,[6] her family becomes invisible and her home disintegrated. "These four walls are no longer my house; the earth beneath it, no longer my home" (75), she repeats and leaves for the U.S. in hope of finding the "disappeared" Geraldo beyond the borders of a military state.

Dramatizing the conditions of political violence and terror in Central America, the story attempts to explain why many Central Americans were forced to flee from their home countries. It also calls attention to the fact that exile begins with an escape from violence that may never end. The Central American woman leaves her homeland fleeing annihilation and destruction. However, her exile in the U.S. does not offer her more visibility or presence. She is confined to her nephew's crowded studio apartment and the filthy locations of her cleaning jobs. On the streets of Los Angeles she is anonymous, knowing no English and having no friends. Debilitated linguistically and socially in the American urban space, she also becomes labeled as an intruder: "[I] hear the lady saying something in Spanish. Right off I know she's illegal, which explains why she looks like a weirdo" (70), comments the owner of the Cariboo Café the first time that he sees her in his diner. This narrative section points out that having been already stripped of integrity and identity in Central America, the exiled is enmeshed in a similar technology of dehumanization in the U.S. Marked by her linguistic difference and class marginality, she faces another protocol of authoritative oppression: the denial of acceptance in the new social space. As Sonia Saldívar-Hull points out, the woman's "Brownness signifies alterity" and exposes how "the dominant marginalize on the basis of color and language" (148).

The Cariboo Café, a gathering place of workers in an industrial part of Los Angeles, is established as a symbolic representation of exile. The remaining *o*'s in its faded name ("oo Café") become read as zeros—the characters in the story dub it as "the zero-zero place" or "the double zero café" (68)—signifying a place of absence and a double exile, from home and from the new location. Desperately sought as a refuge from the immigration police ("*la migra*"), the café turns into a site of betrayal and violence. As Debra Castillo states, the café functions as "an empty signifier, a parody of no-man's land, an illusory crossroads where characters mistakenly believe the shadows that haunt them can be held at bay" (81). Referring to the U.S. immigration policy, the story incorporates an episode where illegal factory workers are targeted in a police raid and are taken to deportation centers. The author calls attention to the poignancy of this experience: after having fled violence and hardships in their native countries, Central American refugees face the same oppression in the U.S. The reader is made to realize the fallacy of the "land of freedom:" the protectiveness of exile is shattered in the same way as was the protectiveness of home. Furthermore, the author warns that the possibility of safety is relativized in any location: violence turns out to be an omnipresent and polymorphous force, easily deterritorialized and turned against the innocent.

Merging different narrative voices and loci, the story continues to emphasize the persistence and invasiveness of political violence in different sociopolitical locations. The unknown mother from Central America is shown experiencing exile in the same way she has experienced violent repression in her homeland. When the police come to take the boy she "kidnapped,"[7] the boundaries between the realities of Central America and Los Angeles merge in her psyche. As Sonia Saldívar-Hull remarks, the woman's confrontation with the U.S. police becomes a continuation of her struggle with the police from Central America (151). However, while in Central America the mother is paralyzed before the indifference of government authorities, in the U.S. she regains agency by refusing to give up the Latino boy to *la migra*. Believing that she is fighting to keep her son, Geraldo, she relives the return of the repressed in all its immediacy and intensity:

> But her legs are heavy and she crushes Geraldo against her, so tight, as if she wants to conceal him in her body again, return him to her belly so that they will not castrate him and hang his small blue penis on her door, not crush his face so that he is unrecognizable, not bury him among the heaps of bones, and ears, and teeth, and jaws, because no one but she cared to know that he cried. (78)

This painful flashback reveals the deepest horror of the sociopolitical reality in Central America. Geraldo is established as one of the numerous victims of state terror, and his mother's pain is described as an expression of a collective trauma: "[s]he begins screaming all over again, screaming so that the walls shake, screaming enough for all the women of murdered children, screaming, pleading for help from the people outside…" (78). Many critics[8] have related this moment to the myth of *La Llorona*, a mother grieving the loss of her murdered children.[9] It is important to emphasize that Viramontes transforms an individual experience of injury and bereavement into a communal condition: the intensity of screaming is amplified to express the pain of all the mothers who have lost their children. The collectivity of grieving mothers spreads across state borders and it is "all children in the Américas," as José Saldívar claims, that are mourned (*Border Matters* 106). This scene suggests solidarity across national borders by denationalizing violence and urging communal resistance. However, in the end, the woman's plea for help remains unanswered as the police violently assert their presence and once again paralyze any public action.

The explosion of pain felt in the final scene dramatizes the return of the repressed: the woman relives the traumatic moment of finding her son killed and mutilated. This flashback merges with the present moment of loss, and the fear of repeated obliteration—both physical and psychological—gives the woman strength to fight the officers until they overpower her. "You can no longer frighten me" (78), she shouts at them, confusing them with the Central American police and continuing to resist them, "I am laughing, howling at their stupidity because they should know by now that I will never let my son go" (79). The mother desperately holds onto the dream of a return to the time and place before the loss: "But I hold onto his hand. That I can feel, you see, I'll never let go. Because we are going home. My son and I" (79). Home embodies a "state of innocence," a condition prior to violation, when one possessed personal safety and integrity. Debra Castillo recognizes this desire to return as a "dream of re-incorporation" (91), of returning the newborn infant to the womb: "She wants to conceal him in her body again, return him to her belly so that they will not castrate him..." (106). The woman's desire for reincorporation reveals again the cathectic and symbiotic dynamics[10]—the complete oneness of mother and son achieved through the ultimate physical unison that happens in the 'pre-symbolic stage.'[11] The womb signifies the originary place and points toward the condition that precedes the symbolic order and entry of the phallic figure. It is interesting to note the reversal of subject positioning: it is the mother, not the child, who experiences their separation, or the distinction between the two subjects, as a traumatic moment. She realizes that the ultimate safety exists only outside of the social realm, away from its protocols of regulation and oppression. In this situation, the entry of the phallic figure comes to suggest a process of not only self-differentiation but also oppression and authoritarian control over women and children. The return to the womb, therefore, signifies a desired state of freedom and protection from violence, and the woman's confrontation with the police, as José Saldívar notices, functions as a symbolic attempt to destroy patriarchy (*Border Matters* 106).

The universality of violence and oppression is portrayed in this scene through a parallelism of the same protocols of force and dehumanization in Central America and the U.S. The American police attack an unarmed woman, with no concern for her true role in the situation. They automatically profile her as a criminal, the one undoubtedly guilty of posing a severe threat to their system. She, on the other hand, perceives their aggressive force as a violent system of no specific national identification: it is just the impersonal "they," who are "swift and cunning and can take your life with a snap of a finger" (76), threatening with "their guns taught [sic] and cold like steel erections" (78). Recognizing the same technology of force and destruction, the Central American woman believes that she is back in the land of oppressive political regime and violence. This slippage in reality conveys the idea that the repressive state is not limited to military regimes, affirming Louis Althusser's argument that the state apparatus is fundamentally repressive. Represented by the government, the police, the army, and the court, the state apparatus functions predominantly as a force of repressive execution and intervention used to ensure its own cohesion and authority.[12] Thus, as dramatized in Viramontes' story, the repressive state asserts its presence in any geopolitical space, demonstrating that forceful state repression is a global phenomenon, unrestricted by national insignias.

In addition, the dynamics of state repression and authoritarianism are revealed as forms of patriarchal power, another cross-national phenomenon. The military system in Central America is represented, as Carl Gutiérrez-Jones notices, through "clichéd manipulations of patriarchal rhetoric" (*Rethinking the Borderlands* 121), while the oppressive U.S. government is presented as taking on a phallic appearance with its aggressive police apparatus: "their guns taught and cold like steel erections" (Viramontes 78). Throughout the story, the images of patriarchal authority and sociopolitical totalitarian power merge with each other to reveal a reciprocal and contiguous relationship, thus providing criticism of both structures of power. Giving a very disturbing, tragic ending to the story, the author adamantly concludes that the inhumane treatment of Central American refugees in the U.S. reveals the cruelty and indifference of the U.S. immigration policy before the plight of innocent victims of political regime.

The story resonates with the crucial problematics of the exilic experience: the distinction between home and exile, as well as between danger and safety, becomes complicated and problematized. Home represents both danger and safety, violence loses national identifications, and the desire to return becomes an obsession. However, the narrative suggests that home in "The Cariboo Café" is not associated with destruction and violence; rather, it is displaced and disassociated from any violation. It symbolizes the familial unity between son and mother and remains manifested as such in the desire to reclaim this unity. This displacement is facilitated by the continuation of violence and dehumanization as traumatic experiences in the new location, and for this reason the Central American mother projects the former location as a desired place. Because it precedes the latest violation, the dangerous site of home paradoxically acquires the meaning of recuperation. The author does not suggest that the woman perceives the violence in Central America as less destructive than the one in the U.S.; rather, the suggestion is that the displaced woman ceases to perceive violence in the home country as she represses it in the act of psychological defense. Moreover, the narrative depiction of the woman's confrontation with the U.S. police is intertextually tied to the historical fact that the U.S. was supporting military dictatorships in Central America at the time and was thus implicated in the murder of Central American civilians. This is why the story utilizes the narrative twist in the end: the violent conflict in Central America is superimposed onto a U.S. terrain and the violence against an innocent woman is executed by the U.S. police. The author presents the violence in the U.S. as a "return of the repressed," an inevitable effect of the U.S. political/military hegemony in Central America.

The question remains whether exile could replace home if it offered personal wholeness and security. Probably yes, but the problem lies in the fact that exile does not erase the trauma of the past experience. It is a constant remainder of the forceful displacement from the temporal and locational site of the unviolated self, the condition of self prior to the loss. This is why one's desire to return becomes so strong: one constantly longs to go back to this "site of innocence" in order to recuperate the loss. In addition, if the country of exile is complicit with violent events in the home country, the exiles are likely to be denied the status and protection of exile, or they are likely to become resentful of their decision to leave home. In this instance, they might prefer to go back when they begin to perceive their life in exile as either a continued peril or an indirect complicity with the perpetrator. Even though it would mean a return to the site of violence and oppression, the determination to leave the space of exile is born out of the psychosomatic need to remove the self from violence.

How the García Girls Lost Their Accents: Creating Presence in the Space of Absence

Julia Alvarez's novel *How the García Girls Lost Their Accents* exposes different degrees of exilic trauma. Focusing on the process of acculturation, it tells a story of a Dominican family who leaves its home because of the father's involvement in the resistance movement. After a planned overthrow of Trujillo's government falls short, the García family escapes to the U.S. before a threat of retaliation. The new country offers them security, but the memory of political terror comes to haunt the father: "[f]or the rest of his life he will be haunted by blood in the streets and late night disappearances" (146). As the story progresses, the reader learns that Carlos García lost his brothers and friends to the dictator and was himself on the list for execution. Because of his political engagement, he was followed and his house was continuously watched.

The narrative development of Carlos García's character illuminates one aspect of exilic existence, allowing Alvarez to impart that the consequences of living in political terror are far reaching. The father's fear of persecution does not disappear with geographic distance; in the U.S. it progresses into an obsession: he cringes at the sight of black Volkswagens or anybody in uniform, imagining the Dominican secret police following him everywhere. The scenes describing the haunting effects of Carlos' past are engaged throughout the novel in order to demonstrate an internalization of violence and a consequent paranoia. For example, the violence on the Dominican streets is superimposed on the American reality: even the person giving out parking tickets, or a museum guard, looks suspicious to Carlos García. As in "The Cariboo Café," two realities merge in the victim's psyche since the fear of political violence ceases to be contained within national boundaries. The self is forever violated and the trauma does not diminish with distance. Ultimately, the presupposed safety of exile is destabilized and ruptured.

The major part of the novel is set in the "post-exile" years, after the fall of the Trujillo regime. Technically, the Garcías are not in exile any longer and could return home. However, the author uses this situation to call attention to the complexity of meaning of exile: the return may be physically possible but not necessarily psychologically attainable, even after the physical danger has been removed. The Garcías manage to go back to their homeland after the fall of the regime, but they never stay for good. After three years in the U.S. and the strong desire of the whole family to go back home, Carlos takes the first trip "for a trial visit" (107) but returns discouraged by the continuing political instability: "It is no hope for the Island. I will become *un dominican-york*" (107). The narrative does not fully describe his first trip back and his experience of the long desired return. However, this narrative silence reflects the feeling of disappointment at the impossibility of such a return, signifying an absence of completion and a lack of closure. Later, the García children go to the island for summer visits, and in spite of their initial homesickness—"we sisters wailed and paled, whining to go home" (107)—they learn that the Dominican Republic does not signify home any longer: after a few years in the U.S. and their quick acculturation, "Island was old hat" (108). The mother slowly adjusts to American life too, finding more personal freedom and affirmation in the new country. The father still feels out place in the U.S., but after his first trip and subsequent disappointment he at last realizes the impossibility of a complete return. With this narrative turn, the author communicates that while temporary returns to the originary place soothe, to some extent, the pain of physical dislocation, they also reveal the illusion of a return to the idealized past. Also, as living in exile inevitably becomes a process of new-identity-acquisition, the former location is re-experienced in reference to the new place: the whole family begins to perceive the Dominican Republic through the lens of American reality, realizing that they do not belong there as much as before. This consequently causes a rupture of the past moment reality and forces the family to think of the future in terms of the new location. The present moment becomes defined by the potentiality of exile instead of by the nostalgia for the absent experience. With the temporal continuum reestablished, the exilic condition of the Garcías is portrayed as acquiring more normalcy and progression.

While the novel demonstrates that exile has a universal meaning of physical and mental displacement, it also makes it clear that this universality is mediated by specific individual and social circumstances. Although, in the beginning, the life in the new country is hard and painful for the entire family, the patterns of adjustment differ according to age and gender. Members of the younger generation embrace assimilation in order to fit in their peers' world, while the older generations resist assimilation in order to maintain their original cultural identity. While the male experience of exile continues to be debilitating and frustrating, the female experience of exile becomes more positive and affirming. The García girls quickly adjust to the American mainstream, which consequently distances them from their Dominican roots. Their mother opposes their Americanization only at first, since later she herself adopts some new practices: she becomes more emancipated and self-reliant, "dreaming of a bigger-than-family-size life for herself" (116). While her husband still debates whether to move back to the Dominican Republic, she is determined to stay: "But Laura had gotten used to the life here. She did not want to go back to the old country where, de la Torre or not, she was only a wife and a mother (and a failed one at that, since she had never provided the required son). Better an independent nobody than a high-class house slave" (143).

Laura's internalization of the American trait of self-reliance is more clearly seen when juxtaposed with the views held by her sister-in-law in the Dominican Republic. While Laura prefers her independence to her social class, her sister-in-law values the opposite. When her nieces try to educate her about women's rights, Tía Flor simply remarks: "Look at me, I'm a queen. [M]y husband has to go to work every day. I can sleep till noon, if I want. I'm going to protest for my *rights*?" (121). Presenting Laura's and Flor's mutually opposing reactions, the novel aims to exemplify the opposing systems of cultural values in the two countries. While both societies value material wealth, they perceive social class differently: in the U.S. one's wealth determines one's social stratum, while in the Dominican Republic one's birth guarantees certain class and reputation. The story of the Garcías' exile points out that their upper social class loses significance in a U.S. context, making their adjustment more difficult and frustrating. On the island, their reputation is built on the fact that they are descendants of the white *conquistadores*; in the U.S., on the other hand, they are defined only as immigrants, or as Laura says, "nobody" (143).

The Garcías' immigrant experience brings out the ambiguity and contradiction of their class consciousness. Their emigration to the U.S. brings them a downward social mobility because they enter the U.S. economic system with no economic power, the major determinant of class positioning. However, they still have cultural capital—social and cultural refinement and education—which is usually a hallmark of a high-class society. With this double social positioning, their class identification becomes ambivalent and confusing, which often happens in the case of exiles from an upper-class rank that lose financial potency in the immigrant location. Both Carlos and Laura cling to their Dominican class consciousness—Laura always emphasizes her last name even in the U.S.—but they soon realize that economic capital dictates class identifications. Even though their cultural capital makes their exilic survival far from the misery of poor, uneducated refugees, their loss of economic potency feels to them rather incapacitating.

Nonetheless, in spite of their relative immigrant hardships, women are portrayed as experiencing affirmation and emancipation in terms of their gender consciousness. The possibility of articulating themselves outside of the domestic space gives them a sense of independence and recognition. They transcend the roles of devoted wives, mothers, and daughters and are able to develop their own careers and interests. Laura García eagerly embraces opportunities for more education and gains more confidence in her intellectual skills. This possibility of women's independence becomes the determining factor for her positive experience of exile.

This narrative development clearly asserts that in spite of the conditions of absence and annihilation, exile also carries a potential for presence and affirmation. In the case of female experience, marginalization and physical dislocation become negotiated more easily if the space of exile offers emancipation and recognition. In her analysis of Latin American women writers in exile, Amy Kaminsky emphasizes that women, too, suffer in exile, but their advantage in exile primarily rests in their [relative] freedom from "the oppressive sexism of the home culture" (39).

In this light, it is home rather than exile that is often perceived as a place of absence and annihilation. Its mechanisms of subordination and confinement parallel, paradoxically, a condition of exile. Besides seeing the Dominican concept of social class as limiting and deluding, Laura feels degraded and marginalized by the patriarchal concept of male superiority. She suffers from the lack of recognition for her motherhood because she "continuously fails" to bear a son. Even her husband is displeased, as manifested when he jokes about "his harem of four girls" (26) and boasts that "good bulls sire cows" (40). His macho sentiments are revealed in an episode where he visits his first-born and long awaited grandson and devotes all attention to him while ignoring his sister. Along with gender discrimination, Carlos exhibits racial preferences: "All the Caribbean fondness for a male heir and for Nordic looks had surfaced" (27).

It is this "Caribbean fondness for males," a regionally acculturated patriarchy, that constructs home as a space of absence and marginalization for women, while it reaffirms the power and control granted to men. Its absence in the space of exile leaves Carlos disempowered while it liberates his wife and daughters. The lack of dominance and control in the public space makes him paralyzed and debilitated. The dinner with the Fannings at a fancy restaurant becomes an uneasy evening for Carlos as he fails to assert control. His diminished financial power and marginalized social status do not allow him to pay for everybody or to buy Barbie dolls offered to his daughters by the waitress. At his home on the island, he was always a generous host and a father who brought home expensive presents. However, in the space of exile his privileged position and power are denied by different protocols of social mobility and gender positioning.

The novel maintains that when in exile in a less male-dominated country than their own, men feel disempowered due to the lack of patronizing patriarchal codes and strict class hierarchy; on the other hand, the less pervasive presence of patriarchy allows women to gain a liberating experience. The more patriarchal social norms guarantee agency and recognition to men, as their regulatory protocols position women in limited and unrecognized roles. Julia Alvarez does not imply that U.S. society is rid of traditional patriarchal norms, but she does maintain that women's agency and emancipation are more pronounced in America than in the strongly macho societies. This claim is made in *The Mixquiahuala Letters,* too, through similar gender and class dynamics. As I have pointed out in the earlier discussion of this book, Ana Castillo allows her novel's main protagonists, Teresa and Alicia, to perceive and experience contrasting values between the U.S. and Mexico in relation to women's emancipation and men's consciousness about female liberation. The author illustrates that the assertion of woman's agency acquires different meanings in these two countries: in the patriarchal space of Mexico, it is regarded as transgressive, while in the less patriarchal U.S. it is accepted as a social process of women's liberation. Similarly, Rosario Morales writes in *Getting Home Alive* that she stops imagining Puerto Rico as her home when she encounters its oppressive patriarchal culture. As I have argued in

Chapter One, women protagonists in these texts recognize the distinct social meaning and decide to inhabit the space that signifies female presence and articulation. This active feminist positioning enables the authors to reinforce positive gender subjectivity of the female experience.

Alvarez's novel demonstrates that in women's experience exilic marginality can be transformed to signify female empowerment. By allowing an easier access to female articulation, visibility, and agency, the exilic absence can provide some form of presence. However, its alienating aspect may not be completely overcome since other dimensions of exilic experience may persist as annihilating and debilitating, such as an unhealed traumatic past, a perpetual nostalgia for homeland, cultural and linguistic exclusion, and possible racism and labor exploitation. It also needs to be stressed that exile into strongly patriarchal countries does not carry a potential for emancipation. In that case, women become doubly marginalized: as exiles and as women.

In men's experience, exile becomes a site of emasculation, or, as Amy Kaminsky notes, feminization. Kaminsky connects exile to femininity, noting that the condition of exile and the condition of women in patriarchy are alike and "both occur with striking frequency, often in the same place" (29). Both conditions signify marginality, lack of agency, and invisibility. As the novel shows, for Carlos García exile is defined by what is missing—male power and recognition—while for his wife and daughters it is defined by what it contains—female emancipation and recognition. This paradoxical condition, where absence becomes presence, stands again as a very specific exemplification of the annihilating power of patriarchy: absence of male domination opens a space for female presence.

Throughout the novel, the dialectics of absence and presence in relation to exile and home takes on a non-traditional signification in the context of female experience: exile carries a potential of presence, while home contains absence and marginality. When translated into feminist terminology, exile relates to the public sphere, where it is usually easier to realize emancipation; while home is strongly connected to the private sphere, where women become defined only in a domestic context. It needs to be stressed again that this paradigm is presented in a very specific context and thus should not be regarded as universal. As I will show in Chapter Four, in politically authoritarian societies, women (and dissenting men) are denied entrance into the public sphere, and in such conditions home is often constituted as a space of safety and personal autonomy, even though that space can be violated too (as

I have illustrated in Chapter One while examining women's lack of safety in both the private and public spheres).

Telling a story of political immigration, Alvarez shows that a gendered experience of exile occurs in two distinct spheres: domestic and sociopolitical. The necessity to participate in the public realm makes exiled women more likely to adopt different gender consciousness. In the private sphere, the values and traditions from the "old country" are not that easily changed. Nevertheless, female emancipation becomes forged in the private sphere when subversions of patriarchy from the public domain enter the Garcías' American home. The García women constantly remind the father that they do not live in a "savage country" (146) any longer, arguing that a challenge of authority and celebration of individualism are not crimes in the U.S. When one of the daughters writes a school speech inspired by Walt Whitman's "Song to Myself," the father condemns her writing for its direct challenge of authority. His concern regarding teachers' authority projects his own fear. The father's patriarchal figure is undermined too, since the speech gives power to the traditionally marginalized and silenced group in both the public and private spheres—the young generation. Thus, the "savageness of the Dominican Republic" carries a double meaning in this context, signifying both a political and a patriarchal oppression. As I have argued in the analysis of "The Cariboo Café," these two kinds of oppression often come together. Based on the same premise—an exercise of phallic power—patriarchy and political regime are mutually conditioned and thus closely related. In this light, the absent home in the space of exile acquires another connotation: it conveys the absence of patriarchal authority, absence that debilitates men and liberates women.

One of the images of absence in exile is established in the very moment of the family's departure from the island. Alvarez describes it as "a hole opening wide inside that would never be filled" (215). This perpetual lack illustrates that the enforced separation from homeland is never completely accepted, even in the case of the young generation's quick assimilation. Yolanda returns to the island as an adult woman, seeking to "remedy her feelings of displacement," as Jacqueline Stefanko states (55). However, her return is not governed by a desire to recover the roots but by a need to make cross-connections. Yolanda's exilic displacement becomes resolved through a negotiation between home and exile, past and present, and memory and assimilation while engaging in a diasporic movement, which I have traced in Chapter Two.

Being members of the younger generation, the García girls' loss is connected to the past and the memory. The past, associated in this text with the island, is first frozen in the moment of the departure and then completely repressed as the girls adopt American identity. As I have mentioned in the second chapter, their memory is what Marianne Hirsch calls postmemory, characteristic for second-generation exiles, who have access only to the imaginary past constructed through their parents' stories. Although idealized and imaginatively recreated, the originary location forever remains elusive and imaginary; while the memory, mediated through time and space, becomes a site of loss and absence. This is why Yolanda decides to go back to the Dominican Republic and reconstruct the lost past through a physical connection with the native place. Asserting her presence at the site of memory and loss, she renegotiates the temporal and spatial deferral and encounters possibilities for the creation of new connections and meanings. This becomes a place where Yolanda begins to write her own stories, reimagining herself and her family's history. Alvarez shows that absence again becomes an impetus for a creation of presence, reflecting the need to remember and create at the site of rupture and loss. Yolanda's diasporic experience of exilic uprooting urges her to fill the inner void, to repair the loss by transforming absence into a meaningful and creative presence.

In *The García Girls*, the complexity and ambiguity of the exilic condition are confronted by creating presence in the space of absence. The experience of the entire family is based on what Mary S. Vásquez identifies as "a dual struggle for connectedness" ("Gender and Exile" 80). As the Garcías struggle with a marginalized social status, nostalgia for homeland, and haunting memory, they learn to survive their dislocation through multiple strategies. The older generation uses the possibility of safe travel between the home and the exile as a mode of cultural preservation. The younger generation embraces assimilation in order to counter the cultural exclusion with a position of insiderness. Women of both generations adopt the available feminist practices as ways of asserting their presence in the public and private spheres. The father finds some gratification as he embraces the American ideal of a self-made man: he succeeds financially in his medical practice and consequently gains more social recognition and presence in the public arena. Yolanda moves even further with her attempt to heal the rupture and loss caused by displacement when she goes back to the Dominican Republic. The "curative return" allows her the possibility to establish cross-connections and articulate her multiple and fluid subjectivity.

Depicting narrative characters caught in a constant negotiation between home and world, inside and outside, memory and forgetting, *The García Girls* presents the challenge of living in exile, in the space that changes its meaning and character depending on different sociopolitical and psychic conditions. While the territorializing forces of distinct social systems—the home and the exile—debilitate agency of displaced subjects by forcing them into a state of outsiderness, the individual will to return into presence becomes a potent force of survival, resistance, and transformation. Agency is restored in everyday struggles for self-definition in a new space, while confronting debilitating exilic absence and seizing on the liberating possibilities of hybrid positioning.

Dreaming in Cuban: Exilic Winter Redefined

Dreaming in Cuban by Cristina García explores displacements and dislocations provoked by the Cuban revolution in the 1960s. Like *The García Girls*, this novel explores the reverberations of political immigration across different generations and in different locations. One of the main characters, Pilar, is established as a member of the younger Cuban-American generation, and like the García girls she, too, is portrayed struggling with diasporic postmemory and a mediated exilic experience. During her first years in exile, she has an immediate and alive memory of her homeland, vividly remembering the day of her family's departure:

> I was only two years old when I left Cuba but I remember everything that's happened to me since I was a baby, even word-for-word conversations. I was sitting in my grandmother's lap, playing with her pearl earrings, when my mother told her we were leaving the country. Abuela Celia called her a traitor to the revolution. Mom tried to pull me away but I clung to Abuela and screamed at the top of my lungs. My grandfather came running and said, "Celia, let the girl go. She belongs with Lourdes." That was the last time I saw her. (26)

Whether Pilar imaginatively recreates this scene or she really remembers it does not matter. What is important is that she perceives this "unhomely moment" (see Chapter Two) as traumatic, as a painful beginning of her unwanted separation from her grandmother and the island. The novel illustrates that this moment of detachment leads to absence and a consequent desire to regain unity. Pilar's longing to go back is revealed through her dreams and telepathic connection with Celia. However, as the years go by, the connection becomes weaker—"Every day Cuba fades a little more inside me, my grandmother fades a little more inside me. And there is only my imagination where our history should be" (138)—which suggests that one's removal from the originary place makes memory more mediated and imaginary. Consequently, as the distance increases, Pilar's anxiety grows and her longing inevitably resurfaces: "Most days Cuba is kind of dead to me. But every once in a while a wave of longing will hit me..." (137). Similar to Yolanda's character in *The García Girls*, Pilar is allowed to retrace the journey back to the origins and reconnect with her past. Portraying Pilar as reestablishing the broken ties and filling the void, the author investigates different possibilities for solving the dilemma of exilic identity. As I have discussed in Chapter Two, the curative return is suggested as a possible way of dealing with the traumatic past and claiming agency in one's identity construction.

Aware of varying effects of exilic trauma, Cristina García develops characters who deal with exilic existence in different ways. As in *The García Girls*, Pilar's parents are presented as first-generation exiles, whose traumatic past followes them to the U.S. However, while Julia Alvarez depicts the character of Yolanda's mother as acculturating slowly and cautiously, García portrays Pilar's mother as assimilating at once and with a great fervor. Both fathers, Carlos García in *The García Girls* and Rufino Puente in *Dreaming in Cuban*, are portrayed as feeling lost in the new land and retaining strong connections with their homelands. However, their reactions to the sense of dislocation are also different: Carlos becomes overly controlling, fighting his lack of authority and self-confidence both at home and in public, while Rufino withdraws from his family, looking for fulfillment in sexual affairs.

Both novels bear out that these different ways of reacting to exile are psychologically conditioned by different experiences of trauma. Carlos García and Lourdes Puente are victims of immediate violence and terror. Carlos was watched and interrogated by the military police in the Dominican Republic, and Lourdes was raped and tortured by the revolutionary soldiers in Cuba. Rufino Puente and Laura García, on the other hand, suffered too, but were not direct victims of violent assaults. As they develop the psychology of the novels' protagonists, Alvarez and García lay bear the severe effects of traumatic events. Being tormented by the memory of psychological and physical violation, Carlos and Lourdes are established as paranoid characters, lacking self-confidence and frequently overreacting and panicking. They are both anxiously worried about their children and obsessively intrusive of their privacy: Carlos reads his daughters' private letters and checks their drawers; Lourdes reads Pilar's diary and gets panic attacks when Pilar is late from school. In these narrative moments, it is clear that they both take on the characteristics of the authoritarian governments from which they have suffered themselves. Repressing their own traumas, they unconsciously perform analogous patterns of mistreatment and thus exchange their victim positions. Both authors call attention to the persevering impact of the violation that has occurred in the past but is not yet healed. Passing of the wound continues in exile too, affecting the generations who, although removed from the site of trauma spatially and temporally, still remain in the circuit. The trauma of a distinct geopolitical source becomes internalized in the space of resettlement and passed on successively.

When the configurations of trauma in García's *Dreaming in Cuban* and Alvarez's *The García Girls* are compared, it can be concluded that 'acting out'[13] of the past trauma is a trans-gender phenomenon, likely to occur in any setting. In exile, it usually becomes intensified since the experience of exilic absence and loss furthers the feeling of victimization. Alvarez's novel maintains that Carlos García's need to assert his authority at home derives from his experience of both the authoritarian oppression in his homeland and the social marginalization in the space of exile. Disempowered in both instances, he is driven to symbolically regain the lost power and 'integrity' in an unthreatening space—his home. In García's novel, Lourdes Puente's compulsive need for control is related to her traumatic experience of rape, another process that violates one's 'integrity.' Because she associates this violation with her homeland rather than patriarchy, exile is projected as a space where she can recuperate her obliterated self. Her reactions of displacement and acting out are facilitated by exilic absence, which Lourdes experiences, as I will demonstrate, not as a continuation of victimization but as a desired affirmation.

Cristina García develops the character of Lourdes Puente by carefully depicting the protagonist's post-traumatic stress disorder. Lourdes is introduced as she is suffering from compulsive eating and insatiable sexual needs, and these character traits are developed as symptoms of her past sexual abuse in Cuba. Her anti-Communist sentiments represent her psychological reac-

tion to this violation: superimposing her pain and anguish on the Cuban sociopolitical reality, she alienates herself from her homeland in order to elude
the troubling past. Like the unnamed Central American woman in "The
Cariboo Café," Lourdes is forced to experience a destruction of "home" and
enter the space of exile in search of physical safety and psychic restoration.
However, Lourdes' departure does not provoke a desire to return. The novel
maintains that the space of home represents a betrayal that she cannot forgive. Its professed security and impregnability turned out to be illusory: she
was violated in the space where violation was not supposed to exist. With
this unconventional rendering of home, the author conveys that the intensity
of trauma and betrayal drives this character to isolate herself from the space
of homeland. Lourdes perceives "home" as an enormous deception, a fake
construct that never offered protection and integrity. While in "The Cariboo
Café" home becomes stored in memory as the condition preceding the experience of violation, in *Dreaming in Cuban* it is situated in memory as a
condition of violence. Hence, a desire to return never resurfaces because its
absence develops into a defense mechanism. The author affirms this claim by
emphasizing Lourdes' refusal to visit Cuba and the moments when Lourdes
relives the violation: any mention of a possible return induces in Lourdes
fear and anguish, and "she smells the brilliantined hair, feels the scraping
blade, the web of scars it left on her stomach" (196). The association of her
rape with her homeland, rather than with political patriarchy, drives Lourdes
into an exilic absence.

The narrative suggests that the space of exile offers Lourdes some ease
and comfort because it removes her physically from the "site of danger."
This removal does not succeed in "The Cariboo Café" because the victim in
this story encounters a continuation of the same danger. Suffering socioeconomic marginalization in the space of exile, the Central American mother
experiences an intensification of victimization and consequently becomes
delusional and psychotic. Lourdes, however, is able to integrate in the new
location as her better economic status and her anti-Communist posture find a
compatible environment. This is why she projects home as a place of destruction and exile as a source of renewal, distancing herself from the former
and embracing the latter. However, even though social class is a significant
determinant of exilic experience—specifically in the process of acculturation
and resettlement—it must be recognized that psychological effects of trauma
are similar in different social strata. In spite of class differences, both of

these characters exhibit delusional approaches to reality since their experience of violation in the space of home has inflicted on them acute pain and suffering.

The narrative section describing Lourdes' arrival in the U.S. demonstrates that physical distancing becomes another defense mechanism, as Lourdes feels the need to disassociate herself completely from anything close to or typical of Cuba:

> "I want to go where it's cold," Lourdes told her husband. They began to drive. "Colder," she said as they passed the low salt marshes of Georgia, as if the word were a whip driving them north. "Colder," she said through the withered fields of a Carolina winter. "Colder," she said again in Washington, D.C., despite the cherry-blossom promises, despite the white stone monuments hoarding winter light. "This is cold enough," she finally said when they reached New York. (69)

The cold of New York City functions in this passage as the polar opposite of the tropical heat of Cuba. Also, it symbolically acts as an anesthetic that helps deaden the past, freeze the emotions, and reduce the intensity of pain. Lourdes embraces the coldness as a protective barrier, seeing the layers of thick, winter clothes as a shield for her vulnerable body: "Lourdes relishes winter most of all—the cold scraping sounds on sidewalks and windshields, the ritual of scarves and gloves, hats and zip-in coat linings. Its layers protect her. She wants no part of Cuba, no part of its wretched carnival floats creaking with lies, no part of Cuba at all, which Lourdes claims never possessed her" (73). Lourdes' intense need to dephysicalize her own body and the space of Cuba refers back to the physical abuse that she has suffered. For the same reason, she gains extra weight: "[m]en's eyes no longer pursued her curves" (21), and she understands her father's obsession with cleanliness: "For her father, conquering the *microbios* required unflagging vigilance" (22). Lourdes' efforts to create a sterile and protected space, devoid of uncontrolled experience and pre-assigned meaning, become her strategy of survival.

The New York winter symbolizes the loneliness and frigidity of exilic condition. However, as the title of this section of the book suggests—'Imagining Winter'—this absence of homelike warmth conveys a different meaning to Lourdes: it signifies the absence of pain and suffering. In this case, exile is imagined to represent safety and the promise of recovery, and as a space of absence it becomes a potential locus for creation of new meanings and beginnings: "Immigration has redefined her. Unlike her husband, she welcomes her adopted language, its possibilities for reinvention" (73). Even the absence of her native language produces a new linguistic territory where she can redefine and recreate her identity. She enters a different signifying frame, which allows her to reinvent herself through the distance from the originary sign.

The novel configures Lourdes' acculturation and assimilation as defense mechanisms that allow her to repress the self that is associated with trauma and suffering. Her wanting "no part of Cuba" stands as an example of her rejection of the troubling past and the disquieting pain. America allows her to live in one time frame and create an ideal, yet false, self-image—a successful business owner who has transcended her past obstacles and has a promising future. Portraying Lourdes as adopting the dominant culture and pursuing the American Dream, the author utilizes the classic American ideal of the self-made woman, a strategy adopted by many exiles that react to their displacement by focusing on the future while trying to forget the difficult past.

The effectiveness of this strategy is destabilized when Lourdes recognizes the difficulty of the task and the impossibility of its completion: "She ponders the transmigrations from the southern latitudes, the millions moving north. What happens to their languages? The warm burial grounds they leave behind? What of their passions lying stiff and untranslated in their breasts?" (73). Loss of the primordial self and the untranslatability of inner reality will haunt Lourdes in spite of her profound denial. Through her well-guarded walls of protection, the suppressed memories and longing ultimately manage to seep in: "Lourdes turns south. Everything, it seems is going south. The smoke from the leaning chimneys in New Jersey. A reverse formation of sparrows. The pockmarked ships headed for Panama. The torpid river itself" (24). Her thoughts travel south too, and she remembers her childhood "mined with sad memories:" "her first winter in Cuba" when she was born and rejected by Celia, and the rides in her father's automobile "traversing the island" (24). Her father's visit to the U.S. stirs up the unwanted memories and brings disquietude. She looks for solace in pecan sticky buns and insatiable sex with her husband, trying to block the resurfaced pain through escapist pleasure. The novel explicates that although assimilation offers possibilities for self-reinvention, it does not eliminate one's trauma. It only temporarily shuts out the inner conflict while offering an illusion of fulfillment

The last part of the novel reinforces this claim by describing an inevitable resurfacing of the "latent material"[14] at the site of violation. In the end, Lourdes does go back to Cuba, and, at first, she feels a profound distance from her native place: even the sugar cane, she remarks, is not as sweet (219). However, upon a visit to the Puentes *finca*, her detachment is weakened and she "longs to dig for her bones like a dog and claim them from the black hooded earth..." (227). While she is revisiting the sites of the past, the repressed resurfaces: she relives the moments of the rape and miscarriage. The acute pain returns, and her bitterness and anger reawaken: "What she fears most is this: that her rape, her baby's death were absorbed quietly by the earth, that they were ultimately no more meaningful than falling leaves on an autumn day. She hungers for a violence of nature, terrible and permanent, to record the evil. Nothing less would satisfy her" (227). The last narrative part suggests that this need for retribution disables Lourdes in her effort to reconcile with the past even though she manages to reestablish some old ties, such as her connection with her nephew. In the end, Lourdes leaves Cuba without being able to forgive her mother for abandoning her as a baby. Nonetheless, the recognition of the past trauma and the new experience of pain shatter her delusion and denial, opening up a possibility for healing and understanding.

Juxtaposing different experiences of exile, *Dreaming in Cuban* asserts that exile is not always defined by a profound nostalgia for home, where hope for return becomes a mechanism of self-motivation in the face of exile's hardships. While psychological and physical effects of displacement may stimulate a desire to return to the originary location, they may as well provoke an aversion toward the past. Thus, the return home is not an automatic desire of every exile, and the curative return, specifically, is not attainable in all cases. However, whether desiring the return or not, exiles cannot evade the effects of displacement; and while they invent different ways of coping with exilic existence, their temporal and spatial positioning in exile is inevitably connected to the previous location. Sociopolitical conditions of both the previous and the present locations determine individual experiences of exile, governing one's psychological response to particularized circumstances. Therefore, an important intervention in an investigation of exilic identities is to identify spatial and temporal aspects of exile in conjunction with the interplay between psychological and material realities.

The Dialectics of Exile and Identity

Edward Said observes that exilic existence is marked by an urgent need "to reassemble an identity out of refractions and discontinuities of exile" ("Reflections" 179). Although dependent upon particularized social conditions and personal psychology, the process of self-restoration in conditions of rupture and fragmentation is generally complicated by the spatial and temporal discontinuity of the exilic condition. As U.S. Latina narratives discussed in this chapter bear out, identity of the exiled is inevitably related back to the past location and time, which are either frozen in the moment of departure or repressed in the act of self-defense. In both instances, subjectivity itself is suspended, disconnected from the present moment, and the challenge that every exile faces is to find ways to reestablish spatial and temporal connections.

However, the reconstruction of self in exile is also an acquisition of a new identity, a process of self-reinvention experienced as liberating and enlightening. Amy Kaminsky connects this process to the experience of endurance in harsh conditions and in an alien space, while Edward Said relates it to contrapuntal awareness, a plurality of vision that profoundly marks one's sense of self and of reality. Reaffirming these claims, U.S. Latina narratives of exile emphasize that the enlightening aspect of exilic survival helps mediate spatial and temporal disconnections that an exiled person experiences in conditions of displacement. However, the development of a new identity is always conditioned by material and psychic configurations of exile as a space of absence.

Self-positioning in exile is complicated via multiple meanings and different articulations of exilic absence. As seen in the discussed Latina narratives, the absence can be both liberating and debilitating, depending on how it is constructed in the interplay between geopolitical and psychic processes. When it represents absence of violence and oppression, whether domestic or public, it acquires positive connotations. Victims of political violence find this absence more or less comforting and reassuring: as they slowly begin to recuperate their violated selfhood, Lourdes is able to repress the memory of sexual abuse and consequently experience the professed safety of exile, while Carlos cannot completely "relax" when the moments of terror revisit his everyday reality. The women of the García household experience exilic absence as emancipation from patriarchal authority and control. The ability to seize more articulation and independence in the new location defines their exilic experience in positive terms.

On the other hand, when exilic absence represents an enforced separation from home, a subsequent uprootedness, and a continual social marginalization, it is experienced as debilitating and oppressive, as the opposite of the promise of salvation and restoration. In all three narratives, the protagonists encounter this form of absence and, as a result, their life in exile is infused with a pleasant memory of the past reality and a strong desire to return. The Central American mother in "The Cariboo Café," particularly, experiences this absence as an act of repression when she is unable to find continuity and healing in the new location. In this story, exilic absence is portrayed in its extreme meaning of the negation of presence—literal, rather than metaphorical, death of a person.

Since they find this multiple-encoded meaning of exilic absence, the displaced are interpolated in a perpetual negotiation between home and exile, the past and the present, memory and forgetting, acculturation and marginalization, and the public and the private. In this negotiation, they encounter further ambiguities and paradoxes: home can signify both safety and danger, assimilation means both gain and loss, memory can haunt and amend, and the public and the private lose distinctness.

Enmeshed in geopolitical complications, the identity formation of exiles undergoes constant transformations, directly related to specific historical, social, and political conditions. They face not only the problems of gender, ethnicity, and class but also of traumatic experiences with political oppression—exile, torture, and disappearance—which further complicates their self-affirmation and definition. Their identity formation becomes defined not only by the interconnections between psychological and cultural processes but also by the interference of the geopolitical in those processes. As demonstrated in the discussed U.S. Latina narratives, political violence and persecution, strong national identifications, and the impossibility of a safe return home trouble the already troublesome subject-positioning of the exiled.

Exilic histories, revealed through diverse experiences of political immigration and resettlement, reveal less pleasant, less jovial aspects of transnational identities as the postmodern passage between different national/sociopolitical contexts is related back to conditions of authoritarianism and military neocolonialism. Foregrounding the role of oppressive social forces in the creation of new individual and communal identities, U.S. Latina narratives of displacement unmask the hybridizing processes of postmodernity as sources of psychic fragmentation, alienation, and suffering. While this criticism of the postmodern age resembles the literary renderings of modernity as an age of individual and social crisis, its literary articulations seek to investigate new configurations of the subjectivity that is placed in transnational spaces and engaged in local/global negotiations. However, even though this new type of subjectivity transcends the notion of a nationally/territorially defined self, it is not completely free of national contexts. While evading self-grounding in a singular national territory, exilic identity is still marked by multiple national narratives and sociopolitical conditions.

Dramatizing the psychic reality of minority immigrant subjects, narratives of exile emphasize that geopolitical conditions need to be accounted for in the study of individual and communal identity. In the specific investigation of hybrid culture and identity of Latino communities in the U.S., the inclusion of the geopolitical gains even more urgency as the effects of political immigrations from Latin America to the U.S. become profoundly felt in new cultural, political, and economic processes of the postmodern age. Just as its new residents are connected to other national locations, the U.S. is inevitably linked to other geopolitical realities while its sociopolitical reality is mediated by the histories of exilic communities.

CHAPTER FOUR

Geopoliticized Identities: Entering the Public Space

*From the signifier of passivity and peace,
mother became a signifier of resistance.*
—Jean Franco, *Critical Passions*

*It is love that can access and guide our
theoretical and political "movidas"—
revolutionary maneuvers toward
de-colonized being.*
—Chela Sandoval, *Methodology of the Oppressed*

In my discussion of exilic conditions in the previous chapter, I have demonstrated that the exiled are defined by their experience of sociopolitical oppression and that their territorial relocation does not necessarily facilitate their individual liberation. In this chapter, I focus on the emergence of oppositional geopoliticized identities as a reaction to conditions of repressive state control and as a movement to end both individual and social oppression. I analyze two U.S. Latina novels, Graciela Limón's *In Search of Bernabé* (1993) and Demetria Martínez's *Mother Tongue* (1994), in an attempt to demonstrate a development of differential identities as well as to identify strategies of resistance and opposition forged in the sites of the personal and the public.

Drawing from Latin American feminist theory and praxis,[1] I investigate these two narratives as texts that resignify the individual as a site of sociopolitical meaning and thus problematize the traditional distinction between the personal and the public. Giving attention to the individual in conditions of authoritarianism, the novels demonstrate the impossibility of a divide between the two realms, while revealing new dynamics in the interaction between the subjective and the social. Through a dramatization of the effects of political violence on individual and collective lives, the authors expose a dialectical, interdependent positioning between the individual and the social, an interdependence that contains both annihilative and liberating potentials. To reveal multiple and shifting meanings of the public and private spaces, both Limón and Martínez portray the socially constructed boundaries between these spheres as being creatively and courageously transgressed by narrative characters and brutally violated by the repressive state. Both authors show that when an oppressive political reality invades the privatized domestic space, individuals are forced to create new locations and strategies of resistance in order to counter objectification and annihilation. The oppressed mobilize modes of existence practiced in the private domain to develop opposition and liberation in the public and geopolitical spaces. Their existence becomes defined by a struggle to simultaneously engender their own emancipation and the liberation of the sociopolitical sphere. Both novels maintain that the entrance of the oppressed and marginalized into the sanctioned public space politicizes their identity and re-establishes their social agency. Reclaiming the exclusive socio-political sphere, the oppressed gain a subversive and non-violent political power that counters authoritarian protocols of subjugation and annihilation.

In their study of the interchange between the subjective and the social, U.S. Latina authors continue to expand and complicate the investigation of identity problematics by portraying the formation of differential and geopoliticized identities in politically totalitarian spaces. They call attention to the fact that identities and lives of those who exist under conditions of military dictatorship and state authoritarianism acquire distinct forms and dynamics. In their narratives, subject positioning in domestic and public spaces meets different challenges as the transgression of boundaries between the private and the public becomes a matter of life and death.

The Personal Enters the Public

Contemporary Latin American feminism bases its practice on the inevitable connection between the private and the public, recognizing the importance of national liberation for the process of individual emancipation. With the advance of oppressive governments in the second half of the twentieth century, the women's movements in Latin America entered the public space and forced the issues of political violence out in the public.[2] They organized around private and communal matters, protesting non-violently against military surveillance and terror, and, by extension, against patriarchal dominance and abuse. During the military regime in the 1970s and 1980s, Argentine mothers organized silent demonstrations, demanding information about their abducted sons in spite of state regulations against large public gatherings.[3] They seized the public space in order to politicize personal issues, exposing the connection between the private and the public. As Jean Franco argues, by focusing the issue of the disappeared into the public, Argentine mothers redefined the public domain and their own roles as mothers and women in the social sphere ("Beyond Ethnocentrism" 503). They represented the image of "private life" publicly, Franco argues, as a contrast to the present reality that destroyed the very family life that the military state had professed to protect (*Critical Passions* 50). In such Latin American political practice, women emerged as social agents, resisting passivity, erasure, and marginalization. As they refused to forget and be silent, they challenged the system of oppressive state power and its aims of social paralysis, alienation, and erasure necessary for the maintenance of authoritarian state supremacy.

Amy Kaminsky notes that this practice asserted presence in the face of erasure and silencing because the disappeared became present in the continued action of others. As she explains, when victims of repression were honored in Latin America—their names were called out as if in rolls and the collectivity then responded "Present"—their presence was at once embodied and represented as individual and historical in a situation when the dominant force deliberately denied it (24). Through this organized and collective form of remembrance, the invisible became visible, rescued from complete obliteration and alienation and brought back into presence.

In their efforts to counter individual and collective annihilation, Latin American women's movements emerged not only as attempts to re-take the public domain but also as efforts to create a new public space where agency and resistant power could be asserted apart from violence and force. Their sociopolitical positioning articulated the need to transform the disciplinary public realm into a democratic, free space that would guarantee individual emancipation. Thus, the women's protests became closely tied to sociopolitical issues, grounding their struggle for gender equality on the idea of national liberation. They comprised efforts to simultaneously feminize and democratize the sphere that was governed by authoritarian and patriarchal control, recognizing, as Sonia Alvarez points out, that militarism and institutionalized violence rested on the patriarchal foundation (7). In this way, women's movements in Latin America brought issues of individual emancipation in a context of geopolitical reality, understanding that personal liberation was conditioned by social transformation.

The women's resistance in Latin America also addressed issues of power and agency in social transformation. Jean Franco points out that the women's opposition and active participation in the sociopolitical sphere revealed "new types of power" as the mothers' public protests interrupted military discourse and exposed its inability to secure democracy and freedom ("Beyond Ethnocentrism" 514). These oppositional activities, of the Argentine and other Latin American women, included the traditionally silent sector of population in "forging politics in ways that no longer subordinated popular culture and women," demonstrating that creativity was not exclusively male but "dispersed among the entire population" (514). The women claimed their indisputable role in the populist movement while demanding an immediate inclusion and recognition in the sociopolitical sphere. Their resistance movement against authoritarian state power generated and legitimized the social agency of the disenfranchised, emphasizing non-violent populist modes of empowerment.

The populist feminist praxis in Latin America is inevitably closely connected to liberation theology, since both social movements advocate the liberation of the oppressed while being highly critical of the existing social hegemony and inequality. Feminist liberation theology, as a specific form of Latin American feminism, actively employs religious faith in its struggle to confront and transform the present conditions of gender oppression in society and in the church order.[4] Emphasizing the importance of moral agency and social responsibility, the feminist practice of liberation theology advocates an emergence of female subjectivities as active participants in and agents of their history. By embracing theology as a liberatory oppositional practice, the populist feminist movements refuse the split between the private and the public, understanding its false and oppressive dichotomy. They reinterpret Biblical teachings to transform, as María Pilar Aquino states, "their so-called weakness into strength" (67) and find inspiration for a sociopolitical transformation of individual and collective reality.

The Intimate as a Political Investment

Both *In Search of Bernabé* by Graciela Limón and *Mother Tongue* by Demetria Martínez connect their stories to the historical context of the civil war in El Salvador (1980–1992) while dramatizing the dehumanizing effects of political brutality on individual and collective being. Drawing from Ellen McCracken's characterization of Limón's novel as a modified testimonial narrative, I recognize the same aspect in Martínez's novel since both texts testify to specific historical events while engaging readers in new interpretative practices.[5] As in *testimonio* literature,[6] the narrator's personal story functions as an account of communal experience of sociopolitical oppression and marginalization as well as a testimony to the abuse of human rights. Its report brings to attention the suffering and struggles of the "foreign Other" and the urgency of their liberation. In a postcolonial manner, this type of narration represents an articulation of subaltern voices and a reconstruction of history from below. While revealing ideological constructions of dominant social discourses, testimonial narration provides "counter-narratives to the official, master-text."[7] In addition, the narrator's personal account integrates a call for social justice, inviting the reader to empathize with the oppressed and oppose their colonization and disenfranchisement.[8] In this fashion, the individual is politicized in order to provide social criticism and initiate sociopolitical transformation. The power of its authentic experience is employed as a means of granting legitimacy to the project of social revolution and liberation.

With emphasis upon the individual and the communal, these narratives also focus on individual strategies of survival and resistance in conditions of oppression to suggest new forms of political opposition and liberation. As Jean Franco and Amy Kaminsky have shown in their studies of Latin American feminist practice, roles performed in the traditionally private sphere can be redefined in the public arena to counter authoritarian practices of the military state. In Limón's *In Search of Bernabé* and Martínez's *Mother Tongue*, privatized concepts—such as love and religious faith—are demonstrated as viable modes of social agency and oppositional populist movement. When mobilized in the public space, their domestic and private designation, imposed by the division between the private and the social, is re-signified into an active social commitment. Both novels reveal subversive and empowering aspects of the intimate as the discourse of love and religiosity reclaims its place in the public sphere and takes a direct, non-violent stance against political oppression.

In addition, the universality of these concepts reaches the common space of experience, affinity, and understanding and thus points at a possibility of new coalitions. Employing an internationalist perspective, these texts aim at cross-national solidarity and identification, and the engaged discourse of love and religion serves as a powerful method of translation between different epistemologies of experience. As it mediates otherness, abstraction, and division, this familiar discourse provides a common point of understanding and coming together, making the power of the testimonial dimension even more pronounced.

The romanticized and abstracted concept of love (in its variant forms: motherly, religious, romantic/erotic, etc.) is presented in a differential mode: borrowed from the domestic arena—traditionally regarded as an apolitical sphere—it is utilized as a political investment and a social action. In Graciela Limón's *In Search of Bernabé*, the author portrays motherly love leading to a differential consciousness that initiates resistance to the dominant center of power—the repressive state authority. In a similar fashion, in Demetria Martínez's *Mother Tongue*, a romantic relationship becomes a site of sociopolitical agency. An interlocking of erotic intimacy and intrusive geopolitics sets into motion the urgency of emancipation and exposes the interconnectedness between the personal and the public.

In Search of Bernabé: A Politicized Motherhood

In Search of Bernabé by Graciela Limón dramatizes struggles of a Salvadoran mother who loses two sons in personal and collective tribulations. Calling attention to the inevitable connection between the private and public realms, the novel builds a parallel between the disintegration of the woman's family and the violent destruction of her country. As the mother searches for her son Bernabé, crossing multiple borders on her way to the U.S., she witnesses the collective suffering of her nation and a continuous legal and human rights discrimination against refugees. Seeing that her story "is not too different from that of many others" (60), she realizes that she is not alone in her pain and suffering. As the novel progresses, the woman's personal condition and plight extend into a collective state of being, reflecting the horrors of the Salvadoran war and pleading for help and solidarity.

In a testimonial and a post-colonial manner, Graciela Limón utilizes voices of the subaltern to re-narrativize the dominant socio-political narrative, as well as to foreground the urgency of global solidarity and liberation. She develops the theme of 'a mother searching for her lost son' in order to integrate the victim's perspective and evince the destructive and dehumanizing effects of political violence and totalitarian authority. Emphasizing the connection between familial and national structures, Limón points out the continuum between the abusive patriarchal domination over women and the totalitarian state control over citizen-subjects.

The novel opens up with a Biblical excerpt on incestual rape, setting the tone for the book's prologue and its theme of patriarchal abuse. The main protagonist, Luz Delcano, is raped by her wealthy and influential grandfather and, after his death, thrown out of the house by the indifferent family. After this account, the first part of the book is introduced by an excerpt from *Time Magazine* reporting the massacre at Archbishop Romero's funeral in San Salvador in 1980. Having established a link between the fictional and the factual, the narration in Part One takes over the sparse and formal journalistic style of the excerpt and imaginatively recreates the moments of the massacre, providing a more immediate and concrete representation. The character of Luz Delcano is again in focus, and this time she is thrown in the midst of political terror and violence. While she is following her son Bernabé in the funeral procession, uniformed soldiers suddenly appear and start shooting at the panic-stricken crowd of people: "Mothers crouched wherever they could in an attempt to protect their babies. Men and women pressed against the cathedral walls hoping to find cover behind a corner or a sharp angle" (23).

The sequence of these segments points at the connection between the forceful exercise of patriarchal power in the domestic sphere and the aggressive authority of the repressive state: the totalitarianism of state power is constituted as an extension of patriarchal domination and its mechanisms of hierarchy, oppression, and violence. This continuum also builds an allegorical meaning for the sociopolitical context: the Salvadoran civil war is translated into an intense physical abuse, or rape, of the civilians, who are in the end outcast by the military social system, having been stripped of humanity and identity. In her own discussion of the novel, Graciela Limón affirms that the rape scene in the prologue functions as a metaphor for the Salvadoran civil war.[9] Corresponding to the logic of the violent act of rape, the political violence, too, may be interpreted as "the final act which obliterates the victims" from the social system and transforms them into "silent, invisible, nonexistent entities" (Herrera-Sobek 249). I make this statement referring to María Herrera-Sobek's argument on the politics of rape in order to reaffirm that state authority is a continuation of the patriarchal exercise of power. I emphasize that in conditions of authoritarianism and militarism both genders become victimized since a military social system maintains its power through subjugation of women and disenfranchised men, who occupy subordinate positions in a hierarchical social structure. Any act against such social organization results in silencing and obliteration, not only in the social but also in the private sphere, illustrating that authoritarian systems attempt to maintain their command over the individual in all social realms.

Throughout the novel, the author underscores the invasiveness of the authoritarian state in an attempt to bring to attention the victimization of innocent civilians. At the same time, as she depicts the horrific conditions of individual and social being under a military regime, Limón shows an emergence of populist resistance. Being denied safety in all social spheres, Salvadoran citizens creatively and fearlessly confront the confinement by forming a new public space that allows resistance and differential movement. The procession that forms for the funeral of Oscar Romero, described at the beginning of the book, can be interpreted as a direct challenge to the dominant center of state power: by disobeying the rule of restricted movement and gathering, the oppressed Salvadorans defiantly assert in public not only their own presence but also the presence of Archbishop Romero. The scene establishes this act as a powerful social protest against military oppression and a call for liberation and social justice articulated in the discourse of liberation theology. By retaking the public space, the civilians not only acknowledge the reality of oppressive conditions but also refuse to be imprisoned by its annihilating weight and mechanisms of control. The subversiveness of this agency is manifested in the counter-action of the Salvadoran government, which utilizes its military apparatus to sabotage the funeral. Although a peaceful and silent gathering, the outdoor burial ceremony becomes "transformed into a tableau of horror: exploding hand bombs, wild gunfire, terrified crowds stampeding in panic" (19), reports the *Time Magazine* excerpt in Limón's book.

As the novel illustrates, when the public space is sanctioned by a totalitarian government, any form of public resistance is punished and erased by force. However, by reincorporating and reaccentuating the issue of liberation (theology) into the public, the oppositional social movement of the oppressed Salvadorans enters the sanctioned public space and transforms it into a place of resistance and survival. By doing this, the oppressed gain politicized identities that contest authoritarian systems of power. They challenge their muted, objectified positions and re-signify them into sites of social resistance and expression. Debra Castillo explains the resemanticization of silence in the context of patriarchal authority as a form of speech, i.e. an expression of female rebellion and independence (*Talking Back* 38). I trace the same process of resemanticization in the silent protests against military regimes in Latin America: the exposure of silence in the public sphere signifies a non-violent stance against state regulations and authority and, at the same time, testifies to the dehumanization and annihilation of the civilian population. Therefore, the objectified Others turn into agents of social change and their own emancipation by using the very semantics of oppression and authoritarianism. Embodying censored speech and silencing, they create a new space of collective expression and visibility that contests the violent military authority.

Limón's book shows that even in conditions of complete helplessness and despair, the will for survival and freedom arises as a powerful force of action. While in the beginning Luz Delcano enters the public space unwillingly and by force, having been thrown out of the Delcanos' house, later on she defiantly remains in it, determined to find her disappeared son Bernabé. Disobeying the rule of restricted movement and refusing to stay confined in her house, she embarks on a risky and dangerous search, first on the streets of San Salvador and then across the borders of Guatemala, Mexico, and the U.S. The narrative traces her multiple border-crossings as an oppositional movement, this time against the regulative protocols of nation-states. At the border between Guatemala and Mexico, Luz stands up to immigration officers when they harass a young Salvadoran man. While his nationality, gender, and age mark him as an offender for the immigration officials—"What have we here? A deserter! That's what you are, aren't you?" (58)—the Salvadoran refugee comes to embody the lost son for Luz. Seeing a gun pointed at the young man's head, she launches herself at the agent. The setting and the psychological dynamics of this incident repeat the pattern of the final scene in "The Cariboo Café," discussed in the previous chapter. Witnessing the threat of physical violence, Luz relives the moment of separation from Bernabé, and as she realizes that "Arturo could have been Bernabé" (58), she panics at the possibility of a repeated loss. Like the mother in "The Cariboo Café," Luz experiences "the return of the repressed,"[10] which transposes her into a defensive mode and gives her enough strength to overpower the immigration officer. Her biological role takes on an oppositional and resistant signification, transforming itself into a social undertaking.

Dramatizing an encounter between a mother who searches for her son and immigration authorities who exercise the power of nation-states, both texts emphasize the entry of women into the public space as a resistant movement against global patriarchy. The subversive power of the maternal emerges in resistance against patriarchal abuse and authority, which are, as the novel shows, exercised beyond the boundaries of a single nation. It asserts itself against international protocols of cross-border movement and in defiance of regulation and authority. The mothers in both stories directly challenge the order of a regulated global space, which is institutionalized in an attempt to protect power structures of nation-states. The women realize that their personal tragedies derive from such order and are manipulated for political interests of dominant power structures.

As in Latin American women's movements, the maternal unmasks authority as both gendered and sociopolitical, demonstrating the necessity of a simultaneous liberation of the individual and the national. In addition, this "politicized motherhood"[11] points out that oppression in conditions of authoritarianism is not limited to only one gender: Luz protects Arturo against patriarchal abuse and authoritarianism, understanding his own objectified and victimized position. Arturo's escape from the Salvadoran military regime also subverts the authoritarian definition of males as expected agents and guardians of patriarchal power. His decision to leave the country signifies not only his refusal to support the military authority but also the impossibility of a safe existence within the system for any dissenting individual.

The symbolism of the 'mother of the disappeared' motif parallels the narrative strategy of Viramontes' short story. As in "The Cariboo Café," the mother's life narrative extends into a history of the country that is engulfed in violence and destruction. The women in both stories lose their sons in the Central American civil wars, and their personal loss reflects the collective state of disintegration and erasure: "[t]he city was under a pall of terror and confusion because a new wave of killings was hitting the streets. Some foreigners and even some of Luz's acquaintances were disappearing. Bodies, mutilated beyond recognition, were being discovered daily" (55). The story of the women's own suffering and tragedy becomes inseparable from the national demise when violence from the streets enters their domestic spaces. It is important to point out here that the division between the personal and the public collapses in the context where the private is expected to be a site of safety and resistance. Although the dichotomy between the two spheres is induced by patriarchal forces from outside and within the private realm with the purpose of maintaining male control and dominance, the division also allows home to be a space of resistance to state regulations and violence. When the public space becomes oppressive and destructive, the private may offer some relief and protection by providing nurturing and affirmation to the self that is endangered by annihilation. As Jean Franco posits, in conditions of state repression, home becomes a refuge and a site of resistance, retaining the traditional meaning of familial unity and power (*Critical Passions* 11). However, the boundary between the two spaces is easily violated, as illustrated by Viramontes' and Limón's stories. State violence invades the safety and privacy of home, asserting the link between the two spheres and exposing the destructive effects that the oppressive social realm has on an individual. Jean Franco sees it as an assault on formerly "immune" and "sacred" territories—the family, the church, and the university—which become appropriated and controlled by the state (9). *In Search of Bernabé* illustrates that even the most intimate and "sacred" concepts of motherhood and religious faith are not spared before political violence. The paradox of this situation is that the invasiveness of the nation-state attacks the very institutions that have been designed as conduits for state power. While the state upholds familial and religious structures as the foundations of its patriarchal order and the proponents of authoritarianism, it also brutally destroys these private spheres when they challenge the dominant authority and its patriarchal rules.

This moment of rupture and destruction of the private realm, however, sets into motion the maternal and religious experiences as modes of individual and collective resistance. The culturally encoded concept of motherly commitment to the family (*Marianismo*, as a cult to *La Virgen María*) is transformed from its underlying notion of female passivity, submissiveness, and selfless sacrifice into a powerful mode of resistance to patriarchal/state authority. Rather than a strictly domestic role, motherhood is presented as a liberation process, committed to social justice and solidarity with the poor and oppressed. In Limón's novel, Luz's devotedness to her son, like the devotedness of the mothers of the disappeared, becomes a potent political force and investment, or, as Franco describes, a "signifier of resistance" (*Critical Passions* 15). By refusing to give up her sons, taken by the patrio-military order, Luz defies the system that has imposed on her the very expectation of sacrificial devotion to the institution of family. Resisting the social protocol of female confinement in the domestic realm, she uses the agency of maternal nurturing in the exclusive sphere of the socio-political to challenge the mechanisms of marginalization and obliteration. Her desperate effort to locate her sons drives her to confront violence in a fearless and persistent way, while giving her the strength to survive its dehumanizing effects. In addition, she practices the principles of motherhood in the communal space by transforming her biological role into a communal solidarity and commitment. Experiencing all disappeared Salvadorans as her own children, she shares her pain with other mothers in a refugee shelter in Los Angeles and helps them in their efforts to locate their disappeared sons. She embraces Arturo as her own child, and at the site of his murder she performs the absent communal vigil by singing "a mournful cradle song for a dead son" (85). To the U.S. police she identifies herself as his mother and mourns the repeated loss "One after another, each of her sons had been taken from her..." (89). The juxtaposition of maternal nurturing—"a cradle song"—and violence in this scene intensifies the criticism of violent state repression and emphasizes its link to the patriarchal order of the domestic space.

Positioning the maternal in a communal context, Graciela Limón portrays motherhood as a subversive and oppositional force to patriarchal regulation of the domestic and public spaces. In this novel, the role of motherhood transcends the domestic space and its essentialist attributes by entering the exclusive public space and becoming a progressive social force. The idea that the motherly "devotedness to children" can be translated into a genuine "commitment to others" dismantles the patriarchal structure that is based on exclusion, subjugation, and alienation; it emphasizes a communal connectedness where one is always positioned in relation to others through common experience and solidarity. As it underscores the concept of humanity in interrelations among individuals and groups, this politicized type of motherhood fights against authoritarian projects of divisiveness, dehumanization, and obliteration. Reaching to the community and pointing toward the urgency of social transformation, motherhood in this novel becomes a philosophy of compassion, alliance, and liberation.

The novel conveys the significance of the communal also through the concept of politicized religion. Highlighting the importance of liberation theology in the resistance movement in Central America, Graciela Limón foregrounds new forms of socio-political agency and solidarity that are based on political activism of the church. The story exposes the dominant social view of the church as an institution that should provide an authoritarian regulation of the social structure. When its progressive religious ethics enters the public space, the church becomes seen as a threat to the patrio-military social order. "Priests had best stay out of politics and confine themselves to mass and forgiveness" (23), the novel's narration captures typical comments of the Salvadoran government on the activism of Central American priests. Religious teachings are allowed to enter public space only when they serve to maintain the existing social structure: by focusing on endurance, patience, obedience, and individual sinfulness, they sustain the status quo and exclude any possibility of social transformation. A politicized progressive religion, as the story illustrates, becomes threatening to authoritarian power structures because it exposes and condemns systemic oppression, subjugation, and exploitation of subordinate groups. With its discourse of equality and non-violence, it directly challenges the dominant social structure based on patriarchal discrimination and militarism. Liberation theology, specifically, counters the dominant power structure with its assistance to the poor and its promotion of liberation and empowerment of the oppressed. In its efforts to contemporize the Biblical teachings on equality and freedom,[12] it brings to light the present conditions of hegemony, oppression, and injustice and points out the urgency of a national liberation that would grant freedom and agency to the disenfranchised.

The influence of liberation theology is marked immediately at the beginning of the book. The first massacre scene is set at the funeral of Archbishop Oscar Romero,[13] a follower of liberation theology who was murdered for his oppositional teachings and activism: "It was a pity, those faces said to Bernabé, that the Archbishop had not heeded his finer instincts, his better judgments" (23). The Archbishop's role in raising awareness about poverty and his effort to change power relations are presented as a direct challenge to the expectations of his complicity with the system of control, discipline, and hierarchy. The narrative conveys that the presence of his differential movement in the public sphere is seen as a serious threat to the military state, a threat that must be eliminated via his own physical annihilation. The Archbishop's dismissal of patriarchal conduct is regarded by the military order as a lack of masculine qualities—"finer instincts, better judgment"—and this emasculation is used to rationalize the act of obliteration. The juxtaposition of religion and militarism in this scene, and throughout the book, intensifies the representation of the authoritarian state as a dehumanizing and destructive social system. Also, while it dramatizes the conditions of living under a military dictatorship, this opposition foregrounds the urgency of communal resistance and empowerment.

The story of seminarian Bernabé carries through the idea of communal liberation as Bernabé is shown as engaging in guerrilla fighting to protect lives of his people. In order to reflect the invasiveness of the oppressive sociopolitical sphere and the intensification of violence instituted by an authoritarian state, the narrative captures the seminarian's inner struggle to reconcile his personal belief in non-violence with his need to actively confront the enclosing destruction. Bernabé himself becomes a victim when the military state attacks his non-violent positioning, first through his feminization—"Better pick up your skirt and find a church to hide with other women" (25), an armed soldier warns him—and then by his physical erasure described at the end of the novel. Other liberation activists working in El Salvador meet a similar end: the narration includes reports of their murder or arrest by the Salvadoran government. The violent counter-action against the practice of liberation theology and peace activism described throughout the novel discloses the full intensity and scope of authoritarian state repression. At the same time, it also reveals the political significance of progressive religious teachings when they are employed to form solidarity and alliances in a populist struggle against oppression.

Addressing the U.S. public, for whom the violent conflict in El Salvador was mostly a removed experience, Limón's book uses the personal and universal concepts of motherhood, love, religiosity, and human suffering to humanize the distant and unfathomable civil war. The novel concretizes an abstracted, depersonalized level of history and politics by effecting affinity through humanity and identification. When Bernabé's fellow fighter, Nestor, tells his life story to Bernabé, the pacifist seminarian feels pain although he himself did not experience Nestor's tragedy. By extension, the removed or the pacifist reader, too, feels sympathy for the man who watched the paramilitary rape his sisters and kill his father. Luz's pain and anguish at the moment of finding the mutilated body of her son reaches all mothers and moves all readers. The horror of the civilian massacres transcends the textual boundaries as an unnerving and alarming experience. This actuality of human suffering breaks through the abstraction of war, asserting that everybody is related on the premise of common humanity. This is why Graciela Limón employs the motif of fratricide, borrowed from the Bible,[14] and insists on international geopolitical connections. As she unmasks the complicity of the U.S. government in the Salvadoran conflict, she also exposes the necessity of a cross-national connection in the process of mourning and healing. The narrative attempts to communicate that the suffering and tragedy of Salvadoran civilians need to be redeemed with an understanding and emotional identification from the American side. This act of bringing different sides together hopes to generate not only sympathy but also a progressive social action, solidarity and alliance with the oppressed nations and a movement to end both local and global oppression.

The personalized narrative of the civil war in El Salvador expands the boundaries of understanding even further by reaching to the side of the oppressor. Besides the voices of the oppressed Salvadorans—represented by Luz, Bernabé, and Arturo—the narration legitimizes voices of the perpetrators, too, in order to create an account that includes both sides. In this fashion, the novel reconfigures the traditional *testimonio* approach—where typically only the voice of a victimized informant provides an account of oppression—in order to demystify and deconstruct the logic of violent national conflicts. In a psychoanalytical manner, Colonel Delcano's drive to control and abuse others is traced back to his childhood, to the traumatic moment of the enforced separation from his mother (he was taken from Luz by the Delcano family) and the resulting feelings of abandonment and betrayal. His obsessive desire to know and control is linked to his "child's terror" and "chronic insomnia" (46), and, while he is building dossiers on his mother and brother, he is also persecuting his countrymen. This connection of one's formative life experiences to the social formation provides an alternative to official interpretations of wars as "habits of less civilized nations," interpretations predominantly used to cover up one's complicity with violence or one's lack of humanitarian concern. The psychoanalytic interpretation asserts again the interlocking of the micro and macro spheres, where an individual is always enmeshed in the oppressive system of a social order that is governed by patriarchal forces. With Colonel Delcano's trauma connected to his mother's annihilation by patriarchy, his exercise of military state power is presented as a direct outcome of patriarchal oppression. This relation confirms patriarchal power as the driving force of authoritarianism and emphasizes the vicious cycle of abuse, where individual victimhood and communal oppression foster each other.

Approaching the connection between the personal and the public from multiple and diverse perspectives, *In Search of Bernabé* exposes both the destructiveness and the political potentiality of the dialectical conditioning between the social and the subjective. Its personal testimonial narration directly engages with sociopolitical reality to unmask the process of communal victimization and simultaneously reveal strategies of liberation. Using the concepts of motherly and religious love, the novel shows that in conditions of authoritarianism the intimate sphere may engender a powerful sociopolitical movement of opposition and resistance.

Mother Tongue: An Interlocking of Desire and Geopolitics

Like Graciela Limón's *In Search of Bernabé*, Demetria Martínez's *Mother Tongue* develops a political element through personalized experience and the concept of love. When political violence of the public, seemingly distant, sphere enters the private space, it becomes apparent that the romantic relationship between two narrative protagonists is interlocked with history and politics. "Love cannot be divorced from history" (44), realizes María, a young Mexican American woman, as she tries to help a Salvadoran refugee deal with his war trauma.

The romantic love story is not utilized in this novel as a camouflaged mode of addressing geopolitical issues. On the contrary, Demetria Martínez develops it into a powerful medium that dramatizes the dehumanizing effects of political violence and the destructiveness of repressive state authority. The young protagonists' intimate and passionate experience is presented as continuously troubled by the oppressive presence of sociopolitical reality. Even in their most intimate and romantic moments, the lovers are unable to flee from the reality of the Salvadoran conflict. As they struggle to preserve their relationship, they witness a deforming impact of war: "War is god that feasts on body parts. It deforms everything it touches, even love. It got to me, too. It cut out my tongue" (161), reads one of María's diary entries. In addition to the portrayal of the dehumanizing effect of war, Martínez uses the dynamics of love to depict a development of oppositional consciousness in conditions of objectification and subjugation. The novel's main protagonists, María (Mary) and José Luis, embrace love as an empowering source that counters the destructive forces of the sociopolitical order. While it allows them to relate to one another on a deep human level, their love also seeks to resist regulation and exclusion that bind their freedom. This profound commitment to each other reveals possibilities for liberation and change. The narrative shows that through their nurturing and caring relation, the young lovers learn to transform their objectified positions into agentic subjectivities while transcending the roles of victims. Lastly, Martínez employs the universal concept of love to also provide positions that are necessary for common perception and action, which enables her to humanize and familiarize the remote and media-manipulated war in El Salvador. The powerful emotional story allows her to break through the abstraction of war and actualize the victimized people and their suffering.

Announcing the importance of remembrance and presence, Demetria Martínez dedicates *Mother Tongue* "to the memory of the disappeared," offering it as a testament to the suffering and tragedy of the Salvadoran people during a twelve-year-long civil war. Using what Linda Hutcheon calls "historiographic metafiction,"[15] she fuses history and fiction to tell a powerful and historically relevant story. In the introductory note, Martínez foregrounds the historical factuality of the novel by creating a connection to the U.S. sociopolitical context: the note cites the amount of military aid that the U.S. government sent to the Salvadoran military regime. This background information unequivocally places the political dimension of the novel in the forefront. Featuring excerpts on love and remembrance from Mayan scriptures and Paul Simon's song, the epigraph establishes a connection that will be elaborated in the novel—the interlocking of history, politics, and love. Describing María's recollection of José Luis' arrival in the U.S., the words 'nation,' 'borders,' and 'love' in the first paragraph strike a strong note for the whole book—the interaction between the intimate, personal realm and the politicized public: "His nation chewed him up and spat him like a piñon shell, and when he emerged from an airplane one late afternoon, I knew I would one day make love with him" (3). As the encounter of the two young protagonists sets up expectations of romance, the oppressive presence of the sociopolitical realm immediately introduces a disruptive element. In the course of the story, the couple's intimate experience will be continuously

ruptured by the ongoing effects of political violence and consequently transformed into a sociopolitically engaged location.

The interlocking of the intimate and the sociopolitical is a constant emphasis in this novel, and Martínez engages it to develop a sociopolitical text
through a personalized account. The opening part of the novel directly demonstrates that the individual always speaks of the social because the social
inevitably informs the individual. José Luis enters María's life as a complete
stranger, but the sociopolitical conditioning of his existence immediately defines his identity. Objectified by and sacrificed for a national cause, identified as "the man who had fled his country" (11), he is marked by the tragedy
and suffering of his people. The novel suggests that this external conditioning becomes María's access to José Luis' troubled being. Learning about the
struggle and agony of the Salvadoran nation, she comes to recognize and
understand his traumatic experience when he avoids explaining it himself. In
this instance, the communal condition testifies to the individual, exposing the
geopolitical appropriation of the subjective. The narrative recreation of a personal history through a national narrative legitimizes the reverse process that
the novel attempts to develop—a reconstruction of social meaning through
personal signification.

By setting up a dialectical positioning between the personal and the sociopolitical, the text demonstrates that individual emancipation and national
liberation are in an interdependent and reciprocal relation. The necessity of
one for the other is obvious in the lovers' relationship. At first, María believes that she can "take a war out of a man" (4), and distance José Luis from
his trauma and pain: "And with the power of love I'm going to help him forget, too. Help him forget the war that he fled from..." (63). However, the
impossibility of such project shows right away as María herself notes that
war is also an internalized reality: "No, he had no warrior's face. Because the
war was still inside him. Time had not yet leached its poisons to his surface"
(4). The boundaries between the personal and the social are erased as the
body manifests its permeability and vulnerability before external, sociopolitical forces. Having become enmeshed in the continuing psychological effects of the Salvadoran war, María herself realizes that "the only way to take
the war out of man is to end the war, all wars" (114). Pointing out the external source of trauma, the author identifies the oppressiveness and destructiveness of a social order that violates the subjective. This correlation foregrounds the urgency of emancipation on both individual and social levels: it

emphasizes that individual liberation is unattainable in isolation from the larger sociopolitical sphere and, therefore, is dependent on social transformation.

From the very beginning of the novel, the body—the most intimate sphere—is exposed as a site of sociopolitical meaning. The connection between the personal and the social is established through the metaphor of 'a body contaminated with political violence,' where war manifests itself as an internal disease waiting to "leach its poisons to [the] surface" (4). The metaphor presents the body as signifying the repressive sociopolitical reality on and through its somatic medium. The individual is inscribed with the topography of the national—José Luis sees "a map of El Salvador" (105) in his image in the mirror—becoming a signifier of national history and politics. In this narrative section, social semantics is expressed through individualized somatics, demonstrating the impossibility of separation between personal narrative and social history. While José is explaining the origin of "the strange markings on his hands and his back" (133), his body becomes a narrative of personal and collective histories: "[...] 1982, someone had branded those numbers into his back. [...] the year he was tortured, that thousands were tortured" (134). As Michel Foucault argues, the body functions as an inscribed surface of events, always imprinted by repressive history.[16] This embodiment of socio-political narration dramatizes the objectification and victimization of citizen-subjects, who are appropriated by state authority and turned into objects of their history. In this instance, the actuality of the physical body is a signifier of the past, always referring back to the traumatic moment and the condition of violation. Its physicality does not connect one to the present reality but, in fact, prolongs the experience of the past victimization and suffering as it continues to expose the oppressive sociotext. In Foucault's terms, history as an "endlessly repeated play of dominations" establishes its mark on and within the body, exposing its own genealogy of destruction and hegemony (150).

María's body, too, serves as a testimony to oppression and abuse, containing an invisible yet unceasingly present narrative of her victimization. The novel explicates that María's fear of abandonment runs "through [her] arteries" (91) as a residue of her repressed memory of sexual abuse. When her body experiences a similar violation, the past resurfaces and a recollection occurs. Haunted by the memory of his girlfriend's murder in El Salvador, José Luis slips back into the reality of the war and attacks María, mistaking her for a soldier. She understands what happens, but her body instinctively reacts by recognizing the traumatic moment from her past. This psychosomatic reaction points back to the sociopolitical sphere and its invasive and colonizing effects on the private, intimate domain. Portraying the young woman as reliving her own victimization in a painful flashback, the scene exposes the connection between state violence and sexual abuse: María's experience of violation in the private space is linked to José Luis' experience of violation in the public space, establishing their seemingly different kinds of victimization as effects of the same exercise of patriarchal oppression. In addition, María's victimization as a seven-year-old is related to the Vietnam war; she remembers war scenes flashing on the TV screen in her room after her abuser "gets up off his knees" and "cancels" her: "Men in baggy clothes that make them look like rocks or trees genuflect, set rifles on their knees, take aim. Helicopter blades shred the sky. Winds beat the jungle down from three dimensions to one. The men in guns have on helmets that look like turtles. They point their guns at small men with almond eyes [...]" (166). In this narrative moment, the dynamics of sexual rape are directly paralleled to the destructive force of war, and political violence in a remote, unrelated site is brought into the domestic space. The destruction of the body comes to signify the dynamics of the patriarchal/military system, which consolidates its power in the act of subjugation and annihilation of the individual.

The novel convincingly demonstrates that psychological effects of war establish a continuum in the private sphere as the victimized are forced to act out aggressiveness in their everyday reality. Like Carlos García in *How the García Girls Lost Their Accents*, José Luis is haunted by images of torture and violence, and his instinctive reaction is so intense that he cannot express it in words. His anger frequently transfers onto María, and he blames her for the tragedy of his people. While reducing her American nationality to her government's complicity with the Salvadoran regime, he also begins perceiving her Mexican origin through the stigmatized mythical figures of *La Llorona* and *La Malinche*.[17] He sees in her, as María comes to understand much later, "not a woman but a beast, a Sphynx... a yanqui, a murderess, a whore" (124). This narrative passage shows that in José Luis' deformed reality, war disfigures María too, and in this state of myopia he misperceives her as a multiple enemy: an American colonizer, a Mexican mother who murders her children, and an indigenous woman who betrays her people. The deforming effect of war is placed again in the site of the body as the victim loses the human form and experiences him/herself and others as monstrous creatures. In a poem that José Luis' girlfriend writes before her murder in El Salvador, José Luis is described as "a man and a monster" (136), while the psychological effects of war become contagious and implanted in one's body as "ticking grenades" (136). The psychological disorder is physicalized in the site of the body in order to expose the invisible injury as visible and continual. This externalization recovers the suppressed signification of violation and reaffirms the process of disfiguration of the individual by hegemonic forces. To recall Foucault, the body becomes a site of social genealogy, revealing the meaning and dynamics of historical processes.

In her study *The Body in Pain* (1985), Elaine Scarry argues that the authority inflicts pain in order to assert its power. In this process, the pain of the body becomes objectified so that it is visible to others and presented as "the insignia of power" (51). As pain is inflicted to destroy a person's "world, self, and voice" (35) human suffering is translated into "an emblem of the regime's strength" (56). However, although the agency of inflicting total pain is perceived and experienced as power, it is a "fraudulent assertion of power" (45), since the authority it strives to declare is "highly contestable and unstable" (27). Thus, the negation of the individual, executed through an attack on the body, is utilized to maintain "the fiction of absolute power" (27). The body is targeted as a territory to be conquered and claimed for sociopolitical purposes; it is emptied of its individual meaning and converted into a medium for the exercise of dominant social narratives.

Demetria Martínez communicates that the expected signification of the body as a site of erotic pleasure and intimacy is violated through its appropriation by the public sphere. José Luis' body carries, not marks of passionate love-making, but a testimony to brutal state violence and dehumanization, to "what was done to your body in the name of politics" (134). The presence of pleasure and intimacy is censored as its original text is overwritten with the sociopolitical script. The sphere of intimate interaction, represented here in the body, is physically colonized by socio-political forces. José Luis' poem written for María states: "[...] my rib throbs beneath / your palm, the rib / they fractured with / a rifle..." (132). Corporeal violation signifies the sanctioning of the individual, which the authoritarian order performs in order to secure its own power and existence. The juxtaposition between the sexual and the socio-political signification testifies to the impossibility of an escape from the social domain which always leaves its mark on the individual. Investigating the place of body in war and torture, Elaine Scarry reaffirms: "The record of war survives in the body" (113) since "injury-as-sign" endures beyond the temporal moment (121).

In the context of state authoritarianism, the process of marking the body represents a totalitarian effort to erase the subject—in Scarry's words "person's self and voice" (35)—in order to obliterate the presence of the subversive. For this reason, to place the body in a sexual context becomes a strategy of resistance to and subversion of authoritarian prohibition. The narrative suggests this subversive meaning by presenting the moments of passion and tenderness between the lovers as healing sessions: as María tenderly massages the scars on José Luis' back, erotic pleasure transforms into a symbolic act of recuperating the obliterated presence. When the sociopolitical sphere colonizes his psychosomatic being, the actuality of the physical connects José back to his present reality. María's body comes to function as José's refuge from nightmare images of civilian massacres, transforming itself into a source of life that gets him "breathing again" (84). The body intervenes in the slippage of reality by concretizing one's temporal and spatial being. Through sexual pleasure, José Luis experiences his body as his own, regaining autonomy and subjectivity against the memory of dehumanizing torture and annihilation. In a similar fashion, María constructs her autonomy in the site of the erotic: through her free practice of sexuality she defies sexual prohibition instituted by traditional Catholic morals and thus challenges authoritarian control and oppression. Her sexualized subjectivity acquires a subversive potential by undermining the system that aims to appropriate and limit her to an asexual and domesticated womanhood.

As the realm of private relationships clashes with the realm of sociopolitical interaction, love asserts itself in this novel as an alternative to patriarchal and state oppression. "Desire was not good enough. Love would ripen in the light of time we spent together" (19), describes María the evolvement of their relationship. While desire motivates the knowledge of the other, love leads to a deep commitment where self is decentered and placed in relation to another. The principles of caring and nurturing developed in such relation disrupt protocols of regulation and exclusion by seeking to reestablish and heal the fractured connections. As profound feelings awaken, one's sense of self deepens and allows connections to others beyond the boundaries of division and difference. In her study of the social signification of love, "Relational Love" (1987), Linell Cady proposes an interpretation of love in which the primary aim is the creation, deepening, and extensions of communal love (142). She argues that love empowers one and others to extend the self beyond the limits of experiential borders. In the process of self-creation through the dynamics of love, the boundaries of identity continually alter, expanding selfhood and deepening community. Linell proposes a concept of relational love that negotiates the private and public realms through principles of connection, unity, caring, and understanding.

Bringing Cady's emphasis upon relatedness and community to my discussion of the connection between the personal and the social, I identify love as a creative and progressive link between the intimate and the political. This potentiality of love is exposed in *Mother Tongue* as María and José Luis' love turns into a revolutionary project. Asserting its presence against the oppressive sociopolitical reality, their love becomes a new mode of resistant power against state regulation and violence. It is utilized in the public space for the purpose of social action, politicizing the lovers' subjectivities and challenging the divide between the private and the public. As María invents different strategies of "shielding José from authorities" (18), he recognizes that her love generates "acts of solidarity" (61). Her connection to José Luis evolves into a commitment to a fight against oppression and objectification. She comes to understand that "the only way to take the war out of a man is to end the war, all wars" (114). The narrative suggests that, as she assists him to become a subject in his history, María herself gains more agency and connectedness to her own history, becoming released from her fear of the traumatic past.

Mother Tongue reveals the political potentiality of love to initiate coalitional and oppositional connections. Being a powerful medium of translation between different epistemologies of experience—"[w]e transcended borders of culture, language, and history" (48)—María and José Luis' love draws them together emotionally and physically while providing an understanding between the self and the other. The novel implies that love, as a condition beyond difference, helps them assert presence before annihilation and dehumanization, motivating their joined struggle against oppression and injustice.

Throughout the novel, love is seen as a powerful mode of aligning different subjects in resistance against repressive authority. It is manifested as an oppositional form of social action, standing against repressive state regulations. As Chela Sandoval argues in *Methodology of the Oppressed* (2000), love can be utilized as a set of practices and procedures that "transit citizen-subjects [...] toward a differential mode of consciousness" (139). Romantic love, Sandoval explains, provides access to a differential mode of consciousness that sets the subject free by breaking through social narratives and releasing one from ideology and hegemony. It leads to a state where the fear from authority disappears and a prospect for transformation arises. In this fashion, love acts as a strategy of resistance and transformation, generating "a higher moral and political mode of oppositional and coalitional social movement" (156).

In *Mother Tongue*, the intimate concept of love is engaged in the public arena as a social project. As in Limón's novel *In Search of Bernabé*, its signification of liberation of oneself and others is deployed against oppression and objectification. Erotic love in Martínez's novel is rendered as a reaction against social appropriation of the subjective and an active confrontation against the invasive forces of patriarchy and authoritarianism. It is presented as a healing force that reconstructs the obliterated presence and fights against personal and historical amnesia. José Luis and María experience it as an act of remembrance that confronts objectification and obliteration and thus allows them to reclaim autonomy and agency. In the end, their love is transformed into a *testimonio* itself, claiming presence and continuation of the disappeared. After José Luis leaves, María saves his diary and personal belongings to materialize his presence. She also travels to El Salvador with her son to find more information about his disappearance. As in the protests of women's movements in Latin America, her search for the truth about her lover's disappearance signifies resistance to alienation and erasure. It reconstructs José Luis' presence as individual and historical against the annihilating forces of authoritarianism and patriarchy.

Depicting the materialization of the intimate into a social action, *Mother Tongue* interrelates the political practice of love with the politicized religion. Like Limón's *In Search of Bernabé*, it foregrounds the importance of liberation theology in oppositional movements in both Central America and the U.S. In the opening chapter, the main protagonists are introduced in reference to the U.S. Sanctuary Movement: fleeing the death squads in El Salvador as a former seminary student, José Luis arrives in the U.S. with assistance of the movement, and Mary, as a member of the movement, is sent to greet him at the airport. Referring to the hostile treatment of U.S. Immigration toward Salvadoran refugees in the 1980s, the scene incorporates a note that another member leaves to Mary instructing her to reinvent José Luis' identity and thus shield him from deportation: "When you are safely out of earshot of anyone remind him that if anyone asks, he should say he's from Juárez. If he should be deported, we want immigration to have no question he is from Mexico. It'll be easier to fetch him from there than from a Salvadoran graveyard" (6). Throughout the narrative, the activism of the Sanctuary movement is consistently mentioned in relation to its efforts to raise consciousness about the situation in El Salvador and help bring the refugees safely across the border.

Inspired by the liberation theology movement in Latin America and the Underground Railroad during the slavery in American confederate states, the Sanctuary movement in the U.S. was formed as an active effort to help Salvadoran and other Central American refugees who were arriving in the U.S. in escape from dictatorships and civil wars. Aware of the U.S. support of military regimes in the region, the movement sought to protect the refugees from deportation, knowing that the government refused to grant asylum to anyone from Central America.[18] Initiated by a group of Quaker activists and progressive church communities in the Southwest, the Sanctuary gathered individual activists and different religious congregations from all over the country.[19] Committed to social justice and liberation of the oppressed, the movement attempted to "awaken the churches of the entire country to the persecution of the church and the poor in Central America" (Crittenden 89). In the first part of the novel, José Luis gives testimony to an activist Quaker meeting by providing evidence of the violent oppression of the poor and the aggressive persecution of religious activists in El Salvador: "One by one, grass roots leaders in the shantytowns around the capital are being disappeared or killed. People are hiding their Bibles. If you are caught with one, the authorities assume not only that you are literate but that you might press for change" (34–35). As in Limón's novel, the progressive politicization of religion is deemed dangerous by the Salvadoran authorities because of its commitment to the liberation of the poor and oppressed. Martínez emphasizes that the same attitude was adopted by the U.S. authorities, who attacked the activism of the Sanctuary movement as "'putting refugees on display,' and 'advocating open violation of the law'" (36). After José Luis' testimony, the local paper reports that an immigration official condemned the gathering by saying: "'Those people are a sanctimonious band of renegades'" (36).

Drawing on specific historical and political events, the novel attempts to focus attention on the importance of differential social movements that utilize the politics of love, compassion, and solidarity in the struggle for social justice and peace. Employing the intimate as a source of resistance and transformation in local and global spaces, *Mother Tongue* presents the oppositional power of love and religion in the process of individual and social emancipation, where agency is gained through populist and non-violent modes of empowerment. As Chela Sandoval asserts, this type of resistant positioning leads to a differential consciousness that breaks citizen-subjects free from authoritarian paradigms and social oppression.

Demetria Martínez writes this romantic love story as a testimony to the lives of the disappeared and as a continuation of their presence. As the line of her epigraph announces, it is a story of remembrance through "the powerful pulsing of love" that refuses to forget those that are gone. Using the motif of love to express protest and resistance, Martínez as a writer actively engages in the literary public space and mobilizes her writing as a potent tool of social criticism and transformation. In addition, by foregrounding cross-ethnic and cross-national connections, she calls for coalitions across difference and promotes international solidarity and assistance in local and global struggles for peace.

Transforming the Public through the Private: An Emergence of New Identities

Investigating the dialectical positioning between the individual and the social in conditions of authoritarianism, *In Search of Bernabé* and *Mother Tongue* locate the emergence of politicized identities at the intersection between the private and public spaces. The novels demonstrate that identities constituted in a repressive sociopolitical reality are forced to occupy this interstetial location: when state violence invades and destroys the private sphere, the oppressed must occupy and transform the repressive public arena that negates their visibility and identity. In addition, by linking the private and the public, the subjects formed under conditions of authoritarianism bring back the empowerment that was taken from them by the authorities, who have enforced the separation between the two spheres as a tactic of control and hegemony.

This type of oppositional praxis is closely tied to the methodology of the oppressed that Chela Sandoval theorizes in her study of social agency in postmodernity. As their methods of survival and resistance develop in response to authoritarian practices of nation-states, the oppressed citizen-subjects adopt tactics and locations that grant them subversive and liberative agency in their particularized contexts. Their modes of empowerment are generated in the process of differential social positioning and via the strategies of resistance from below. This politicization of identity through lived experience illustrates that the process of conscientization of oppressed subjects occurs through a social praxis that emerges on both individual and national levels while transforming the public sphere through the private.

Denied presence in both the private and public spaces, the oppressed gain subjectivity in reaction to this exclusion. As illustrated in the two U.S. Latina novels, when the subaltern enter the exclusionary space of sociopolitical interaction, they often mobilize the practices from the intimate location in order to resist oppression and subjugation. They adopt strategies that are available and familiar to them and re-configure them into tactics of survival and resistance in the space of exclusion and subjugation. When the mother of in Limón's novel enters the public space, she breaks the boundaries set by the dominant discourse and affirms motherhood as a public and political investment. She transforms her essentialized identity into a differential and politicized subjectivity, applying the maternal as a liberation project in her community and across national borders. When the social appropriates and colonizes the site of lovers' intimate relationship in Martínez's novel, the young protagonists are forced to embrace their intimacy as a location of resistance to oppression and objectification. The progression of their love parallels the development of their political consciousness and builds up their relationship into a united political struggle that crosses national borders.

Asserting their presence and subjectivity in the public arena, the oppressed and marginalized Others subvert the imposed silence and transform the space of authoritarian political regulation into a space of resistance and emancipation. Their identity develops as a communal expression and practice of opposition against marginalization and dehumanization, and in this process the selfhood defined by victimization alters into an identity of survival and transformation. Both Luz Delcano and José Luis use their subaltern positions to tell a story of their people—Luz shares her life-narrative with Arturo and Father Hugh, and José Luis testifies to peace groups in the U.S.—asserting their own victimization in public as a counter, subaltern version to the dominant narrative and a challenge of the authoritarian project of silencing and annihilation. In this act of bearing witness, positions of victimhood are transformed into positions of individual and communal resistance. In addition, individual subjectivities form in relation to others who share the experience of oppression, and this interaction advances a communal sense of self and a deep commitment to others. This relational identity also negotiates the division between the private and the public and thus affirms the interdependence between the individual and the national in sociopolitical processes of liberation and democracy.

Foregrounding the connection between familial and national structures, the U.S. Latina writers discussed in this study portray identities that assert agency and resistant power in both of these structures. In order to become subjects of their history, oppressed citizen-subjects use the site and practices of the private sphere in their struggle to reclaim the national space, from which they have been absent and by which they have been subjugated. With the repressive nation-state territorializing their individual spaces and bodies, the identities of the oppressed become politicized in conditions that aim to paralyze their geopolitical subject-positioning. Set in motion by the need to survive and resist, their oppositional movement emerges from particularized contexts and extends into global geopolitical spaces, fearlessly defying restrictions and boundaries that have been enforced by national structures.

CONCLUSION

Hybridity and Marginalization in U.S. Latina Literature: Politicization of the Postmodern

Writing in the age of postmodernity and engaging in aesthetic and philosophical projects of postmodernism, U.S. Latina writers provide an insightful cultural critique of postmodern socioeconomic and political reality. While focusing on the questions of identity, they criticize positivist, homogenous, and ahistorical notions of the human subject by emphasizing the dialectical relationship between the individual and the social. At the same time, they present these two spheres as ambiguous, fluctuating, heterogeneous, and shaped by power relations. Foregrounding subjective fragmentation in their literary representations of the self and in their narrative strategies, the U.S. Latina texts discussed in my study demonstrate complex and multifaceted relations between the subject and the world of postmodernity: the relations that rest on forms of oppression and at the same time entail modes of empowerment.

In his study of the correlation between the postmodern condition and U.S. minority identity, *Framing the Margins* (1994), Phillip Brian Harper asserts that subjective fragmentation has always been an experience of minority groups in the U.S. due to their "socially marginalized and politically disenfranchised status" (3). He borrows this statement from bell hooks, who claims that "the overall impact of postmodernism is that many other groups now share with black folks a sense of deep alienation, despair, uncertainty, loss of a sense of grounding even if it is not informed by shared circum-

stances" (4).[1] Harper states that the aim of his study is to corroborate hooks'
claim and "more importantly—to suggest that marginalized groups' experience of decenterdness is itself a largely unacknowledged factor in the 'general' postmodern condition" (4). The marginalized positions of U.S. minority
groups demonstrate the social effects of difference in the context where it is
constructed as negative, posits Harper, and this experience of marginality
thus complicates the "general" disorientation characteristic of the postmodern condition. The social forces of postmodernity produce not only fragmented and unstable identities but also "ineffective subjectivities" impaired
by specific forms of social oppression, such as gender, race, and sexual discrimination. Calling for the inclusion of the marginalized minority experience in the theoretical debates on postmodern subjectivity, Harper emphasizes not only the importance of social marginality in the development of
subjectivity but also the necessity to specify the sources of marginalization
and fragmentation. He rightly points out that although postmodernist debates
focus attention on subjective decenterdness and attribute it to technological
and economic development, they continue to obscure forces of oppression
that affect subjects according to their racial, ethnic, gender, class, and sexual
identity.

   In order to demonstrate that the psyche's decenteredness—a phenomenon theorized as a crucial aspect of the postmodern condition—parallels the
experience of social marginality of U.S. minority groups, Harper's study
traces the presence of subjective fragmentation in U.S. novels written prior to
the postmodern period. Interestingly, there are no U.S. Latino/a novels included in his study, although, as I have stated in Introduction, the early
phases of U.S. Latino/a literary production foreground both individual and
communal struggles for self-definition in the conditions of multiple social
oppression and marginalization. Foregrounding the psyche's fragmentation
in relation to specific social conditions, U.S. Latino/a novels often present
"ineffective subjectivities" marked by cultural and political exclusion and
struggling with the resulting alienation, disorientation, and crisis of the self.
Recent U.S. Latina narratives continue to deploy the theme of social marginality, but as I have shown in the previous chapters, they reconfigure the marginal subjectivities in positive terms by demonstrating effective forms of
agency emerging in oppressive circumstances. Voicing their criticism against
specific forms of oppression and subjugation, they foreground new emancipated subjectivities that are engaged in oppositional forms of enunciation and

committed to differential and resistant subject-positioning. In this way, contemporary U.S. Latina writing "*re*-frames the margins" and thus further complicates what Harper calls "the general postmodern condition."

Initially placed on the margins of literary and national/cultural discourses, Latina writers in the U.S. seize the epistemological and ontological potency of marginalized positions to explore and articulate the specificity of women's experience in the age of postmodernity. Although they focus attention on what Harper identifies, in his readings of works by black female authors, as a "female experience of psychic fragmentation," U.S. Latina writers seek effective ways to counter the debilitating fragmentation effected by patriarchy. As I have shown, they assert that liberating female agency and self-definition can be engendered in spite of cultural and political forms of patriarchal oppression.

Engaging with the questions of female minority identity, the discussed U.S. Latina authors problematize not only the traditional masculinist and nationalist paradigms of self-definition but also the current theories on identity politics in the U.S. As I have argued, their literary narratives investigate and reconfigure subject-constitution and subject-positioning as effects of cultural and geopolitical conditioning in the age of mass migrations, globalization, and post-coloniality, unmasking both the patterns of oppression and the potentials for resistance embedded in postmodern conditions. Focusing on material conditions in the U.S. and Central America/the Caribbean, the U.S. Latina texts have shown that the awareness of global connections is fundamental for the understanding of identity politics in a specific national context. The history of economic and political oppression, like any history of repression, plays a prominent role in identity articulation of minority groups, and the narrative of displacement—so typical of postmodernity—needs to be recovered and included in contemporary debates on identity politics.

Criticizing the celebratory and detached narratives on postmodern hybrid identities, the selected U.S. Latina texts expose the other side of postmodern reality where identities are formed and transformed under the forces of patriarchy, racism, colonialism, and the repressive state apparatus. They assert that the processes of postmodern displacement and re/de-territorialization are grounded in the dynamics of social domination and objectification and that, consequently, identities are hybridized through hegemonic, authoritarian practices. Thus, postmodern hybridization is inevitably historical, enforced via sociopolitical forces and often enacted via force, and as such it is not a new process. However, the formation and the positioning of subjectivity under these processes have received new configurations.

With this claim, the U.S. Latina writing discussed in my study calls attention to the fact that female minority identity is marginalized and constituted under conditions of multiple oppression, which is present not only in the dominant culture but also within the culture of the subjugated. The territorializing practices of cultural patriarchy and state authoritarianism, as I have demonstrated in my textual analyses, place women in objectified and inferior positions in both the private and public spaces; the spaces identified as the domestic and the public, the family and the nation, the home and the exile, the body and the socius. Furthermore, these regulating practices often reterritorialize these spaces in their attempts to intensify the protocols of control and authority: using acts of physical violence, they attack the individual in order to repress or annihilate it. The U.S. Latina narratives discussed in the final chapters foreground this violent nature of authoritarian reterritorialization by dramatizing the processes of exile and "disappearance" of those who refuse to conform to social regulation.

Enmeshed in multiple discourses of subjugation, the oppressed encounter hybridity's potential of liberatory resistance as they are forced to occupy the creases between these discourses. The "maneuver in-between" becomes their refusal to be (re)territorialized and, as they adopt fluidity and multiplicity to counter multiple territorialization, the minority female subjects learn to assert enunciative agency through a differential and hybrid positioning. U.S. Latina texts emphasize this type of positioning as coalitional and cross-national, insisting on forms of hybridity that address cultural and sociopolitical disjunctions and the resulting physical and psychological dislocations.

Hybridity, in these texts, emerges out of postmodern displacement, and as a product of colonizing practices of nation-states, it turns into a site of contestation, resistance, and transformation. In this way, as U.S. Latina narratives demonstrate, a hybridized minority identity is produced by objectifying social forces but is also potentially geared toward an agentic enunciation and a conscious differential subjectivity. Deconstructing postmodern cultural practices, U.S. Latina authors express an unambiguous political agenda of resistance and empowerment by using postmodern politics: they simultaneously embrace and subvert the postmodern methodology of fragmentation and hybridization in order to identify strategies of resistance against oppressive social forces.

Because of its double-coded politics of subversion and complicity, Linda Hutcheon defines postmodernist representation as politically ambivalent: while it interrogates domination, it does not propose "an unproblematic position from which to speak" (153). In her influential study *The Politics of Postmodernism* (1989), she exposes the postmodern as "both complicitous with and contesting of the cultural dominants within which it operates" (142) while it engages in a de-doxification (de-naturalization) of the dominant representation and a de-totalization of the historiographic metanarrative. Hutcheon reasserts this political ambivalence of the postmodern strategy in her examination of the correlation between "feminisms"[2] and postmodernism. While feminisms and postmodernism share similar concerns in their problematization of the traditional representations of the body and sexuality, their engagements differ: feminisms have distinct and unambiguous political agendas of resistance and transformation, while postmodernism does not adopt political agency in fear of totalization and centeredness. Hutcheon, however, states that the postmodern does have a potential to be political when it engages in practices of contestation and deconstruction. Revealing the problematic sites of social discourse, postmodernism points at what needs to be questioned and, at the same time, provides tools of interrogation and criticism.

U.S. Latina narratives exploit the political potential of the postmodern by employing deconstruction and subversion of social metanaratives, such as cultural and political patriarchy, and by de-essentializing dominant representations and paradigms, for example, gendered and national identity. Furthermore, they politicize postmodern conditions of dislocation and hybridization as they transfigure these concepts into forms of resistance and empowerment. In their texts, hybridity and the in-between maneuver are portrayed as modes of individual and communal emancipation in conditions of patriarchal and political oppression. Invested in postmodern methodology of liberation, the discussed U.S. Latina writing engages feminist, postcolonial, and psychoanalytic models of self-empowerment in order to reinforce the politicization and conscientization of postmodern subjectivity. Drawing from and expanding on the theories of Gloria Anzaldúa, Chela Sandoval, Homi Bhabha, Amy Kaminsky, Jean Franco, and Jacques Lacan, the selected U.S. Latina narratives mobilize the "social marginality" entailed in postmodern sociopolitical conditions to suggest new sites and modes of political resistance and empowerment. Also, they transform the modern crisis of self into a creative postmodern reinvention of subjectivity, while they foreground decentered and pluralized identities as positions of survival and resistance in conditions of social oppression and marginalization.

NOTES

Introduction—U.S. Latina Literature: Mobilizing and Reconfiguring Postmodern Subjectivity

1. The ethnic label 'Latino' is an umbrella term that covers diverse ethnic groups of Latin American descent and thus erases differences and varieties among individual groups (for an excellent discussion of ethnic labels, see Suzanne Oboler's *Ethnic Labels, Latino Lives*). However, it would be hard to use specific terms—such as, Chicano, Puerto Rican, Cuban American, Dominican American, etc.—when referring to the entire range of the ethnic grouping. I use it with no intention to lump and disregard difference but for the purpose of a more practical usage. In addition, its unifying connotation serves my argument for a more interactive and unified conception of Latino/a literary production.

2. I take these historical moments as beginning points of U.S. Latino/a literature because they mark the emergence of diverse Latino communities within the U.S. nation-state. However, early writings expressing the identity problematics of *mestizaje* can be traced back to Alvar Nuñoz Cabeza de Vaca's *Naufragios* (Madrid: Catedra, 1989), chronicles written in the sixteenth century for Spain's colonial court. De Vaca's chronicles are regarded by many literary critics as the earliest narrative expression of the Chicano/Latino quest for identity. See, for example, Luis Leal and Juan Bruce-Novoa.

3. Common themes of Latino/a literature—such as discrimination (racial, ethnic, class, linguistic, etc.), immigration, labor exploitation, acculturation, and exile—derive from similar experiences of sociocultural and political oppression in the U.S. The experience of Mexican Americans is profoundly marked by the 1848 annexation, when the territory and population of the northern Mexican regions were granted to the U.S. upon the signing of the Treaty of Guadalupe Hidalgo. Although promised legal rights and protection, the "male citizens of Mexico" who chose to accept U.S. citizenship immediately experi-

enced racial and legal discrimination as their lands became illegally and permanently ex-
propriated by Anglo settlers (see Hine and MacFaragher's *The American West: A New
Interpretative History*). Ever since, Mexican Americans have suffered social marginalization and discrimination: they have been regarded as the "foreign Other" in spite of the
fact that they were the indigenous population in what is now considered the American
Southwest. In addition, the economic immigrants from Mexico are allowed to enter the
U.S. only when the American economy suffers from deficit in labor force; otherwise,
they are denied immigration and are treated as "illegal aliens" if they manage to cross the
border. The Puerto Ricans share a similar experience of annexation: their island was
ceded to the U.S. in 1898 after the Spanish-American war and they were granted U.S.
citizenship, but no right to vote, in 1917. Although Puerto Ricans in the U.S. do not have
to struggle with the immigration law like Mexican immigrants, they too are seen as the
"foreign Other" on the American mainland, while on the island they continue to struggle
with U.S. imperialism and a challenge to define their national and cultural identity. The
experience of Central American immigrant groups in the U.S. is primarily defined by
their escape from the turbulent political upheavals in the region during the 1970s and
1980s. Military regimes and civil wars forced Guatemalan, Salvadoran, and Nicaraguan
refugees to enter the U.S., illegally in most cases, and to face a repeated dehumanization
in exile, being usually denied political asylum and regularly deported to their countries of
origin. Their persecution by immigration police was instigated by the U.S. government,
which at the time supported the dictatorships in Central America. Similarly, the Cuban
American experience is marked by the political exile of a large number of Cubans after
the socialist revolution in 1959. However, these political refugees were immediately
granted asylum since they opposed the Revolution and its leader, Fidel Castro. Coming
predominantly from the white upper-class groups, they were able to successfully integrate in the economic mainstream of the U.S. and avoid racial and class discrimination.
However, they lost the elite status they had enjoyed in Cuba and became a minority in the
U.S. The later waves of immigration from Cuba brought poor and non-white Cubans,
who shared the experience of economic and racial marginalization with other economically disempowered Latinos. The contradiction of the Cuban American position has been
the fact that they have become a strong and internally well-connected diaspora but without any support of their native country. The problem of their identity augments with the
impossibility of claiming the present moment in Cuba, since for many exiled Cubans the
return is not attainable. For a detailed history of these groups, see for example Martin N.
Marger's *Race and Ethnic Relations: American and Global Perspectives* and Ronald Takaki's *A Different Mirror: A History of Multicultural America*

4.   Literary themes of modernist literature are undoubtedly diverse and complex, but the
predominant one focuses on an individual and his/her struggle to achieve or retain self-
awareness and wholeness in the face of the turbulent social changes of modern times,
changes brought about by industrialization, modern nation building, and the Great War.
Seeing modernity as an age of individual and social crisis, some of the most noted modernist writers in Europe and the U.S.—such as Virginia Woolf, James Joyce, Gertrude
Stein, Franz Kafka, Willa Cather, Scott Fitzgerald, and Ernest Hemingway—engage the
notion of an alienated subject as the main focus of their writings, looking for sources of

stability and coherence in the chaotic world of modern society. In the context of minority experience in the U.S., efforts to find or preserve cultural, linguistic, and racial identity are formed, as I state, in reaction to sociocultural and political marginalization enforced by the dominant culture.

5. In his book *Our America*, Walter Benn Michaels forms an argument on American nativism around the nationalist commitment to identity prevalent in the 1920s. He names this period "nativist modernism" and uses John Higham's definition to describe it as "an opposition to an internal minority on the grounds of its foreign connections" (2). While Michaels sees this difference in cultural/racial terms rather than political, the experience of Californian Mexicans after the U.S. annexation proves that political difference was an inevitable consequence of racism: although they were formally given political rights and citizenship, Mexicans in California were abused through a flagrant legal discrimination, and their difference rooted in their racial/cultural otherness justified the political discrimination. Michaels also argues that identity is disconnected from citizenship, and this separation specifically posed a problem in the process of self-definition of Mexican Americans.

6. See Hine and MacFaragher's *The American West: A New Interpretative History*.

7. Luis Leal and Pepe Barrón identify this phase of Chicano literary production as 'literature of transition' (1848–1920), perceiving the encounter between two cultures, traditions, and languages as a moment that marks the beginning of Chicano literary expression in the U.S. For a detailed analysis, see Leal and Barrón's "Chicano Literature: An Overview."

8. *Indigenista* (indigenous, Spa.) movements were primarily literary movements which reimagined the history of the indigenous ancestors in mythical and poetic terms. See, for example Chicano poetry that evokes the Aztlán myth and celebrates the indigenous roots, such as Alurista's *Floricanto en Aztlán* (1971) and Rodolfo "Corky" Gonzales's "I am Joaquín: An Epic Poem" (1972); and the Puerto Rican poetry of the Nuyorican movement that claims strong ties with the Puerto Rican island as the homeland of the Taíno Indians, such as poetry by Miguel Algarín, Miguel Piñero, Pedro Pietri, Sandra María Esteves, and Lucky Cienfuegos.

9. Aztlán was a land where the Aztec tribes lived before the foundation of Tenochtitlán (present day Mexico City) in 1325. No one knows for sure what territory the region originally occupied, but in the Chicano movement it was used to signify the whole territory of the Southwest, which originally belonged to Mexico prior to the 1848 annexation by the U.S. Boricua (or Borinquen) was a pre-Colombian name of the Puerto Rican island and a homeland of indigenous tribes of Taíno Indians. In order to reclaim cultural and national autonomy of the island, the nationalist Puerto Rican movements—the Young Lords Party and Nuyorican Movement—deployed the indigenous identity as an affirmative source of identification. For a detailed analysis, see the chapters on Chicano and Puerto Rican literature in *Handbook of Hispanic Cultures in the U.S.: Literature and Art*, ed. Francisco Lomelí (Houston: Arte Público Press, 1993).

10. See, for example, Chicano works such as Raymond Barrio's *The Plum Plum Pickers* (1969), Richard Vásquez's *Chicano* (1970), Tomás Rivera's *... y no se lo tragó la tierra* (1971), Oscar Zeta Acosta's *The Revolt of Cockroach People* (1973), Alejandro Morales'

Caras viejas y vino nuevo (1975), and poetry by Alurista, Ricardo Sánchez, Abelardo Delgano, and Sergio Elizondo. Puerto Rican works include Piri Thomas' *Down These Mean Streets* (1967), Nicholasa Mohr's *In Nueva York* (1977), Lefty Barreto's *Nobody's Hero* (1977), and poetry by Miguel Algarín, Pedro Pietri, and Tato Laviera. Cuban-American writing in this phase is represented by Octavio Armand's *Piel menos mia* (1973), Lino Calvo Novás' *Maneras de contar* (1970), and José Sanchez-Boudy' poetry collection *Poemas de otoño e invierno* (1967).

11. The list of those works is too long to be cited here, but I suggest several authors whose writings define this literary phase: (Chicanos/as) Rudolfo Anaya, Ana Castillo, Denise Chavez, Sandra Cisneros, Rolando Hinojosa, Arturo Islas, Graciela Limón, Demetria Martínez, Alejandro Morales, Helena María Viramontes; (Puerto Ricans) Martín Espada, Sandra María Esteves, Tato Laviera, Nicholasa Mohr, Rosario Morales, Aurora Levins Morales, Judith Ortiz Cofer, Ed Vega; (Cubans) Roberto Fernandez, Cristina García, Oscar Hijuelos; (Dominican) Julia Alvarez and Junot Díaz.

12. For an excellent discussion of U.S. Latina writing in the 1980s, see "At the Threshold of the Unnamed: Latina Literary Discourse in the Eighties" by Eliana Ortega and Nancy Saporta Sternbach in *Breaking Boundaries: Latina Writing and Critical Readings*, edited by Horno-Delgado et al.

13. See Chela Sandoval's articles and book on the "methodology of the oppressed."

14. Modern humanist reconstruction of subjectivity foregrounds an authentic and unified individual subject (see, for example, philosophical theories of Kant and Descartes), while postmodern critiques of subjectivity emphasize a fractured and unstable individuality.

15. "Deterritorialization" is originally Deleuze and Guattari's term developed in *Anti-Oedipus*, where they theorize subject-formation as modes of abstraction regulated by certain discourses, such as the family, the state, and the law.

16. The term "Third World" was used first by Alfred Sauvy, French demographer who opposed the Cold War rhetoric and applied it in his description of economic, political, and social relationships in the world (see Sauvy's *General Theory of Population*, New York: Basic Books, 1970). The term has come to define the underdeveloped and formerly colonized nations, and while many contemporary critics challenge its reductive and ethnocentric designation (Aijaz Ahmad, for example), some use it strategically in order to emphasize the economic and political difference (third-world feminists, for example). I employ this term in my analysis as a specific referent that defines female experience in the context of multiple oppression and disenfranchisement. I myself oppose its reductive and imperialist configuration but find its strong connotation of colonization and marginalization to be a helpful specification of the notion of multiple subjectivity, which can assume numerous and diverse meanings within different discourses.

17. See, for example, Sandoval's "New Sciences: Cyborg Feminism and the Methodology of the Oppressed."

18. See Sandoval's "U.S. Third World Feminism."

19. As in "subaltern studies," the dominant historical text is read against the grain in order to allow for the agentic voice of the subaltern to emerge. In the context of Latin American writing, this subaltern narration is present in the tradition of *testimonio* literature; and in the context of U.S. Latina writing, Ellen McCracken identifies the tradition of "modified

testimonial narratives" in works that deal with the Central American experience, such as Graciela Limón's *In Search of Bernabé*.

20. See, for examples, writings by Jean Franco, Marguerite Guzman Bouvard, Sonia Alvarez, Beatriz Sarlo, Laura Rossi, and Nelly Richard.

21. There are just a few studies that perform a comparative analysis of U.S. Latino/a literature and approach it as a unified literary production. *New Latina Narrative: The Feminine Space of Postmodern Ethnicity* (1999) by Ellen McCracken discusses a large number of U.S. Latina narratives through feminist and cultural studies approaches. John S. Christie's *Latino Fiction and the Modernist Imagination* (1998) explores how Latino/a literature adopts modernist techniques. Marc Zimmerman's essay "U.S. Latinos: Their Culture and Literature" (1992) provides a discussion of U.S. Latino literature and culture through a brief survey of Chicano, Puerto Rican, Cuban and other Latino literatures in the U.S., also including an annotated bibliography. In addition to these longer studies, several articles engage in critical and comparative analyses of U.S. Latino/a writing; see, for example, Suzanne Bost, Ellen McCracken, Fatima Mujcinovic, and Jacqueline Stefanko. In the last two decades, an increasing number of literary collections and anthologies portray Latino/a literature as a unified literary production. The first to be published were *Cuentos: Stories by Latinas* (1983) edited by Alma Gómez, Cherrie Moraga, and Mariana Romo-Carmona; and *Compañeras: Latina Lesbians* (1987) edited by Juanita Ramos. *In Other Words* (1994) by Roberta Fernandez presents creative writing by a wide range of U.S. Latina writers, insisting on a recognition and inclusion of less known ethnic groupings of Latina authors.

22. According to U.S. Census Bureau, the number of "Hispanic Origin Persons" grew from 22,372.000 in 1990 to 29,348.000 in 1997, with the net growth rate of 35.8 (compared to 7.4 for the total U.S. population, and 33.6 for Asians and 12.7 for Blacks). It is estimated that in 2050, Latinos will grow to 96,508.000, around 25% of the projected number for the total U.S. population (393,931.000). For more detailed statistics, see *Statistical Abstract of the United States: 1998*.

23. 'Biculturalism' refers here to the coexistence of Latin American tradition and dominant Anglo culture in a U.S. context. However, it also implies that there are multiple cultural influences and traditions within these two cultures. I use the term 'biculturalism' rather than 'multiculturalism' in order to emphasize the tension and negotiation between the dominant culture vs. minority/ethnic tradition, the binarism informed by the practices of domination and exclusion. This dialectic allows me to approach cultural identity as a site of contentation that is infused with the problematics of gender, race, class, sexuality, and age, and is permeated with the dynamics of an "in-between positioning" foregrounded in U.S. Latina identity politics as a strategy of resistance to domination and objectification. The term multiculturalism would be misleading since it has come to represent, in the most general meaning, a cultural movement in the U.S. that struggles for the recognition of multiple cultural centers by promoting egalitarian cultural politics.

24. The cultural conservatives argue that the American nation is becoming fragmented and disunited due to the disregard of American core culture and the insistence on multiple cultural centers. They defend assimilation as the way of securing national unity and strengthening the idea of '*e pluribus unum*.' See, for example, the following writings:

Alvin J. Schmidt, *The Menace of Multiculturalism: Trojan Horse in America* (Westport, CT: Praeger, 1997), Dinesh D'Souza, *Illiberal Education: The Politics of Race and Sex on Campus* (New York: Free Press, 1991), and Arthur Schlesinger Jr., *The Disuniting of America* (Knoxville, Tenn.: Whittle Direct Books, 1991).

25. See, for example, Freud's theory on the unconscious in his *Three Essays on the Theory of Sexuality* and *The Interpretation of Dreams* and Lacan's explanation of "the Other" in "The Agency of the Letter in the Unconscious" and *The Four Fundamental Concepts of Psychoanalysis.*

26. In Lacanian usage, 'the other' designates the opposing reference to 'the self' in the 'subject vs. object' binarism, or to alterity in general. As an exterior form/image of one's self-differentiation, it is a source of the subject's secondary identification ("ego ideal") through which one affirms its sense of self, its existence and agency. Distinct from this is the (capitalized) "Other," which Lacan defines as the "second degree of otherness," that which is constructed as the "Ideal Ego" in the process of the subject's primary identification. This identification is misperceived since it is based on an imaginary projection of the totality and autonomy of the self. Because the subject is dependent on the field of the Other, as it is involved in an infinite search for the unattainable self-totality, its constitution is always based on lack, absence, and incompleteness. The Other also parallels the unconscious, the internal other of the subject that is repressed and that may resurface in the form of aberrations, phobias, dreams, jokes, verbal slips, etc. (when defense mechanisms are weaker or completely off). This resurfacing, argues Lacan, demonstrates the unconscious as the discourse of the Other and the manifestation of the Other's desire for recognition. The definition of the o/Other may be much more elaborate than this, and the difficulty lies in the fact that Lacan refused to be specific about it. This is why it is necessary to read Lacan's sources directly and carefully. Consult, for example, Lacan's "The Mirror Stage," "The Agency of the Letter in the Unconscious," *The Seminar of Jacques Lacan, Book II* , and *Four Fundamental Concepts of Psychoanalysis.* Outside of psychoanalytic criticism, the "Other" is used to refer to a person or a group of people that are placed in opposition to the dominant social group or culture. Often, racial, ethnic, class, gender, and sexual minorities are named or portrayed as "the Other." Hegel's explanation of the 'master vs. slave' dialectic in "Lordship and Bondage" provides a useful explanation of the connection between the self and the other (see *Hegel's Dialectic of Desire and Recognition.* Ed. John O'Neill. Albany: SUNY Press, 1996. 29-36).

27. Freud defines the 'return of the repressed' as the involuntary irruption into consciousness of unacceptable derivatives of the primary impulse.

28. Lacan rewrites Freud's psychoanalytic theory by reading it through structuralism and Ferdinand de Saussure's linguistics. He perceives the unconscious to be structured like a language, based on deferral and absence. Linguistic signs designate absence of real objects and evade full signification. Since the signifier and the signified are asymmetrical, the linguistic signs cannot convey a complete meaning. The signifier cannot provide a full representation of the signified, argues Lacan in "The Agency of the Unconscious," and it consequently requires multiple reference. This movement of the signifier forms an infinite "chain of signifiers" as the full meaning is always deferred and multiply layered.

29. Homi Bhabha's term that generally refers to the space of encounter between binary concepts.

30. It is important to note a distinction between subjectivity and consciousness. In his article "What is Cultural Studies Anyway?," Richard Johnson posits that "subjectivity includes possibility... that some elements or impulses are subjectively active... without being consciously known," while consciousness "embraces the notion of a consciousness of self and an active mental and moral self-production" (44). Johnson bases this distinction on the concept of conscious versus unconscious agency. In the context of postmodern identity dynamics, I see subjectivity in the postmodern conditions as constituted through the process of resistance to social objectification and subjugation, the process of agency that is not, as Johnson argues, necessarily conscious and premeditated. Similarly, I understand one's consciousness as an awareness of self always based on an active, deliberate agency in self-formation under the conditions of objectification and subjugation. Therefore, both subjectivity and consciousness are gained through the process of acting against objectification, and the distinction lies in the awareness of one's action, or strategy of resistance.

31. See endnote 26 for more explanation of the Other.

32. See Franco's introduction to Roberta Fernández's anthology *In Other Words*.

33. "Stranded objects" represent Eric Santner's psychoanalytic notion of the "transitional objects" devoid of their meaning. When these substitutive figures used in the process of mourning lose their symbolic meaning of absence, they block the mourning and thus impede the task of transition to the resolution of a traumatic loss. For a detailed analysis, see Santner's first chapter in *Stranded Objects*.

34. Drawing from examples of populist, and specifically women's movements in Latin America, Jean Franco, Amy Kaminsky, Sonia Alvarez, Laura Rossi, Julieta Kirkwood, Nelly Richard and many other critics have argued that Latin American feminism foregrounds joined struggles for female emancipation and national liberation.

35. See texts by Jean Franco, Amy Kaminsky, Sonia Alvarez, Marguerite Guzman Bouvard, Mary Beth Tierney-Tello, Julieta Kirkwood, and Laura Rossi.

36. See Alvarez's *Engendering Democracy in Brazil*.

37. See Bhabha's "The Commitment to Theory" (*New Formations* 5, Summer 1988: 5-23).

38. "Women-of-color" as a form of identification signifies in this context an alliance formed around common experience of female oppression by patriarchy, racism, and classism (see, for example, writings of Gloria Anzaldúa, bell hooks, Trinh Minh-ha, Chandra Mohanty, and Chela Sandoval). It establishes female solidarity and political unity through an inclusive label whose racial, gender, and economic denotation serves to foreground a difference from the hegemonic Anglo feminism and a specificity of political agenda. On the other hand, racial specificity of this grouping obstructs the unifying factor of social class since it excludes, for example, white women living in poverty. Also, the emphasis put on color becomes problematic in the context of politics of visibility, where color is not always rendered as visible. This is why Chandra Mohanty insists that "this is a term which designates a political constituency, not a biological or even sociological one," foregrounding *"common context of struggle* rather than color or racial identifications," (7, Mohanty's emphasis). With this modification, third-world feminism comes to signify

ideological positioning towards oppression and objectification and thus allows for political links across class, racial, ethnic, gender, and national boundaries.

39. See, for example, Gloria Anzaldúa, Cherríe Moraga, Kimberlé Cranshaw, bell hooks, Chandra Mohanty, and Trinh Minh-ha.

40. As Chela Sandoval and others argue, this term is employed in a feminist context to emphasize a new category for social identity, the third gender category that is formed at the interstices of cultures and social markings and in response to binary structures and divisions. See, for example, Sandoval's "Feminist Forms of Agency and Oppositional Consciousness: U.S. Third World Feminist Criticism."

41. Kaminsky's description of exilic displacement in *Reading the Body Politic*, 32.

42. See Bammer's introduction to *Displacements*, ed. Angelika Bammer.

43. "The dirty war" (in Spanish, *"la guerra sucia"*) refers to the period of Argentine military regime from 1976–1983, inducted with the military coup in 1976 by three commanding officers of the armed forces. The military junta and their leader General Jorge Rafael Videla displaced Isabel Perón's civilian government by suspending the Congress and establishing their own government. In order to preserve their power and eliminate already weakened guerrilla groups, they began "antisubversive operations" directed not only against guerrillas and other oppositional groups but also against innocent civilians. Around 30,000 Argentines permanently disappeared during the six years of the regime, abducted, tortured, and brutally murdered by military and paramilitary groups. The security forces dragged men and women, young and elderly, to detention centers where they were subjected to sadistic sexual abuse. Most of the raids were carried in secrecy (some occurred in broad daylight) and were categorically denied by the authorities. For a detailed description and testimonial information, see, for example, Marguerite Guzman Bouvard's chapter on "the dirty war" in *Revolutionizing Motherhood*.

44. For a detailed analysis, see Franco's "Beyond Ethnocentrism."

45. See Hall's article "Who Needs Identity?"

46. See Freud's discussion of the "Oedipal Stage" in *Three Essays on the Theory of Sexuality* and Lacan's "Mirror Stage" in *Ecrits*.

Chapter One—Gendered Hybrid Identities: Maneuvering Between Two Cultures

1. Difference has become one of the key concepts of the postmodern discourse, finally becoming legitimized in the mainstream ideology as it is celebrated through the trend of global heterogeneity that has been fostered by the free flow of capital, labor, goods, and people. However this is not a humanist or liberalist incorporation, since difference becomes just another commodity that sells well on the market and assists further development of consumerism in the postmodern age. Stuart Hall alertly explains: "[...] in order to maintain its global position, capital has had to negotiate and partly reflect the differences it was trying to overcome. It has had to constitute a world in which things are dif-

ferent. Some seem to take pleasure in that, but, for capital, differences do not matter" (182). Hall is aware that the seeming inclusion of difference is governed solely by economic forces and that capital has had to negotiate and incorporate difference not because of the populist pressure for inclusion but because a new profitable commodity was needed on the market saturated by sameness. Symbolized by ethnic food and music, promoted as pluralism, and advocated by multicultural trends, difference ultimately becomes divorced from its humanist referent—the marginalized, post-colonial subject. For an excellent discussion, see Hall's article "The Local and the Global: Globalization and Ethnicity."

2. Chela Sandoval, "New Sciences: Cyborg Feminism and the Methodology of the Oppressed," in *The Cyborg Handbook*, ed. Chris Hables Gray; and *Methodology of the Oppressed*.

3. See Donna Haraway's "A Cyborg Manifesto: Science, Technology, and Socialist-Feminism in the Late Twentieth Century," in *Simians, Cyborgs, and Women*.

4. One of the frequently posed questions in regards to the epistolary form of this novel addresses the absence of Alicia's voice, as the letters go in only one direction, from Teresa to Alicia. (See, for example, articles by Erlinda Gonzales-Berry, Yvonne, Yarbro-Bejarano, and Hector Torres.) I interpret this absence through the novel's emphasis on self-reflexivity. The letters represent Teresa's dialogues with her own self, and the narration of the past events is her reconstruction of the quest for self-meaning. Alicia is the "other" from whom Teresa distances herself and at the same time identifies with in her process of introspective self-examination and projection.

5. It has to be emphasized that *machismo* is not limited to Mexican culture only, since its patriarchal code of traditional gender roles is present across cultures. For a detailed analysis of *machismo* and its different and shifting meanings, see, for example, Matthew C. Gutmann's anthropological study *The Meanings of Macho: Being a Man in Mexico City* (Berkeley: U of California P, 1996).

6. I modify this term by using its original etymological meaning [*integritas*, L; *integrité*, Fr.—entirety, wholeness] to convey the concept of wholeness of selfhood distinct from the psychoanalytic notion of unified self. This wholeness is grounded in dignity, humanity, and affirmation of the self gained through the experience of belonging and recognition. I relate this argument to Charles Taylor's "Politics of Recognition," which links identity formation to social recognition and individual/communal rights.

7. Herrera-Sobek analyzes *Giving Up the Ghost* by Cherríe Moraga and "Silver Lake" by Sylvia Lizarraga.

8. Norma Alarcón, "The Sardonic Powers of the Erotic in the Work of Ana Castillo."

9. At her book signing at the University of California, Santa Barbara (May 10, 2001), Sandoval pointed out that 'methodology of emancipation' would be a more accurate name for this set of oppositional practices.

10. In her book *Gender Trouble*, Judith Butler theorizes gender as performance, demonstrating performative character and ideological construction of gender roles.

11. Clearly, rather than a racial concept, whiteness is presented in the text as the symbol of economic privilege and of the removal from multiple oppression in American society. Coming from a higher economic stratum and a European family, Alicia is privileged, or

"white;" yet, it is a relative privilege since, as a woman, she is exposed to patriarchal oppression, which makes her "partially white" and closer to the social marginalization that
Teresa experiences as a "woman of color."

12. In her follow up novel *¡Yo!*(1997), Julia Alvarez continues to foreground the issue of
social class, and in one of the stories she discusses sexual abuse of maids in the Dominican Republic.

13. *Bildungsroman* [Ger: *Bildungs*-formation, *Roman*-novel] is a coming of age novel, tracing the processes of development of the main hero/heroine.

14. English translation: "My husband does not let me."

15. "He doesn't let me."

16. "But you let him not to let you."

17. While Aurora's parents had grown up and lived most of the time in the U.S., she was
born in Puerto Rico, where the family had temporarily relocated because of her father's
fear of the draft to Vietnam. She arrived in the U.S. for the first time when her family returned home after eleven years. This is why she says in her poem "Child of the Americas" that she is "an immigrant and the daughter and granddaughter of immigrants."

18. *Getting Home Alive* was published in 1986, while *Borderlands/La frontera* came out of
press in 1987, and the writers apparently read and shared each other's works before publication.

19. A line from Aurora Levins Morales' piece "Old Countries" used as the title in the second
section of the book.

Chapter Two—Diasporic Identities: At the Frontiers of Nations and Cultures

1. See Homi Bhabha's description of the post-colonial condition in *The Location of Culture*.

2. See Stefanko's analysis in her article "New Ways of Telling," 66.

3. In his article "Mexican Migration and the Social Space of Postmodernism," Roger Rouse
examines the effects of Mexican migration on the reorganization of social space. He emphasizes the limitations and reconfigurations of the traditional socio-spatial images, such
as community and center/periphery, in the postmodern conditions of displacement, technological development, and globalization of capital. He builds his argument on the an-
thropological/sociological case-study of Aguililla, an agrarian community in Mexico,
whose population is half relocated in the Silicon Valley, mostly in Redwood City. Rouse
records a continuous circulation of people, money, goods, and information between these
two locations: while the Mexicans in the U.S. are listening to popular *corridos*, their relatives in Mexico are consuming U.S. goods and spending U.S. dollars; via the means of
modern transportation and telecommunication, Aguilillans actively maintain relationships in both locations; and young generations are prepared to operate on both sides of
the border with bilingual and bicultural skills. Combining different forms of economic
and cultural experience, the Aguilillan model represents a "transnational migrant circuit"
that challenges the dominant ways of reading spatial organization and migratory patterns.

Rouse argues for new spatial images, border-zone and peripherialized center, which more adequately explain dynamics and contradictions of the postmodern social space and the globalized sociocultural and economic order.

4. This term is originally developed by Gilles Deleuze and Félix Guattari in *Anti-Oedipus*. Néstor García-Canclini modifies it in his *Culturas híbridas* to describe the processes of cultural displacement and hybridization. Drawing from the examples of Roger Rouse's study, García-Canclini defines deterritorialization as a disconnection from a specific territory or as a loss of self-definition on the basis of a [singular] territorial origin.

5. Many studies of postmodernism have a celebratory tone in their descriptions of cultural hybridization and transnationalization as effects of migrations, but they overlook the material conditions that produce territorial displacement and border-crossing, such as poverty and political violence. They frequently fail to mention the miserable conditions of living and working in the migrant ghettos, and they ignore the repeated political dehumanization on "this side" of the border.

6. The paradox is that (post)modern conditions both reinforce and negotiate displacement by providing the means of crossing and re-mapping the space. In this way, in both instances, postmodernity works against the homogenizing project of nation-state as it initiates de-territorialization, erosion of borders, and fusion of center and periphery.

7. See José David Saldívar's *Border Matters: Remapping American Cultural Studies*.

8. Homi Bhabha uses Henry James' *The Portrait of a Lady*, Toni Morrison's *Beloved*, and Nadine Gordimer's *My Son's Story*.

9. The author borrows the concept "moments of being" from Virginia Woolf's memoir *Moments of Being* written in 1940 (New York: Harcourt Brace Jovanovich, 1985).

10. See the introductory part of the chapter for more explanation of the "looking-glass monster."

11. Freud defines 'defense mechanism' as a technique used to protect the ego from neurosis or emotional disturbance.

12. Freud defines 'repression' as a defense mechanism, or a process by which an unacceptable impulse or idea is rendered unconscious.

13. See Bakhtin's *Problems of Dostoevsky's Poetics* (1929), "Discourse in the Novel" (1934-35), and *Rabelais and His World* (1965).

14. In "Discourse in the Novel," Bakhtin states that discourse is governed by two forces: centripetal and centrifugal. Centripetal force pushes linguistic elements toward a single, unified center of utterance, while centrifugal force pushes the elements in different directions and away from the center.

15. In her analysis of this novel, Rocío Davis notes that Pilar's last name, Puente, "highlights her role as a bridge between the place and the people of the past and the future" ("Back to the Future" 62).

16. In her emphasis on the metaphorical significance of language in this text, Mary S. Vásquez points out that the novel's title implies "an idiom of belonging, a collective, ever-imperfect antidote to isolation and estrangement" ("Cuba as Text" 23).

17. See Aurora Levins Morales' poem "Old Countries" in *Getting Home Alive*.

18. See Luis' argument in *Dance Between Two Cultures*, 230.

19. *'Künstlerroman'* [Ger: *Künstler*-artist, *Roman*-novel] is a novel that traces coming of age of a young artist as he/she searches for a creative voice.

20. Lacan explains the "Ideal-I" as part of a subject's primary imaginary identification that takes place before the self is objectified in the dialectic of identification with the "other." In the mirror stage, an infant discovers a total unity which replaces its former experience of fragmentation and becomes the basis for all subsequent secondary identifications. Since this totality is misperceived, it can never be achieved. For more, see Lacan's "The Mirror Stage" in *Ecrits*.

21. Conducting research on Holocaust survivors and their children and also relating her own experience, Hirsch notices that second generation memory differs from survivor memory, being recreated only indirectly and imaginatively through stories and memory of the parents. The children feel exiled and removed from the place of origin, which propels an even greater need to know and rebuild. See Hirsch's "Past Lives: Postmemories in Exile," in *Exile and Creativity*, ed. Susan Rubin Suleiman.

Chapter Three—Exilic Identities: The Interplay Between Time and Space

1. I refer to the wave of sociopolitical upheavals in Central America and the Caribbean that took place mostly in the second half of the twentieth century: the military regime of General Rafael Trujillo from 1930–1961 in the Dominican Republic, characterized by severe repression of oppositional movements and imprisonment and liquidation of political dissidents; the socialist revolution in Cuba, which ended the Batista dictatorship in 1959 but provoked a wave of emigration in the following decades; a 12-year civil war in El Salvador that erupted in 1980 after a decade of the disappearance, torture, and murder of thousands of civilians by the paramilitary groups of the right and with support of the government army.

2. In Introduction, I specifically quote the numbers of refugees from Central American and Caribbean countries, which amounted to two million in the period from 1950–1983 (the statistical data taken from Robert Pastor's article "Migration and Development," 300).

3. As I have mentioned in Chapter One, I modify this term by using its original etymological meaning [*integritas*, L; *integrité*, Fr.—entirety, wholeness] to convey the concept of wholeness of selfhood distinct from the psychoanalytic notion of a unified self. This wholeness is grounded in dignity, humanity, and affirmation of the self gained through the experience of belonging and recognition. I relate this argument to Charles Taylor's "politics of recognition," which links identity formation to social recognition and individual/communal rights.

4. In psychoanalytic use, 'denial' is a defense mechanism used to block painful or depressive feelings and to deny the inner significance of experience.

5. 'Cathexis'—the Freudian term for energy attached to an object/representation and used as a defensive strategy of investing in one process in order to facilitate repression of another.

6. Mothers of the disappeared children in Argentina (Las *Madres de la Plaza de Mayo*) organized silent protests against the regime in defiance of orders prohibiting public demonstrations. In this way, they focused the issue of the disappeared into the public and, as Jean Franco notes, redefined the social space (for further explanation, see the analysis in Chapter Four). The absence of this kind of communal resistance in "The Cariboo Café" can be interpreted as a public paralysis effected by the regime.

7. The semantic exchange between "kidnapping" and "disappearing" in this story reinforces the idea of the fundamental repressiveness of the state apparatus. While the government authorities in Central America cover up the violence of their system by categorizing the kidnapped/murdered civilians as the "disappeared," the U.S. immigration authorities justify their brutality against refugees by criminalizing them as "kidnappers."

8. See, for example, Debra Castillo, Carl Gutiérrez-Jones, and José David Saldívar.

9. The myth of *La Llorona* tells a story of a woman who drowns her children in a river after she finds out that her husband has been unfaithful. She does this to punish him, but immediately afterwards she feels guilty. In her desperation, she goes to the river every night and weeps loudly while calling out for her children. The myth explains that ever since, cries of the "weeping woman" (*la llorona*) can be heard at night.

10. 'Symbiosis'—Mahler's term describing the psychological process of the dependence between the mother and the infant.

11. 'Pre-Symbolic Stage'—Lacan's concept defining a phase in child's development prior to child's acquisition of language and entry into the social order, or 'symbolic stage.' In the pre-symbolic stage, a child at first does not recognize its independence from its mother, and thus there is no distinction yet between the self and the other. Its subjectivity begins to emerge in what Lacan names the 'mirror stage,' when the child begins to perceive itself as an independent self, separate and distinct from the mother. However, this self-identification is imaginary because it is based on an imagined totality and unity of the subject. It is also still within the pre-symbolic, or imaginary order, since it is pre-linguistic and pre-oedipal (it precedes the entry of the father–figure). The symbolic stage follows with the child's acceptance of the sexual and gender difference conveyed by the father. In this stage, the child assimilates the symbolic order of language and society and completely separates from the mother and others. This separation is marked by loss and absence because it is based on the repression of the child's desire for a complete unity with the mother and the harmony of the imaginary order. This is when the child's unconscious forms to store all of the socially unacceptable desires, which splits its identity between the conscious and the unconscious. For a detailed explanation, see Lacan's "The Mirror Stage" in *Ecrits*.

12. See Louis Althusser's "Ideology and Ideological State Apparatuses" in *Lenin and Philosophy and Other Essays*. Althusser draws from the Marxist-Leninist theory that defines the state as a "machine of repression" that functions in the interest of the ruling classes. In addition to the repressive state apparatus, Althusser identifies another reality that supports the state apparatus: the ideological state apparatuses (ISA), which are distinct and specialized institutions belonging to the private domain and functioning predominantly by ideology. In his essay on ISA, Althusser analyzes connections between state power and ISA and discusses the specific role of ISA in class struggle.

13. According to Freud, action of reliving the repressed contents in the present without recognizing their source. It is an impulsive and often aggressive action directed at either oneself or others.

14. Freud distinguishes between 'manifest' and 'latent' content in his theory of dreams. The manifest content is the distorted expression of the unconscious, or latent, material in dreams. For a detailed explanation, see *The Interpretation of Dreams*.

Chapter Four—Geopoliticized Identities: Entering the Public Space

1. As I have explained in Introduction, the analysis in this chapter relates to Latin American feminist theory and praxis that is based on connections between the private and the public in conditions of authoritarianism. I will specifically refer to the rise of women's movements in Latin America during the period of totalitarian state regimes and will draw on theories of Jean Franco, Amy Kaminsky, and Sonia Alvarez.

2. See, for example, studies on Latin American women's movements done by Sonia Alvarez, Marguerite Guzman Bouvard, Jean Franco, and Mary Beth Tierney-Tello.

3. Argentine mothers, known as *Las Madres de la Plaza de Mayo*, began their organized gatherings in the aftermath of the political coup in 1976 (that ushered the period of the "Dirty War" in Argentina; see endnote 43 in Introduction). They first met in 1977 as a small group of women, and soon their number grew to include hundreds of women who dared to demand information about their disappeared children. As Marguerite Guzman Bouvard states, they were the only group that dared to confront a repressive military government and gather in public, before the presidential palace in the Plaza de Mayo, to demonstrate against state violence. In 1977, they also openly constituted themselves as an organization promoting democratic values, and by the time a constitutional government replaced the military junta in December 1983, they "transformed the Plaza de Mayo so that it not only reflected power and dissent but also celebrated their unique battle for human rights and their radicalized, collective version of maternity" (2). For a detailed analysis, see Bouvard's *Revolutionizing Motherhood: The Mothers of the Plaza de Mayo*.

4. For an excellent discussion on feminist liberation theology, see María Pilar Aquino's study *Feminist Theology From Latin America*.

5. See Ellen McCracken's discussion in *New Latina Narrative*, 61.

6. A unique Latin American genre of "testimonial" literature that joins oral and written media and privileges, as Myriam Yvonne Jehenson argues, the truth value of its account over artistic coherence. It captures the voice of the native informant with the help of an editor who records, organizes, and edits the narration. For excellent discussions of *testimonios*, see John Beverly and Marc Zimmerman's *Literature and Politics in the Central American Revolutions* and Myriam Yvonne Jehenson's *Latin American Women Writers: Class, Race and Gender*.

7. In her reading of *In Search of Bernabé*, Ellen McCracken states that Graciela Limón reconfigures a number of biblical motifs and thus presents "a counter-narrative to the master text of organized religion" (*New Latina Narrative* 61). I expand this to include a

counter-narrativization of not only dominant religious discourses but also of dominant sociopolitical and historiographic texts.

8. In her analysis of *testimonio* genre, *Latin American Women Writers: Class, Race, and Gender*, Myriam Yvonne Jehenson states that "the reader is asked to empathize with the marginality of the uneducated native informant" and "to join in the struggle to overcome an oppressive class of which he/she is a member" (140–41). I see this call in more communal terms and more inclusive of other forms of oppression: in addition to class, I recognize racial, ethnic, linguistic, and gender oppression.

9. From Limón's interview given to Ellen McCracken for the biographical entry in *Dictionary of Literary Biography: Chicano Writers*.

10. As I have explained in the previous chapter, Freud defines "the return of the repressed" as the involuntary irruption into consciousness of the unacceptable impulse that has been repressed into unconsciousness in the process of psychological defense.

11. Analyzing the women's movements in Brazil, Sonia Alvarez describes the phenomenon of mothers' demonstrations as a "politicization of motherhood." For a detailed analysis, see Alvarez's *Engendering Democracy in Brazil: Women's Movements in Transition Politics*.

12. The most significant practice of liberation theology was reading and interpreting of the Bible, conducted by parish priests who challenged the dominant interpretation of Biblical teachings that advocated fatalism and submission to social inequality and hierarchy. The Scripture discussions were adopted by "base communities" (*comunidades de base*), informal gatherings that practiced religious service and political forums. Specific passages were related to parishioners' daily lives and interpreted in an emancipatory populist mode. For a detailed analysis of liberation theology, see James Schall's *Liberation Theology in Latin America* (San Francisco: Ignatius Press, 1982) and Phillip Berryman's *Liberation Theology: Essential Facts about the Revolutionary Movement in Latin America and Beyond* (Philadelphia: Temple UP, 1987).

13. Oscar Arnulfo Romero (1917–1980) was ordained to priesthood in 1942 and appointed archbishop of San Salvador in 1977. Although, in the beginning, he was quite conservative in doctrinal matters and very traditional regarding authority, he emerged as a populist leader who aligned himself with the poor and the disenfranchised and openly denounced state autocracy and violence. In his final pastoral letter, for example, he condemns the doctrine of national security that places "the individual at the total disposal of the state, denies him political rights and creates inequality in the fruits of development" (Keogh 78). It is believed that the murder of Rutilio Grande, Romero's very close friend and one of the most respected pastors in El Salvador, forced the Archbishop to change his views on hierarchy and authority and become open to more progressive and liberationist ideas. Romero was shot to death on March 24, 1980, at the alter in the chapel of the Divine Providence Hospital, a cancer hospital in San Sebastian. For a detailed analysis of Romero's life and work, see Keogh's study *Romero: El Salvador's Martyr*.

14. Archbishop Oscar Romero often used this motif in his explanations of the Salvadoran civil war. For example, when he appealed to the government soldiers to disobey the orders and stop the repression, he spoke: "Brothers, each one of you is one of us. We are

the same people. The campesinos you kill are your own brothers and sisters" (Erdozaín 78).

15. In her critical work *The Politics of Postmodernism*, Linda Hutcheon defines "historiographic metafiction" as a paradoxical postmodern form that includes both history and fiction in its narrative representation, having its "historical and socio-political grounding sit uneasily alongside its self-reflexivity" (15). The fusion of history and fiction is developed to recreate the past and reinterpret history in a more vivid, immediate, and powerful way. This is a postmodernist effort that answers to the impossibility of objective recording and the arbitrariness of historical meaning. It privileges the value of experience and representation over historical facts, recognizing that historical accounts are always ideologically constructed.

16. In his essay "Nietzsche, Genealogy, History," Michel Foucault uses Nietzsche's philosophy to trace connections between genealogy and history and to argue for the inclusion of the body in philosophical discourse. He posits that genealogy, as an examination of the descent, is situated within the articulation of the body and has a task of exposing a body "totally imprinted by history and the process of history's destruction of the body" (148).

17. The myth of *La Llorona*, a woman who drowns her children, is explained in the previous chapter, endnote 10. The myth of *La Malinche* goes back to colonial days, recounting a story of a Native woman, Malintzín, who became Cortés' interpreter and mistress. The woman helped Cortés advance through the unknown territory and thus conquer the land of the Aztecs. Both women have come to symbolize negative female figures of Mexican folklore: a murderess and a traitor. However, their meaning and symbolism have been deconstructed and resignified by contemporary feminist writers and theorists. See, for example, Gloria Anzaldúa, Norma Alarcón, and Sandra Cypess.

18. In her book on the Sanctuary Movement, Ann Crittenden provides statistics on asylum cases filed with the INS from June 1983 to September 1986. The approval rate for the Salvadoran nationals is quoted as 2.6%: out of 19,207 cases only 528 were approved. The Guatemalans have even a lower rate (0.9%), while the Nicaraguans fare a little bit better (14%). The highest approval rates are quoted for the nationals of Iran (60.4%), Romania (51%), Czechoslovakia (45.4%), Afghanistan (37.7), and Poland (34%), refugees from Communist countries or the Middle East that the U.S. regarded at the time as enemies and thus was eager to support their dissenters. For a complete statistical chart and a detailed analysis of the Sanctuary movement, see Crittenden's *Sanctuary: A Story of American Conscience and the Law in Collision.*

19. The first church to declare itself a public sanctuary for Central American refugees in the U.S. was Southside United Presbyterian Church in Tucson. The declaration took place in March 1982, and by the end of the year there were fifteen other churches—including Catholic, Quaker, Unitarian, Presbyterian, Lutheran, Episcopelian, and Methodist congregations—that had publicly joined the Sanctuary, while there were around 150 others that supported the movement with money, food, and clothing. For a detailed analysis, see Crittenden's study.

Conclusion—Hybridity and Marginalization in U.S. Latina Literature: Politicization of the Postmodern

1. The statement is borrowed from bell hooks' *Yearning: Race, Gender, and Cultural Politics* (Boston: South End Press, 1990).
2. Hutcheon rightly insists that feminism needs to be approached as a multiplicity of feminist theories and practices.

BIBLIOGRAPHY

Primary Sources

Alvarez, Julia. *How the García Girls Lost Their Accents*. New York: Plume, 1992.

———. *¡Yo!* New York: Plume, 1997.

Castillo, Ana. *The Mixquiahuala Letters*. 1986. New York: Anchor / Doubleday, 1992.

García, Cristina. *Dreaming in Cuban*. New York: One World / Ballantine, 1992.

Limón, Graciela. *In Search of Bernabé*. Houston: Arte Público P, 1994.

Martínez, Demetria. *Mother Tongue*. New York: One World / Ballantine, 1994.

Morales, Rosario, and Aurora Levins Morales. *Getting Home Alive*. Ithaca, NY: Firebrand Books, 1986.

Ortiz Cofer, Judith. *Silent Dancing: A Partial Remembrance of a Puerto Rican Childhood*. Houston: Arte Público P, 1990.

Viramontes, Helena María. "The Cariboo Café." *The Moths and Other Stories*. 1985. Arte Público P, 1995.

Secondary Sources

Abraham, Nicolas, and Maria Torok. *The Shell and the Kernel: Renewals of Psychoanalysis*. Chicago: U of Chicago P, 1994.

Acosta-Belen, Edna. "A MELUS Interview: Judith Ortiz Cofer." *MELUS* 18.3 (Fall 1993): 83–97.

Alarcón, Norma. "The Sardonic Powers of the Erotic in the Work of Ana Castillo." *Breaking Boundaries*. Ed. Horno-Delgado et al. 94–107.

Alarcón, Norma, Ana Castillo, and Cherríe Moraga, eds. *The Sexuality of Latinas*. Berkeley: Third Woman P, 1993.

Althusser, Louis. *Lenin and Philosophy and Other Essays*. Trans. Ben Brewster. London: NLB, 1971.

Alvarez, Sonia. *Engendering Democracy in Brazil: Women's Movements in Transition Politics*. Princeton: Princeton UP, 1990.

Anzaldúa, Gloria. *The Borderlands/La Frontera: The New Mestiza*. San Francisco: Spinsters / Aunt Lute Book Company, 1987.

Aquino, María Pilar. *Feminist Theology From Latin America*. Maryknoll, N.Y.: Orbis Books, 1993.

Bakhtin, Mikhail. "Discourse in the Novel." *The Dialogic Imagination: Four Essays by M.M. Bakhtin*. Ed. Michael Holquist. Trans. Caryl Emerson and Michael Holquist. Austin: U of Texas P, 1981. 259–422.

Bammer, Angelika, ed. *Displacements*. Bloomington: Indiana UP, 1994.

Barak, Julie. "'Turning and Turning in the Widening Gyre:' A Second Coming into Language in Julia Alvarez' *How the García Girls Lost Their Accents*." *MELUS* 23.1 (Spring 1998): 159–76.

Benítez-Rojo, Antonio. *The Repeating Island: The Caribbean and the Postmodern Perspective*. Trans. James E. Maraniss. Durham: Duke UP, 1996.

Benmayor, Rina. "*Getting Home Alive*: The Politics of Multiple Identity." *The Americas Review: A Review of Hispanic Literature and Art of the USA* 17.3–4 (Fall/Winter 1989): 107–17.

Bennet, Tanya. "No Country to Call Home: A Study of Ana Castillo's *Mixquiahuala Letters*." *Style* 30 (Fall 1996): 462–78.

Beverly, John, and Marc Zimmerman. *Literature and Politics in the Central American Revolutions*. Austin: U of Texas P, 1990.

Bhabha, Homi. *The Location of Culture*. London: Routledge, 1994.

———, ed. *Nation and Narration*. London: Routledge, 1992.

———. "DissemiNation: Time, Narrative, and the Margins of the Modern Nation." *Nation and Narration*. Ed. Homi Bhabha. 291–322.

Bost, Suzanne. "Transgressing Borders: Puerto Rican and Latina *Mestizaje*." *MELUS* 25.2 (Summer 2000): 187–211.

Bouvard, Marguerite Guzman. *Revolutionizing Motherhood: The Mothers of the Disappeared*. Wilmington, Delaware: SR Books, 1994.

Bruce-Novoa, Juan. *Retrospace: Collected Essays on Chicano Literature*. Houston: Arte Público P, 1990.

Butler, Judith. *Gender Trouble: Feminism and the Subversion of Identity*. New York: Routledge, 1990.

Cady, Linell. "Relational Love: A Feminist Christian Vision." *Embodied Love: Sensuality and Relationship as Feminist Values*. Ed. Paula Cooye, Sharon A. Farmer, and Mary Ellen Ross. San Francisco: Harper and Row, 1987. 135–49.

Calderón, Hector, and José David Saldívar, eds. *Criticism in the Borderlands: Studies in Chicano Literature, Culture, and Ideology*. Durham: Duke UP, 1991.

Castillo, Debra. *Talking Back: Towards a Latin American Feminist Literary Criticism*. Ithaca: Cornell UP, 1992.

Christie, John S. *Latino Fiction and the Modernist Imagination*. New York: Garland Publishing, 1998.

Corpi, Lucha, ed. *Máscaras*. Berkeley: Third Woman P, 1997.

Craft, Linda. *Novels of Testimony and Resistance from Central America*. Gainesville, FL: UP of Florida, 1997.

Crenshaw, Kimberlé. "Mapping the Margins: Interdisciplinarity, Identity Politics, and Violence Against Women of Color." *Critical Race Theory*. Ed. Kimberlé Crenshaw. New York: The New Press, 1995. 357–83.

Crittenden, Ann. *Sanctuary: A Story of American Conscience and the Law in Collision*. New York: Weidenfeld and Nicholson, 1988.

Davis, Rocío G. "Back to the Future: Mothers, Languages, and Homes in Cristina García's *Dreaming in Cuban*." *World Literature Today* 74.1 (Winter 2000): 60–68.

Deleuze, Gilles, and Félix Guattari. *Anti-Oedipus: Capitalism and Schizophrenia*. New York: Viking P, 1977.

Díaz-Briquets, Sergio, and Sidney Weintraub, eds. *Determinants of Emigration from Mexico, Central America, and the Caribbean*. Boulder: Westview P, 1991.

Erdozaín, Plácido. *Archbishop Romero: Martyr of Salvador*. New York: Orbis Books, 1981.

Eysturoy, Annie. *Daughters of Self-Creation*. Albuquerque: U of New Mexico P, 1996.

Fernández, Roberta, ed. *In Other Words: Literature by Latinas in the United States*. Houston: Arte Público P, 1994.

Flores, Juan. *Divided Borders: Essays on Puerto Rican Identity*. Houston: Arte Público P, 1992.

Flores, Lauro, ed. *The Floating Borderlands: Twenty-five Years of U.S. Hispanic Literature*. Seattle: U of Washington P, 1998.

Foucault, Michel. "Nietzsche, Genealogy, History." *Language, Counter-Memory, Practice: Selected Essays and Interviews by Michel Foucault*. Ed. Donald F. Bouchard. Trans. Donald F. Bouchard and Sherry Simon. Ithaca: Cornell UP, 1977. 139–64.

Franco, Jean. *Critical Passions: Selected Essays*. Ed. Mary Louse Pratt and Kathleen Newman. Durham; London: Duke UP, 1999.

———. *Plotting Women: Gender and Representation in Mexico*. New York: Columbia UP, 1989.

———. "Beyond Ethnocentrism: Gender, Power, and the Third-World Intelligentsia." *Marxism and the Interpretation of Culture*. Ed. Cary Nelson and Lawrence Grossberg. Urbana: U of Illinois P, 1988. 503–15.

Freud, Sigmund. *Three Essays on the Theory of Sexuality*. Ed. and trans. James Strachey. Basic Books, 2000.

———. *A General Selection from the Works of Freud*. Ed. John Rickman. New York: Liveright Publishing Co., 1957.

———. *The Interpretation of Dreams*. 1900. London: Hogarth P, 1968.

García-Canclini, Nestor. *Culturas híbridas: Estrategias para entrar y salir de la modernidad*. Mexico City: Grijalbo, 1990.

Gómez, Alma, Cherrie Moraga, and Mariana Romo-Carmona, eds. *Cuentos: Stories by Latinas*. New York: Kitchen Table, Women of Color P, 1983.

Gonzales-Berry, Erlinda. *"The* [Subversive] *Mixquiahula Letters*: An Antidote for Self-Hate." *Chicana (W)rites on Word and Film.* Ed. Herrera-Sobek and Viramontes. 115–24.

Gonzalez, Rey, ed. *Currents from the Dancing River: Contemporary Latino Fiction, Nonfiction, and Poetry.* San Diego: Harcourt Brace and Company: 1996.

Gordon, Avery, and Christopher Newfield, eds. *Mapping Multiculturalism.* Minneapolis: U of Minnesota P, 1996.

Grobman, Laurie. "The Cultural Past and Artistic Creation in Sandra Cisneros' *The House on Mango Street* and Judith Ortiz Cofer's *Silent Dancing.*" *Confluencia: Revista Hispanica de Cultura y Literatura* 11.1 (Fall 1995): 42–49.

Gutiérrez-Jones, Carl. *Rethinking the Borderlands: Between Chicano Culture and Legal Discourse.* Berkeley: U of California P, 1995.

———. "Desiring (B)orders." *Diacritics* 25.1 (Spring 1995): 99–112.

Hall, Stuart. "The Local and the Global: Globalization and Ethnicity." *Dangerous Liasons: Gender, Nation, and Postcolonial Perspectives.* Ed. Anne McClintock, Aamir Mufti, and Ella Shohat. Minneapolis; London: U of Minnesota P, 1997. 173–87.

———. "Who Needs Identity?" Introduction. *Questions of Cultural Identity.* Ed. Stuart Hall and Paul du Gay. London: Sage Publication, 1996. 1–17.

Haraway, Donna. *Simians, Cyborgs, and Women: The Reinvention of Nature.* New York: Routledge, 1991.

Harper, Phillip Brian. *Framing the Margins: The Social Logic of Postmodern Culture.* New York: Oxford UP, 1994.

Herrera-Sobek, María. "The Politics of Rape: Sexual Transgression in Chicana Fiction." *Chicana Creativity and Criticism.* Ed. Herrera-Sobek and Viramontes. 245–56.

Herrera-Sobek, María, and Helena María Viramontes, eds. *Chicana Creativity and Criticism: Charting New Frontiers in American Literature.* Albuquerque: U of New Mexico P, 1996.

———. *Chicana (W)rites on Word and Film.* Berkeley: Third Woman P, 1995.

Hicks, Emily. *Border Writing: The Multidimensional Text.* Minneapolis: U of Minnesota P, 1991.

Hine, Robert V., and John Mack Faragher. *The American West: A New Interpretive History.* New Haven: Yale UP, 2000.

Hirsch, Marianne. "Past Lives: Postmemories in Exile." *Exile and Creativity.* Ed. Susan Rubin Suleiman. 418–46.

Hoffman, Joan M. "'She Wants to Be Called Yolanda Now:' Identity, Language, and the Third Sister in *How the García Girls Lost Their Accents.*" *Bilingual Review / Revista Bilngüe* 23.1 (Jan–Apr 1998): 21-27.

Hollinger, David. *PostEthnic America: Beyond Multiculturalism.* New York: Basic Books, 1995.

hooks, bell. *Feminist Theory from Margin to Center.* Boston: South End P, 1989.

Horno-Delgado, Asunción, Eliana Ortega, Nina M. Scott, and Nancy Saporta Sternbach, eds. *Breaking Boundaries: Latina Writing and Critical Reading.* Amherst: U of Massachusetts P, 1989.

Hutcheon, Linda. *The Politics of Postmodernism.* New York: Routledge, 1989.

Jameson, Fredric. *The Political Unconscious: Narrative as a Socially Symbolic Act.* Ithaca: Cornell UP, 1981.

JanMohamed, Abdul. "Worldliness-without-World, Homelessness-as-Home: Toward a Definition of the Secular Border Intellectual." *Edward Said: A Critical Reader.* Ed. Michael Sprinker. Oxford: Blackwell Publishers, 1992. 96–120.

Jehenson, Myriam Yvonne. *Latin American Women Writers: Class, Race and Gender.* Albany: State U of New York P, 1995.

Johnson, Richard. "What is Cultural Studies Anyway?" *Social Text* 16 (Winter 1986/87): 38–80.

Kaminsky, Amy. *Reading the Body Politic: Feminist Criticism and Latin American Women Writers.* Minneapolis: U of Minnesota P, 1993.

Kanellos, Nicolas, ed. *Hispanic American Literature: A Brief Introduction and Anthology.* New York: Harper Collins, 1995.

Kattán-Ibarra, Juan. *Perspectivas culturales de · Hispanoamerica.* Lincolnwood: National Textbook Company, 1994.

Keogh, Dermot. *Romero: El Salvador's Martyr.* Dublin: Dominican Publications, 1981.

Kirkwood, Julieta. "Femenistas y políticas." *Nueva Sociedad* (julio/agosto, 1985): 62–70.

———. "El femenismo como negación del autoritarianismo." Essay. Santiago de Chile: FLASCO, 1983.

Lacan, Jacques. *The Four Fundamental Concepts of Psychoanalysis.* Ed. Jacques-Alain Miller. Trans. Alan Sheridan. New York: Norton, 1998.

———. *The Seminar of Jacques Lacan, Book II: The Ego in Freud's Theory and in the Technique of Psychoanalysis, 1954–1955.* Ed. Jacques-Alain Miller. Trans. Sylvana Tomaselli. New York: Norton, 1988.

———. *Ecrits: A Selection.* Trans. Alan Sheridan. New York: W.W. Norton, 1977.

———. "The Mirror Stage as Formative of the Function of the I. " *Ecrits.* 1–7.

———. "The Agency of the Letter in the Unconscious or Reason Since Freud." *Ecrits.* 146–78.

———. "The Signification of the Phallus." *Ecrits.* 281–91.

Laplanche, Jean. *The Language of Psycho-Analysis.* Trans. Donald Nicholson-Smith. New York: Norton, 1974.

Leal, Luis, and Pepe Barrón. "Chicano Literature: An Overview." *Three American Literatures.* Ed. Houston Baker. New York: MLA, 1982. 9–32.

Lindstrom, Naomi. *Women's Voices in Latin American Literature.* Washington, DC: Three Continents P, 1989.

López, Iraida H. "Formas femeninas de la biculturación: *Borderlands/La frontera* y *Silent Dancing.*" *Letras Femeninas* 27.2 (Fall 2001): 85–101.

———. "'… And There Is Only My Imagination Where Our History Should Be:' An Interview with Cristina García." *Michigan Quarterly Review* 33 (1994): 605–17.

López, Kimberle S. "Women on the Verge of a Revolution: Madness and Resistance in Cristina García's *Dreaming in Cuban.*" *Letras Femeninas* 22.1–2 (Spring/Fall 1996): 33–49.

Luis, William. *Dance Between Two Cultures: Latino Caribbean Literature Written in the U.S.* Nashville: Vanderbilt UP, 1997.

Marger, Martin N. *Race and Ethnic Relations: American and Global Perspectives*. Belmont, Ca: Wadsworth Publishing Co., 1991.

McCracken, Ellen. *New Latina Narrative: The Feminine Space of Postmodern Ethnicity*. Tucson: U of Arizona P, 1999.

———. "Graciela Limón." Biographical Entry. *Dictionary of Literary Biography: Chicano Writers*. Ed. Francisco Lomelí and Carl R. Shirley, vol. 209. Detroit: The Gale Group, 1999. 127–32.

———. "Rupture, Occlusion, and Repression: The Political Unconscious in the New Latina Narrative of Julia Alvarez and Ana Castillo." *Confrontations et Metissages*. Ed. Elyette Benjamin-Labarthe, Yves-Charles Grandjeat, and Christian Lerat. Bordeaux, France. 1995. 319–28.

Michaels, Walter Benn. *Our America*. Durham: Duke UP, 1995.

Minh-ha, Trinh. *The Woman, the Native, the Other*. Bloomington: Indiana UP, 1989.

Mitchell, David T. "National Families and Familial Nations: Communista Americans in Cristina Garcia's *Dreaming in Cuban*." *Tulsa Studies* 15.1 (Spring 1996): 51–60.

Mohanty, Chandra Talpade. "Cartographies of Struggle." Introduction. *Third World Women and the Politics of Feminism*. Ed. Chandra T. Mohanty, Ann Russo, and Lourdes Torres. Bloomington: Indiana UP, 1991. 1–47.

Moi, Toril. *The Sexual/Textual Politics: Feminist Literary Theory*. London: Methuen, 1985.

Moraga, Cherríe, and Gloria Anzaldúa, eds. *This Bridge Called My Back: Writings by Radical Women of Color*. New York: Kitchen Table P, 1983.

Mujcinovic, Fatima. "Multiple Articulations of Exile in U.S. Latina Literature: Confronting Exilic Absence and Trauma." *MELUS* 28.4 (Winter 2003): *forthcoming*.

———. "Hybrid Latina Identities: Strategic Positioning In-Between Two Cultures." *CENTRO Journal for Puerto Rican Studies* 13.1 (Spring 2001): 45–59.

———. "In Search of Bernabé: Politicized Motherhood." *Ethnic Studies Review* 24.1–3 (2001): 29–47.

Muller, Gilbert. *New Strangers in Paradise: The Immigrant Experience and Contemporary American Fiction*. Lexington: U of Kentucky P, 1999.

Murphy, Dervla. *Tibetan Foothold*. London: Pan Books, 1969.

Neate, Wilson. *Tolerating Ambiguity: Ethnicity and Community in Chicano/a Writing*. New York: Peter Lang, 1998.

Oboler, Suzanne. *Ethnic Labels, Latino Lives: Identity and the Politics of (Re)presentation in the United States*. Minneapolis: U of Minnesota P, 1995.

Ocasio, Rafael. "The Infinite Variety of the Puerto Rican Reality: An Interview with Judith Ortiz Cofer." *Callaloo* 17.3 (Summer 1994): 730–42.

Omi, Michael, and Howard Winant. *Racial Formation in the United States: From the 1960s to the 1990s*. New York: Routledge, 1994.

Ortega, Eliana, and Nancy Saporta Sternbach. "At the Threshold of the Unnamed: Latina Literary Discourse in the Eighties." *Breaking Boundaries: Latina Writing and Critical Readings*. Ed. Horno Delgado et al. 2–23.

Pastor, Robert. "Migration and Development: Implications and Recommendations for Policy." *Determinants of Emigration From Mexico, Central America, and the Caribbean*. Ed. Díaz-Briquets and Weintraub. 295–318.

Payant, Katherine B. "From Alienation to Reconciliation in the Novels of Cristina García." *MELUS* 26.3 (Fall 2001): 163–82.

Pérez Firmat, Gustavo. *The Cuban Condition: Translation and Identity in Modern Cuban Literature.* New York: Cambridge UP, 1989.

Quintana, Alvina. *Home Girls: Chicana Literary Voices.* Philadelphia: Temple UP, 1996.

Ramos, Juanita, ed. *Compañeras: Latina Lesbians.* New York: Latina Lesbian History Project, 1887.

Rebolledo, Diana Tey. *Women Singing in the Snow.* Tucson: U of Arizona P, 1995.

Richard, Nelly. *Margins and Institutions: Art in Chile since 1973.* Melbourne: Art and Text, 1986.

Rivero, Eliana. "From Immigrants to Ethnics: Cuban Women Writers in the U.S." *Breaking Boundaries.* Ed. Horno-Delgado at al. 189–200.

Rossi, Laura. "¿Cómo pensar a las madres de la Plaza de Mayo?" *Nuevo texto crítico* 4:2 (1989): 145–53.

Rouse, Roger. "Mexican Migration and the Social Space of Postmodernism." *Diaspora* 1.1 (Spring 1991): 8–23.

Rycroft, Charles. *A Critical Dictionary of Psychoanalysis.* New York: Basic Books, 1968.

Said, Edward. "Reflections on Exile." *Reflections on Exile and Other Essays.* Cambridge: Harvard UP, 2000. 173–86.

———. *The World, the Text, and the Critic.* Cambridge: Harvard UP, 1983.

Saldívar, José. *Border Matters: Remapping American Cultural Studies.* Berkeley: U of California P, 1997.

———. *The Dialectics of Our America: Genealogy,Cultural Critique and Literary History.* Durham: Duke UP, 1991.

Saldívar, Ramón. "The Borderlands of Culture: Américo Paredes's *George Washington Gómez* and Chicano Literature at the end of the Twentieth Century." *American Literary History* 5.2 (Summer 1993): 272–93.

———. *Chicano Narrative: The Dialectics of Difference.* Madison: U of Wisconsin P, 1990.

Saldívar-Hull, Sonia. "Feminism on the Border: From Gender Politics to Geopolitics." Diss. U of Texas at Austin, 1990.

Sandoval, Chela. *Methodology of the Oppressed.* Minneapolis: U of Minnesota P, 2000.

———. "Feminist Forms of Agency and Oppositional Consciousness: U.S. Third World Feminist Criticism." *Contemporary Feminist Theory: A Text/Reader.* Ed. Mary F. Rogers. Boston: McGraw-Hill, 1998. 53–65.

———. "New Sciences: Cyborg Feminism and the Methodology of the Oppressed." *The Cyborg Handbook.* Ed. Chris Hables Gray. New York: Routledge, 1995. 407–21.

———. "US Third World Feminism: The Theory and Method of Oppositional Consciousness in the Postmodern World." *Genders* 10 (Spring 1991): 1–24.

Santner, Eric. *Stranded Objects: Mourning, Memory, and Film in Postwar Germany.* Ithaca; London: Cornell UP, 1990.

Sarlo, Beatriz. "Women, History, and Ideology." *Women's Writing in Latin America.* Ed. Sara Castro-Klarén, Sylvia Molloy, and Beatriz Sarlo. Boulder: Westview, 1991. 231–48.

Scarry, Elaine. *The Body in Pain.* New York: Oxford UP, 1985.

Schrimer, Jennifer. "The Seeking of Truth and the Gendering of Consciousness: The Co-Madres of El Salvador and the CONAVIGUA Widows of Guatemala." *'VIVA:' Women and Popular Protest in Latin America*. Ed. Sarah A. Radcliffe and Sallie Westwood. London: Routledge, 1993. 30–64.

Schwartz, Marcy. *Writing Paris: Urban Topographies of Desire in Contemporary Latin American Fiction*. Albany: State U of New York P, 1999.

Spivak, Gayatri. *The Spivak Reader: Collected Works of Gayatri Spivak*. Ed. Donna Landry and Gerald MacLean. New York: Routledge, 1996.

Steele, Cynthia. *Politics, Gender, and the Mexican Novel, 1966–1988: Beyond the Pyramid*. Austin: U of Texas P, 1992.

Stefanko, Jacqueline. "New Ways of Telling: Latinas' Narratives of Exile and Return." *Frontiers* 17. 2 (1996): 50–70.

Suleiman, Susan Rubin, ed. *Exile and Creativity: Signposts, Travelers, Outsiders, Backward Glances*. Durham: Duke UP, 1998.

Takaki, Ronald. *A Different Mirror: A History of Multicultural America*. Boston: Little, Brown and Co., 1993.

Taylor, Charles. *Multiculturalism and "The Politics of Recognition:" An Essay*. Princeton, NJ: Princeton UP, 1992.

Taylor, Kathy. *The New Narrative of Mexico: Sub-Versions of History in Mexican Fiction*. Lewisburg, PA: Bucknell UP; London: Associated UP's, 1994.

Tierney-Tello, Mary Beth. *Allegories of Transgression and Transformation: Experimental Fiction by Women Writing Under Dictatorship*. Albany: State U of New York P, 1996.

Torres, Héctor A. "Story, Telling, Voice: Narrative Authority in Ana Castillo's *The Mixquiahuala Letters*." *Chicana (W)rites on Word and Film*. Ed. Herrera-Sobek and Viramontes. 125–45.

Torres, Lourdes. The Construction of the Self in U.S. Latina Autobiographies." *Third World Women and the Politics of Feminism*. Ed. Chandra T. Mohanty, Ann Russo, and Lourdes Torres. Bloomington: Indiana UP, 1991. 271–87.

Vásquez, Mary S. "Cuba as Text and Context in Cristina García's *Dreaming in Cuban*." *Bilingual Review / Revista Bilingue* 20.1 (1995): 22–27.

———. "Gender and Exile: Mothers and Daughters in Roberto G. Fernandez's *Raining Backwards*." *The Literature of Emigration and Exile*. Eds. Whitlark and Aycock. 79–85.

Walter, Roland. "The Cultural Politics of Dislocation and Relocation in the Novels of Ana Castillo." *MELUS* 23.1 (Spring 1998): 81–97.

West, Cornel. *Beyond Eurocentrism and Multiculturalism*. Monroe: Common Courage P, 1993.

Whitlark, James, and Wendell Aycock, eds. *The Literature of Emigration and Exile*. Lubbock, Tx: Texas Tech UP, 1992.

Wiegman, Robyn. *American Anatomies: Theorizing Race and Gender*. Durham: Duke UP, 1995.

Yarbro-Bejarano, Yvonne. "Chicana Literature from a Chicana Feminist Perspective." *Chicana Creativity and Criticism*. Ed. Herrera-Sobek and Viramontes. 213–19.

———. "Gloria Anzaldúa's *Borderlands/La Frontera*: Cultural Studies, 'Difference,' and the Non-Unitary Subject." *Cultural Critique* (Fall 1994): 5–28.

Zimmerman, Marc. U.S. Latino Literature: An Essay and Annotated Bibliography. Chicago: MARCH/Abrazo P, 1992.

INDEX

MODERN AMERICAN LITERATURE
New Approaches

Yoshinobu Hakutani, *General Editor*

The books in this series deal with many of the major writers known as American realists, modernists, and post-modernists from 1880 to the present. This category of writers will also include less known ethnic and minority writers, a majority of whom are African American, some are Native American, Mexican American, Japanese American, Chinese American, and others. The series might also include studies on well-known contemporary writers, such as James Dickey, Allen Ginsberg, Gary Snyder, John Barth, John Updike, and Joyce Carol Oates. In general, the series will reflect new critical approaches such as deconstructionism, new historicism, psychoanalytical criticism, gender criticism/feminism, and cultural criticism.

For additional information about this series or for the submission of manuscripts, please contact:

Peter Lang Publishing
P.O. Box 1246
Bel Air, MD 21014-1246

To order other books in this series, please contact our Customer Service Department at:

800-770-LANG (within the U.S.)
(212) 647-7706 (outside the U.S.)
(212) 647-7707 FAX

Or browse online by series at:

www.peterlangusa.com